Landscaping Egypt
From the Aesthetic to the Productive

تنسـيق المـواقع
في مصر
من الجمـالي
إلى المنتِج

Cornelia Redeker and Monique Jüttner (eds.)

Preface

Allah has promised to the believing men and the believing women gardens, beneath which rivers flow, to abide in them, and goodly dwellings in gardens of perpetual abode; and best of all is Allah's goodly pleasure; that is the grand achievement.

Qur'an 9.72

Al Azhar Park, Cairo

Photo: Sites International

Preface
مقدمة

Laila ElMasry Stino

In their book, *Landscaping Egypt – From the Aesthetic to the Productive*, editors Cornelia Redeker and Monique Jüttner examine the state of landscape architecture in Egypt. They pay particular attention to water as a design element, and the challenge posed by its scarcity to agriculture and landscape architecture. What most distinguishes this book is its compilation and presentation of relevant academic articles, supported by successful applications of design principles and concepts to landscape architecture projects in Egypt.

The Chapter *Learning from..* provides examples of a range of projects effectively designed and constructed in Egypt, each differing in location, scale, function, aesthetic aspects, productivity, design constraints, and available resources. The projects include a number of parks and productive orchards designed to take into account the environmental factors of the region, water limitations and user needs.

The editors also examine the concerning large scale sprawl of urbanism in Egypt, and the attempts to rehabilitate agricultural lands. They offer lessons that can be learned from the past by presenting examples of historical gardens, Islamic gardens and desert gardens in Egypt. They emphasize the often forgotten vital role of gardens in food production.

The book includes valuable resources in the form of a list of productive plants in Egypt and a plant dictionary that provides both the Arabic and English names, which I believe is particularly useful and beneficial to the reader.

I believe that Cornelia Redeker's and Monique Jüttner's book has great significance and value to designers, including architects, landscape architects, professionals in the field of environmental design and sustainability, academicians, and even the casual reader in the Middle East, where research and publications addressing the field of landscape architecture in Egypt are rare.

Cornelia Redeker is an architect and urban planner focusing on landscape-based urban design strategies. With her office Cities on Rivers / Cities On Sand, she has worked as a consultant for urban development and upgrading projects in the flood plain of the Rhine and the Nile and, more recently, in the desert. She studied architecture and urban planning at the University of Applied Sciences Cologne, Germany and the Berlage-Institute in the Netherlands and holds a PhD on Urban Flood Integration along the Rhine from TU Delft. In parallel to developing her PhD research, she was teaching and research associate at the Chair for Urban Design and Regional Planning at TU Munich. Since 2012 she is associate professor for architecture and urban design at the German University in Cairo. In 2013, she co-founded the Nile Islands Initiative, an interdisciplinary platform to map, protect and activate the spatial qualities of Nile islands in the context of increasing urbanization. In this context, Dahab Island in Cairo, where she also lives, is serving as the main case study also for action-based research formats.

Monique Jüttner is an architect, urban designer and researcher. She studied architecture at the University of Applied Sciences Lausitz in Cottbus, Germany and at the Accademia di architettura – Università della Svizzera italiana in Mendrisio, Switzerland. Working in architectural offices in Switzerland, the US and Germany, she managed the design and construction of various housing and large-scale urban development projects. She was teaching and research associate at the Chair for Urban Design and Regional Planning, TU Munich, and lecturer at the Architecture and Urban Design Program of the German University in Cairo. She currently holds a position as a PhD researcher at the Institute of Urban Planning at Brandenburg University of Technology Cottbus. Her interests revolve around urban transformation processes, innovative strategies and typologies in housing, as well as urban and landscape design. Her current research focusses on urban food production seeking to address issues of social justice, food security and climate change in the European city and the MENA region.

Cornelia and Monique's shared interest in more productive open space design and their fascination for Egypt's landscapes led to the foundation of Landscaping Egypt. As a research and teaching platform it involves lectures, workshops, design studios, the international conference in 2017 held at the German University in Cairo together resulting in this publication.

We would like to thank all those whose projects inspired us to make this book and whose generous support in terms of sharing their knowledge, graphics and photos actually made it happen. A special thank you goes out to Laila ElMasry Stino for not only sharing her ground-breaking work with us, but for writing our preface and advising us along the way. We would further like to thank Hala Barakat, Faris Farag, Undine Giseke, Thomas Löffler, Dunja Karcher, Hanaa Nazer, Mohie El-Din Omar, Mohamed Refaat, Mohamed Salheen, Antje Stokman, and Aurelia Weintz for their consultancy and the project team at the GUC Architecture and Urban Design Program for all their contributions. Without the many excursions to the landscapes of Egypt with Khaled Aziz and Carola Fricke many photos in this book would not have been taken. We would also like to thank Theresa Hartherz and Doris Kleilein and the team at JOVIS Publishers, Markus Otto and Karolina Hettchen at b-tu Cottbus, as well as all who hosted us in Cairo and Berlin over the course of four years. A very special thank you to Prince Naguib Abd Allah for so generously hosting us at Dahab Island Palace, its magical gardens providing an endless source of inspiration, to the wonderful work environment at Spreefeld Berlin, to our friends and our families for their eternal support. We could not have done this without all of you.

Photo: NASA

This book is dedicated to the beauty of Egypt.

Pyramid Plateau and Nile Valley, Giza

Photo: Monique Jüttner

Table of Contents
فهرس

03 Preface / *Laila ElMasry Stino*
05 Acknowledgements
10 Introducing the Narrative
21 Editorial

24 **01 Landscape Conditions** أحوال المناظر الطبيعية
27 Evolving Landscapes / *Hanaa Nazer, Cornelia Redeker*
35 Landscaping Practices — From Symbiosis to Commodification / *Eman Farouk, Cornelia Redeker*
38 Timeline / *Eman Farouk, Monique Jüttner, Cornelia Redeker*

40 *Essays* **Water** المياه
41 Water Conditions in Egypt / *Mohie El-Din Omar*
47 Designing for Global Water Challenges / *Antje Stokman*

52 **02 Learning From** التعلم من
54 Al Azhar Park
58 Khalifa Heritage and Environment Park
62 Geziret El Dahab
66 Desert Afforestation
70 Wadi Agriculture
74 Orchard Park
78 Water-Sensitive Open Space Design
82 Urban Microfarms
86 Constructed Wetlands
90 Aquaponic Farming
94 Ten Medjool Date Palms

98 *Essays* **Urbanization** تمدّن
99 The Larger Scale — Urbanization, Agriculture, Land Reclamation / *Kareem Ibrahim, Deena Khalil, Salwa Salman*

104 **03 Revisited and Projected** إعادة التفكير و التصور
106 Ancient Gardens
110 Islamic Gardens
114 Desert Gardens

118 *Essays* **Food** الطعام
119 Planning for Egypt's Food System and Heritage / *Monique Jüttner, Hala N. Barakat, Undine Giseke*

124 **04 Productive plants** النباتات المنتجة
126 Doum Palm
130 Date Palm
134 Egyptian Sycamore
138 Pomegranate
142 Olive
146 Banana
150 Sweet Orange
154 Grape
158 Prickly Pear
162 Moringa
166 Papyrus
170 Bamboo
174 Reed
178 Tamarisk
182 Argoun Palm
186 Weeping Fig
190 Acacia ehrenbergiana
194 Acacia nilotica
198 Acacia tortilis subsp. raddiana

202 Dictionary
206 Endnotes
211 References
218 Authors and Consulting Experts
220 Imprint

Photo: Alia Mortada

Aswan High Dam, Lake Nasser

During the flood, the "Arrival of Hapi", Egyptians would place statues of Hapi in the cities and villages and throw offerings into the river at places sacred to the god. These rituals were to ensure that the inundation was not too low leaving insufficient water for the crops nor too high risking the destruction of their mud-brick homes.[1]

Water

**Egypt – a hydraulic civilization
formed by the changing courses of the Nile
and water scarcity in the desert**

Photo: Monique Jüttner

Egypt's annual water supply dropped to an average of 663 cubic metres per person in 2013, down from over 2,500 cubic metres in 1947. Egypt is already below the United Nations water poverty threshold, and by 2025 the UN predicts it will be approaching a state of "absolute water crisis" with a predicted annual quota dwindling to 582 cubic meters per person.[2]

Dahab Island, Giza

"Agricultural cropland habitats have been diminishing since late 1980s. These declines are thought to be connected to changes in land use and agricultural practices. Agricultural land remains to be lost to human settlements. It is estimated that some 47,700 feddans are lost every year. The introduction and wide use of high yielding varieties led to the neglect and disappearance of traditional varieties and the erosion of crop plant genetic diversity. Currently, Egypt depends on four crops (wheat, corn, rice and potato) for 50% of its vegetarian food and 14 mammal and bird species for 90% of animal proteins."[3]

Food

A culture deeply rooted in agricultural practice,
growing food in contrasting environments
of barren desert and the rich,
fertile Nile Valley and Delta

Photos: Monique Jüttner

Never plant a tree that does not grow fruit.

Bedouin Saying

Photo: Monique Jüttner

Fish Garden, Zamalek

Urban Egypt has one of the lowest green area ratios per inhabitant globally. Whereas the more affluent Cairenes may have between 4–7 sqm, the urban poor have as little as 0.1 square meters of green space per capita.[4] For Egypt's New Urban Communities materializing in the desert this is changing. With a building footprint of around 50%, green areas define the new counter model to Central Cairo's hyperdensity calling for water-sensitive design solutions.

Urban Green
Commodfied landscapes producing habitat and defining land value

Photo: Peter Blodau

Private Garden, New Cairo

"The Insatiable Human Desire to Imagine, Explore, And Create...Today's trends of urban development also raise questions about the ethics of these activities in desert locations or other challenging environments. This kind of awareness is fundamental to the conceptualization and implementation of new large-scale urban infrastructure projects."

Jerry Van Eyck, !Melk Landscape Architects NYC,
chief designer Green River Park, New Administrative Capital

Photo: Peter Blodau

Lake Manzala, Alexandria

"A SUCCESS STORY: Lake Manzala is a shallow brackish lake on the north-eastern edge of the Nile Delta, separated from the Mediterranean Sea only by a sandy beach ridge. The lake has high inputs of pollutants from industrial, domestic, and agricultural sources. Other problems include a substantial reduction in both fish and bird species as well as absence of irrigation water for crops cultivation. The Lake Manzala Engineered Wetland Project is a constructed wetland facility to treat 25,000 cubic meters per day of wastewater from the Bahr El Baqar Drain and demonstrates a low-cost innovative water treatment solution. Treatment of wastewater via engineered wetlands is a new low-cost technology to the Middle East. The success in reducing water pollution has led national authorities to explore the reuse of treated water via engineered wetlands in irrigation, fish farming, and decentralized wastewater treatment technology in remote areas."

Ahmed Rashed, National Water Research Center, Ministry of Water Resources and Irrigation

Blue-Green

Natural and constructed ecosystems
between water and land

Photo: Yosra Malek

In the Red Sea, mangroves are relied on for food or as a nursery ground by 35 species of fish and also provide a wildlife sanctuary out of the water to numerous insects and birds. Mangroves protect from coastal erosion and store carbon. A filtration system in their roots prevents most salt from being taken up by the trees, and that which is absorbed is later excreted through the leaves and branches. 75 percent of the world's tropical commercial fish spend a portion of their lives in mangroves. All of the Red Sea mangrove areas were declared as protected areas in 1986 before the urban development of the coast. For a true systemic impact, the mangroves of Egypt would have to be 4–5 times the area. Initiatives to increase the areas by planting seedlings with the local community have proven successful in the past.[5]

Photo: Monique Jüttner

Tunis Village, Fayoum Oasis

The Siwan embroidery has four main colours, those of the different phases of ripeness of a date while growing on the tree. On the seventh night of a wedding the groom cuts a palm tree from his orchard to serve its heart to the mother of the bride.

Omar Hamza Ahmed, archaeologist, Siwa Oasis

Green-Gold
The oasis and its reinterpretation in the context of new urban developments in the desert

Photo: Peter Blodau

It is not only new urban developments that lead to habitat loss, but also the transformation of existing or remaining green areas through plantation of non-native plant species, managed lawns, and removal of the mid-story canopy.[6]

Dahab Island, Giza

Photo: Peter Blodau

Editorial
إفتتاحية

Cornelia Redeker and Monique Jüttner

With LANDSCAPING EGYPT – FROM THE AESTHETIC TO THE PRODUCTIVE we want to look at responsive models for the rapidly and very diversely urbanizing landscapes of Egypt through the eyes of local and international practitioners, researchers and design professionals engaged in new emerging practices. With the aim to explore hidden potentials and given obstacles for landscape design to become productive in both formal and informal contexts, we even dare to build on the hypothesis that new landscape models may have the potential to bridge the societal gap by being applicable in various realms.

Egypt is one of the oldest civilizations, rich in natural and man-made landscapes of genuine beauty. Despite the long tradition and history of productive landscapes both in the Nile Valley and its arid regions and the productive nature of paradisical gardens, the majority of contemporary open space designs rarely respond to the climatic, geographical and economic conditions on the ground in a productive way. Based on a conception of landscape as scenery a main feature are lush, extensive lawns. Due to a lack of shade and often missing consideration of the human scale, open spaces today do not instigate physical movement and thus do not contribute to health and well-being to their full capacity. In favour of a car-friendly environment, open spaces are rarely walkable or cyclable. Between the oases of the upper and middle class in the new urban communities that are evolving as a parallel band in the adjoining desert of existing cities and the countryside we find a dialectic between the strictly aesthetic vs. the richness of agrarian landscapes that are, as of yet, rarely considered culturally relevant. New urban developments transport certain lifestyle values, but hardly respond to the cultural practice and urgencies that revolve around water scarcity, food security, rapid urbanization, desertification and the accelerating impacts of climate change. The planet needs to cut its emissions from today by more than half to get on a path to limit global warming to 1.5 degrees Celsius in this century. The world may only have until 2030 to reach that milestone. As we are urbanizing on rapidly diminishing resources, how we live and eat plays a pivotal role. In this context, a circular approach to urban landscape design becomes paramount. Moving from a predominantly modernist, sectoral and market-steered planning culture towards a design practice of open systems, the focus moves beyond typologies and land use to include flows and processes. We find ourselves in an environment of continuous experimentation responding to unforeseen or ignored adverse impacts. These are largely produced by large-scale anthropogenic and often seemingly irreversible transformations of natural landscapes in the name of development and growth as we are currently most impactfully experiencing with Covid-19. Global urgencies, as a combined result, are triggering a radical shift and thus innovation, ideally supported by institutional and market incentives, but often evolving bottom-up. As we begin to embrace biophysical complexity, the regional scale, defined by ecosystems such as watersheds, but also habitats and man-made networks, is becoming increasingly pivotal. In this context, Egypt's geographic specificity exemplarily opens up an arena for a new landscape understanding and design.

WATER-SENSITIVE OPEN SPACE DESIGN Water scarcity in Egypt is a rising challenge that is receiving increasing attention. Large amounts of drinking water in new urban communities are used to irrigate private gardens. Water loss through leakage, damage caused by rising ground water levels, and a general lack of awareness regarding the use of water are prevalent. In this context, it is not simply a question of adapting landscape and urban design practices to become more resourceful. The built environment, and in this context, parks and open space designs also serve as educational landscapes. Recent projects showcasing native, drought-tolerant and productive plants, reintroducing vernacular and traditional elements, for example of Islamic garden design, planting according to hydrozones, implementing resource-efficient irrigation systems and water-recycling mechanisms are currently creating a promising body of knowledge for future users and planners to build on. LANDSCAPE CONDITIONS are of course framed by the dialectic development between the Nile Valley and the vast desert. But, looking beyond the fundamental question as to where the country will develop, the question here is: how? We find two main approaches that we are "LEARNING FROM…": Working with given arid resources like the sun, the available space and the waste water of the desert's growing population can create recreational landscapes that contribute ecosystemically, while site-independent solutions such as constructed wetlands, rooftop farming or aquaponics show us how accumulatively, on a small-scale, urban micro-climates and the overall spatial quality can be improved while growing food or treating waste water. We are also learning from new and very inspiring socio-economical models to make these projects happen. To move away from foreign models of landscape aesthetics and design, we go on to look at the EVOLUTION of both agricultural and aesthetic LANDSCAPES in Egypt and major events, innovations and agendas that influenced these. We then exemplarily REVISIT garden typologies that are historically, culturally and geographically rooted in the Egyptian context. Ancient and Islamic gardens as well as Desert Gardens are explored by PROJECTING these models onto contemporary urban open spaces as potentially more sustainable alternatives to the current design practice. The plant atlas offers an alternative repertoire of beautiful indigenous and PRODUCTIVE PLANTS and explores how they can produce distinctive spatial qualities within garden designs. It also provides specific information about each plant to understand its ecosystemic potentials and needs.

As we researched the content for this book with the presented best practices at the LANDSCAPING EGYPT – FROM THE AESTHETIC TO THE PRODUCTIVE conference at the German University in Cairo in May 2017, but also with GUC architecture and urban design students in different course formats over the past three years, we realized that formulating new approaches is not only an exploration of genuine spaces and potentials, but also a representational and a linguistic question. Many landscape-related terms are not known in Arabic and are replaced with English words and vice versa. With the selective DICTIONARY we collected those that crossed our path and translated them to the best of our ability.

With this publication, we are of course building on a very rich body of existing knowledge. In the last century, the rich collection of Orman Gardens and its Herbarium, Vivi Täckholm and Mohamed Drar's Students' *Flora of Egypt* (1956) and Nabil Hadidi's, Loutfy Boulos', Samy Makar's and Magdy Gohary's illustration of the common *Street Trees of Egypt* in 1968 have provided a botanical scholarly perspective. In response to the rising challenges of landscape designers to cope with water scarcity, in her book *Desert Garden – A Practical Guide* from 2006, Irina Springuel celebrates the beauty and splendour of indigenous plants in arid environments. She offers guidelines for planting in new desert developments, not just in cities, but also for the emerging tourist developments along the coasts. Laila ElMasry Stino's *Plant Guidebook For Al Azhar Park* and *The City Of Cairo and Landscape Architecture and the Planting Design of Al Azhar Park* from 2014 illustrating Al Azhar Park marks a turning point in Egyptian landscape design. As a green lung, a neighbourhood and city park, and an experimental garden that is simultaneously a water infrastructure for the city, Al Azhar Park is documented by its chief designer elaborating the integrated approach taken and offers a detailed manual that has become the reference for all practitioners in the field.

We are learning from and building on this data base to explore and share practices and tools within the current Egyptian context for architects, urban planners, landscape architects and other disciplines with an interest in integrated open space design on different scales. We aim to expand the visual and spatial beauty of current garden design practices to include the magic that is rooted in the eco-systemic potential of integrated design approaches on multiple scales and for different contexts and responsive to the their environment and hope to make these more accessible. We see Egypt as exemplary for a globally emergent change in design practices and hope to contribute to a rising consciousness and discourse by documenting these.

Humbled and grateful for the opportunity to explore the divine landscapes and emerging landscape practices of Egypt, we want to thank all of the contributors to this book who have so generously shared their expertise and experience in support of expanding the horizon of what is possible when we design open spaces. The past four years have been a learning experience. We want to explicitly thank our students who have explored these practices together with us and hope to have planted a seed.

Evening leisure, El Corniche Alexandria

01

Landscape Conditions
أحوال المناظر الطبيعية

Egypt's landscapes are often reduced to the Nile Valley and Delta and its vast surrounding desert. With its coastline to the Northern Mediterranean and the Red Sea surrounding the mountainous Sinai Peninsula it is of course much more diverse. As the new national urban agenda is defined by urban development away from the hyperdense and highly polluted megapolises of Cairo and Alexandria, with new cities outside of the Nile Valley, and increasingly along the given coast lines, this diversity creates new design parameters when aiming to design landscapes that are productive and resilient.

From the urban morphology that defines our open spaces to the materials we use today, we have created city models that are lacking resilience and are rarely productive. In this context, landscape design becomes the tool to create more livable cities within the anthropogenically transformed landscape conditions and given the limited resources at hand.

The paradigm shift from a rural to an industrial agricultural practice shaped by the modernist perception of controlling nature has not only framed current landscape conditions, but also reflects on the sectoral approach to landscape and garden design within the urban realm. This shift was enabled by large-scale water infrastructure, most prominently the Aswan High Dam, and a change in irrigation techniques, and continues with the yet not foreseeable impacts of the Grand Renaissance Dam. Therefore, it is crucial to understand the current water regime when considering a new role for landscapes within the highly dynamic urban development corridors expanding east and west of the Nile Valley and along the coast lines of the Mediterranean and Red Sea.

The climate of Egypt and the advent of climate change and its impact on this highly vulnerable region further frame the question of how to design open spaces to mitigate and to adapt, also to future conditions. We are challenged both by too little water, with one of the highest desertification rates globally, as well as too much water as heavy rains result in flash floods, and coastal areas will be impacted by sea level rise. These extreme landscape conditions, both in terms of temperature amplitudes and water availability, are redefining the systemic role of landscapes as environmental buffers and habitat for the urban realm.

In this chapter and with the timeline, we want to give an overview of Egypt's natural and man-made landscape conditions to understand how they evolved over time to have arrived at current agricultural and landscape design practices.

أحوال تحولات
المناظر الطبيعية

Agricultural Land Reclamation, Western Desert, Egypt

Photo: Monique Jüttner

Evolving Landscapes

Hanaa Nazer, Cornelia Redeker

Landscapes and Climate Zones

The diversity of Egyptian landscapes offers habitat and hospitable microclimates to a wide array of local communities and species. On an area of roughly 1000 square kilometers with coastlines along the Mediterranean and Red Sea of roughly 1000 km each, we find four physiogeographic regions: The Nile Valley and Delta, the Western Desert, the Eastern Desert, and Sinai. Together they host five main habitat systems with desert, pasture land, agricultural crop land, marine habitat and mountain habitat. Egypt can be divided into four bioclimatic zones: the Eastern desert, which is hyper arid with mild winters, hot summers and extremely rare rainfall; the Southern Sinai region which is also hyper arid but has cool winters, hot summers, and less than 30 mm/year of rainfall; the coastal belt along the Mediterranean Sea; and the sub-coastal belt and the wetlands in the Nile Valley and Delta. 99% of the current population is living on less than 4% of the land due to the fact that 92% of the country is arid.[1]

The Red Sea and the Nile Basin are two main routes along the Palearctic-tropics journey of migrating birds, for which the Mediterranean wetlands make up vital resting stations.[2] Together with climate change, urbanization is considered one of the largest threats to wildlife (including many bird species) due to habitat loss and fragmentation. It is not only new urban developments that lead to habitat loss, but also the transformation of existing or remaining green areas through the planting of non-native plant species, managed lawns, and removal of the mid-story canopy.[3]

Climate (Change) in Egypt

Beyond severe temperature differences between day and night and summer and winter, Egypt, due to its rapidly increasing population and urbanization, is vulnerable to climate change. Agriculture, coastal zones, aquaculture and fisheries, water resources, human habitat and settlements, and human health are the most affected sectors in order of severity and certainty of results.[4] For the most part, it is not too much but too little water that urges for a water-sensitive approach to urban and landscape design to accommodate a burgeoning population increasing by approximately 1 million inhabitants every 10 months. Increasing temperatures due to climate change resulting in higher evaporation and higher water demands as well as a potential increase in the water claimed by upstream riparian countries will lead to decreasing water levels and, thus, a greater water stress.[5] At the same time, sea level rise from the Mediterranean will severely impact the Alexandria region as well as new urban developments along the North coast. An assessment of the vulnerability of Alexandria alone suggests that a rise of only 50 cm may demand the evacuation of more than 2 million people.[6] In addition, the lowering of ground water tables through increasing extraction will allow rising sea waters to enter the aquifers and lead to further salination of the already scarce fresh water. Yes, it hardly rains in Egypt, but when it does, there is often heavy rainfall over a short period of time. As a consequence of urbanization, resulting flash floods have created enormous economic damage in recent years. Failure to consider topography, the increase of impervious surfaces such as asphalt and concrete, and a street section that does not include canalization correspondingly produce run-off. At the same time, flash floods do, however, offer enormous potential in terms of rainwater harvesting. This ancient practice is currently being explored as an additional freshwater source or directly for irrigation.[7] Throughout Egypt, spring and autumn are the seasons with a mild climate, except for some days in April, when the general wind direction changes from the prevalent Northern winds to the warm Southern winds often resulting in sand storms known as Hamseen. This is another context in which green buffers can make communities more resilient to conditions of heat, dust formation, erosion and resulting desertification. A previous project to alleviate related impacts is the 'Green Belt Greater Cairo' (around 100 km in length) planned by the Ministry of Environment.[8] During the summer months, most regions in Egypt suffer from heat stress. Overall well-being and economic performance are therefore reliant on active cooling through air-conditioning to ensure thermal comfort inside of buildings, producing a major economic and environmental burden due to the amount of energy consumed as well as heat emissions from the ACs which lead to a rise in outside temperatures in the direct vicinity.[9] So, how can one make use of climatic factors when planning cities and villages while preserving the native environment and minimizing the negative impacts of a highly incompatible modernist urbanization practice?

Climate Adaptation – The Vernacular

Traditionally, inhabitants of the Egyptian Desert overcame local climate problems by creating a comfortable living environment suitable for stability and survival by carefully choosing sites and building materials such as mud, sand and salt bricks, but also by designing a responsive urban morphology according to prevailing winds.[10] Urban squares and open courtyards of traditional houses, partially covered with green surfaces and a central water fountain, regulate the heat by taking advantage of the large difference in temperature between night and day and the differential pressure between the narrow shaded alleys and entrances and the open square or courtyard in the early hours of the day and evening hours. Rows of trees and green spaces work as windbreakers and filters to rid the air of dust particles and sand and to reduce temperatures. When ventilation and moisture are increased, the walls respond by absorbing the moisture from the air that passes through the building or, indeed, the city. Air intake through a wind catcher in combination with organic materials used in traditional construction purify and moisturize the air. Mud brick buildings are able to maintain a constant temperature between 21 – 23° C, whereas, in a comparable setting, concrete brick buildings, with their high conductivity, exceed outside temperatures by 9 degrees. The thickness of mud brick walls of up to 75 cm enables the delayed arrival of high temperatures by ten to twelve hours, and thus the thermal resistance of the mud brick wall is 13 times greater than that of the concrete wall.[11]

Anthropogenic Landscapes

The severe upheaval the Nile ecosystem underwent with the large-scale hydro construction of the Aswan Low and High Dam led to Egypt's cut with the natural cyclic water provisions the seasonal floods supplied. This paradigm change from living with nature to the modernist concept of controlling nature impacted Egypt far beyond the advent of a new industrialized agricultural practice. It gave rise to a new

Schematic section (horizontal scale 1:10 000)

urban planning and building practice and consequently a change in life style.
When considering the built environment today, cities account for 2/3 of global energy consumption and more than 70% of CO_2 emissions. The majority of currently used building materials, be it for their economic advantage (such as red brick and concrete), usability (asphalt) or their appearance (steel-glass constructions) do not prove resilient in extreme weather conditions such as heat stress, sand storms or heavy rains, and neither does the contemporary urban layout of new cities. Specifically in the summer months, thermal comfort is rarely achieved for outdoor spaces and fully relies on artificial cooling of the interior. Due to lacking shade and a lack of continuous networks, open spaces today are for the most part unwalkable and also not cyclable. In addition, streetscapes, urban layouts and regional development are prioritizing cars. This not only creates a hostile environment for pedestrians, but also produces car reliance. A recent study looking at air, noise and light pollution together, considered Cairo, where roughly 20% of Egyptians live, the most polluted city in the world.[12] Combined with one of the lowest green area ratios per inhabitant and highest population and building densities globally, this creates detrimental effects on human health and well-being.

Vulnerability and Threat – The Importance of Landscape

Beyond the creation of Egypt's 30 protectorates (Law 102, 1983), landscape today is rediscovered in its integrative capacity to reduce our ecological footprint while creating livable environments in the urban context. Environmental buffers on different scales, for example the planting of trees and greening rooftops or facades, is therefore a crucial and doable strategy to improve living conditions for the vastly urbanizing landscapes of Egypt. Walkable environments demand new, more shaded and more green street sections, as well as short-distance cross-connections between blocks and attractive and safe open areas that make walking more attractive. Coupled with the continuous improvement of public transportation, this would create more healthy ways of movement which would not only reduce CO_2 emissions, but incentivize physical movement contributing to an overall improvement of health and well-being. With its urbanized agricultural land, large-scale infrastructures, and reclaimed desert land for new cities and agricultural production, as well as its vastly urbanizing coastlines partially below the expected rising sea levels, as in many countries, the anthropogenic landscapes of Egypt are currently highly vulnerable and pose a future threat to the livelihood of its inhabitants. This risk places strategic importance on the role of landscape and open space design to provide environmental buffers, sponges, habitat, humidity, and clean air, as well as to provide for water filtration, carbon sequestration, and as a source of food and resources. Landscapes have the potential to improve microclimates and mitigate the adverse impacts of the extreme desert climate, as well as the increase in temperatures, and other extreme weather conditions and events while simultaneously creating new livelihoods. This calls for an integrated, multi-scalar approach to strategic planning and urban design where landscape architecture becomes pivotal in multiple ways.

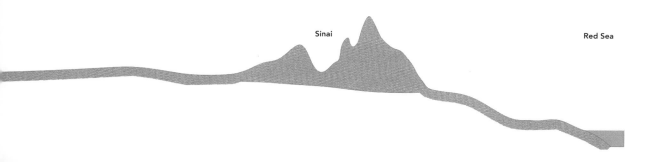

Sinai   Red Sea

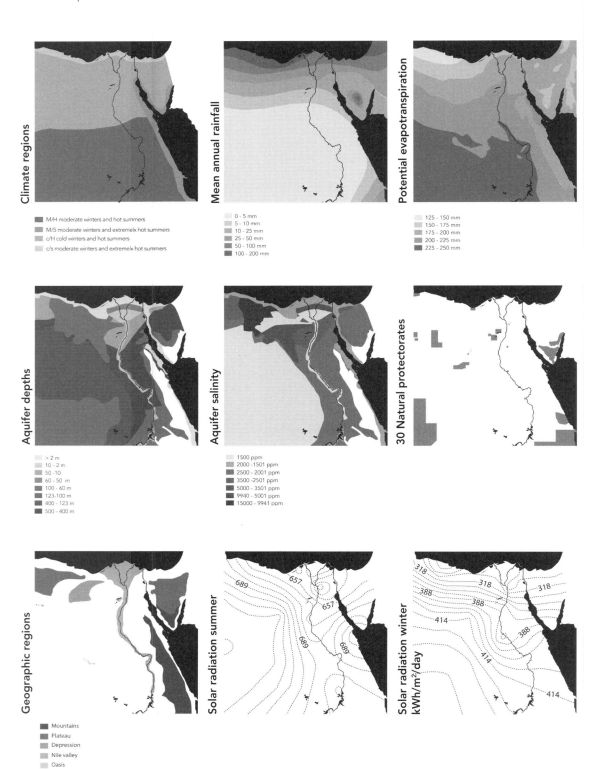

Climate regions

- M/H moderate winters and hot summers
- M/S moderate winters and extremelx hot summers
- c/H cold winters and hot summers
- c/s moderate winters and extremelx hot summers

Mean annual rainfall

- 0 - 5 mm
- 5 - 10 mm
- 10 - 25 mm
- 25 - 50 mm
- 50 - 100 mm
- 100 - 200 mm

Potential evapotranspiration

- 125 - 150 mm
- 150 - 175 mm
- 175 - 200 mm
- 200 - 225 mm
- 225 - 250 mm

Aquifer depths

- > 2 m
- 10 - 2 m
- 50 -10
- 60 - 50 m
- 100 - 60 m
- 123-100 m
- 400 - 123 m
- 500 - 400 m

Aquifer salinity

- 1500 ppm
- 2000 -1501 ppm
- 2500 - 2001 ppm
- 3500 -2501 ppm
- 5000 - 3501 ppm
- 9940 - 5001 ppm
- 15000 - 9941 ppm

30 Natural protectorates

Geographic regions

- Mountains
- Plateau
- Depression
- Nile valley
- Oasis
- Desert

Solar radiation summer

Solar radiation winter
kWh/m²/day

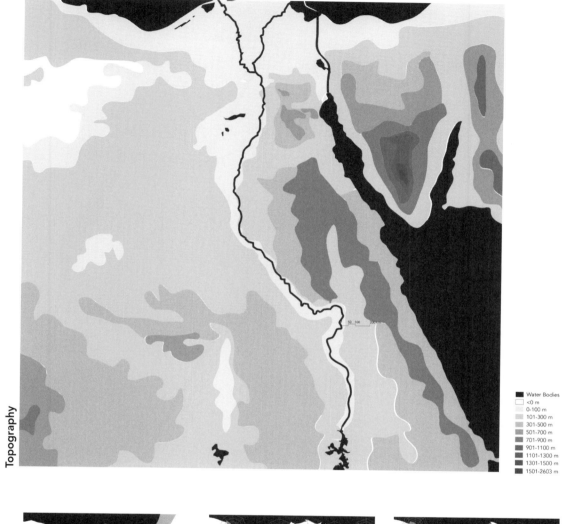

Topography

Water Bodies
<0 m
0-100 m
101-300 m
301-500 m
501-700 m
701-900 m
901-1100 m
1101-1300 m
1301-1500 m
1501-2603 m

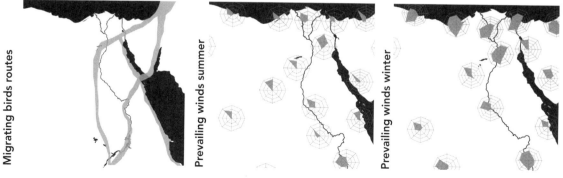

Migrating birds routes

Prevailing winds summer

Prevailing winds winter

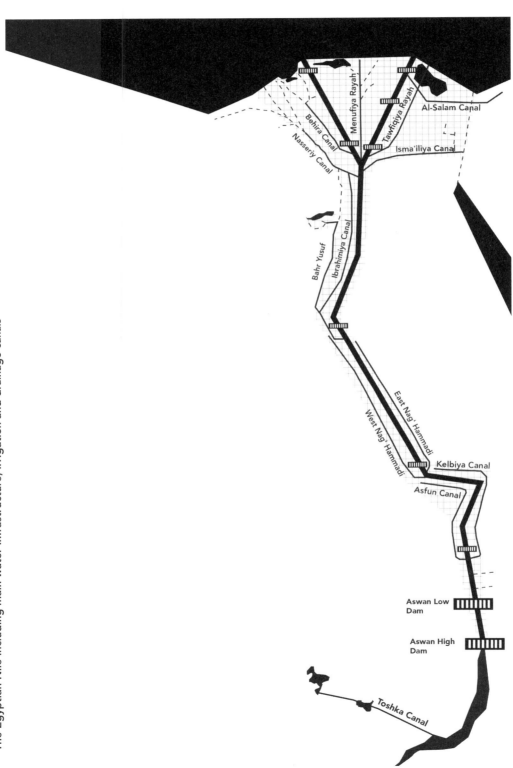

The Egyptian Nile including main water infrastructure, irrigation and drainage canals

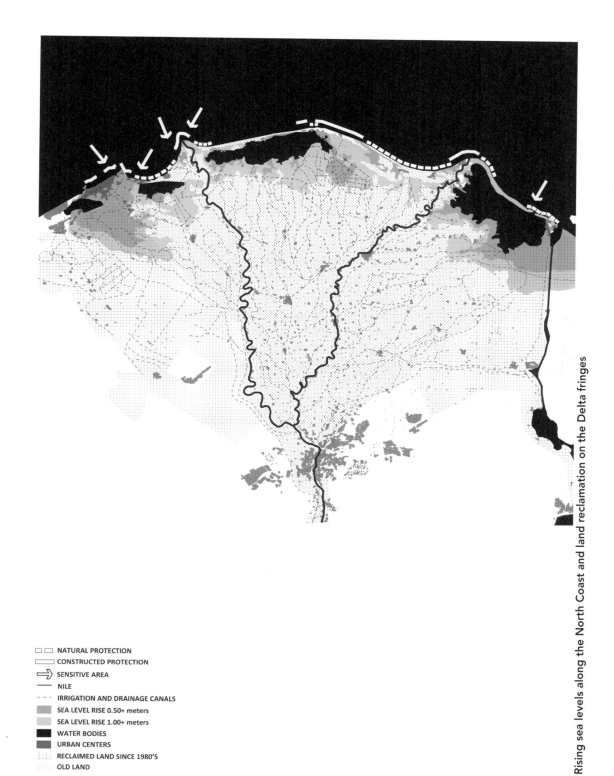

Rising sea levels along the North Coast and land reclamation on the Delta fringes

☐ ☐ NATURAL PROTECTION
☐☐ CONSTRUCTED PROTECTION
⇒ SENSITIVE AREA
— NILE
- - - IRRIGATION AND DRAINAGE CANALS
▨ SEA LEVEL RISE 0.50+ meters
▨ SEA LEVEL RISE 1.00+ meters
■ WATER BODIES
▨ URBAN CENTERS
▥ RECLAIMED LAND SINCE 1980'S
▨ OLD LAND

أحوال تحولات
المناظر الطبيعية

Real Estate Advertisement Ringroad, Cairo

Photo: Peter Blodau, Urs Walter

Landscaping Practices
From Symbiosis to Commodification

Eman Farouk, Cornelia Redeker

Pharaonic Hieroglyphs glorified productive landscape elements present in the Egyptian context at the time. Today's billboards glorify an appealing landscape dream that is, however, incompatible with the urgencies of contemporary Egypt. The following is an exploration of evolving landscaping practices from the Pharaonic period until today. As an ancient agrarian society, Egypt has brought forth cultural landscapes as distinctive as its extreme environments, further impacted by the severity of their anthropogenic transformations. These specific geographic and climatic conditions, framed by a lack of rain and, since more than a century, the suspension of Nile floods are making any kind of cultivation reliant on artificial fertilization and engineering to transport water both horizontally and vertically.

Symbiotic Landscapes of the Past
Pharaonic Landscapes
During Pharaonic times, Egyptians associated Nile floods with the onset of the Sirius Calendar and the god Hapi, holding festivals in his honour. Retained by dikes, basins were filled from the Nile during flooding. Due to the annual supply of natural silt as a natural fertilizer, the basin irrigation system did not tax the agricultural land.[1] Typically, lands at higher elevations were supplied through water-lifting techniques such as the shaduf and the saqiya.[2] Primary crops included date palms, sycamores, papyrus and wheat. Also, gardens included water storing elements that were filled during flooding periods. The Pharaonic Empire was defined by the rhythm of the flood both spiritually and socio-economically. Some historians assume that slaves and workers may have been working seasonally by dividing their time between agriculture and construction. With Nile water level fluctuations of up to twelve meters,[3] Nilometers were used to estimate forthcoming harvests and to define according taxes. The abundance and excess of crops harvested in the fertile Nile Valley with its rich, natural silt deposits further enabled export and trade (during the Ptolemaic and Roman Rule also), and its provision of wheat coined Egypt the granary of the Roman Empire.

Given the difficulties of excavating gardens, archaeological remains and inscriptions in tombs and temples picturing garden design elements have helped to determine Pharaonic garden construction, function, and symbolism. Tombs of temple garden caretakers give detailed records of the layout and description of the plants through murals.[4] Ancient Egyptian religious culture manifested in both architectural and landscape design. Certain native plants were considered sacred: the date palm represented Re, Papyrus represented Horus, etc.[5] Myths were manifested by adding a plant or building in the place where mythological events were believed to have happened.[6] In the temple gardens, a sacred building was erected wherever a spiritual being was believed to reside. In both domestic and palatial gardens, Egyptians included sacred productive plants as a reminder of their beliefs.[7] Despite the abandonment of polytheism by Akhenaten, the use of plants and garden layouts persisted throughout 3,000 years of Dynastic Pharaonic and Ptolemaic rule followed by the Roman Empire.[8]

Islamic Landscapes
Rulers of the Early Islamic Empire as well as merchants and farmers were motivated to improve the agricultural sector given its apparent economic benefits, yet without making any significant changes or investments in the existing water infrastructure. Instead, rulers focussed on maintaining the canal and basin system inherited from previous times.[9] The production of manuals and calendars was subsidized by the Caliphate. Some sources were based on Pharaonic and Hellenistic records, others included comparing, verifying and documenting current agricultural methods. The manuals described crop types, crop rotation, mixed cropping (polyculture), pollination, etc. In addition, some manuals describe the optimum location to start farming or establishing a garden. These manuals rarely included a description of gardens as they were primarily concerned with farming methods.

Land tenure in Egypt during the first five centuries of Islamic Rule (7th-12th century) was framed by improved assessment and taxation methods to increase the state share, at that time diminished by lacking control over unentitled shares by the collecting agencies and repeated tax revolts by the peasants.[10] By Ottoman times, property relationships in Egypt had transformed to include forms of private land ownership framed by a hierarchy of shared claims both of the land itself and its produce. The sultan was the legal owner of most agricultural land, while the state was authorized to tax the land and responsible for the infrastructure maintenance work through the use of the *corvée*. This included a layer of intermediaries who were responsible for individual villages and received partial revenue shares or private sections from the land. The peasants held traditional rights to cultivate and live on the land. In years of droughts or extreme floods, taxes would be adapted.[11]

To understand Islamic gardens, researchers rely on maps, travelogues and archaeological remains. Generally, Islamic garden culture began as a secular response to the needs of organizing space, controlling nature and enhancing crop yield. Earlier Roman and Persian models with four-quadrant geometrical layouts sub-organized by axial water courses and walkways became an inspiration for the main Islamic garden form, the *chahar bagh*, in all its variations throughout the Orient. Symbolism was attached to the gardens later in history by relating qur'anic metaphors of paradise to these layouts, as well as the ruler's success and divine blessing.[12]

Unlike existing misconceptions of Islamic cities as fortified and barren cities within the desert, they were "a unique blend of nature and human settlement. Low building density was maintained in order to preserve a strong relationship with greenery".[13] As the maps of Piri Reis[14] show, Cairo and Alexandria were fortified. They were, however, surrounded by fruit orchards and agrarian fields towards the Nile. In 1046, traveler Nasir Khusraw witnessed orchards and gardens between the palaces in Cairo, although he does not mention specific features. He also talks of orchards between Fustat and Qahira that are submerged during flooding season – with the exception of the ruler's gardens, which are situated on a higher plateau. Other travelers indicate that farming was also practiced within the city walls.[15] Archaeological excavations in Fatimid Cairo show that most houses were built around courtyards. Some of these courtyards contained shrubs, garden beds and low trees along with fountains and watercourses. Also, many mosques contained courtyard gardens.

Khusraw speaks of Cairo as a vibrant city with 7-14 story high buildings describing one rooftop garden containing orange and banana trees, as well as herbs and flower beds.[16] Archaeologists have found wall flues and stairwells for wastewater which indicate the presence of upper stories or roof gardens.[17] Many of these practices faced deterioration during the late Ottoman rule. This changed with the arrival of the French in 1798 and the beginning of viceroy Mohamed Ali's tenure in 1805, which marked the advent of modernization in Egypt. An important Islamic public water feature found throughout the Islamic world is the sabil, a drinking fountain charitably endowed with the intention by a donor seeking to gain a reward in the

Water Conditions
in Egypt

Mohie El-Din Omar

Introduction

In Egypt, the per capita water share has dropped below the threshold of water poverty. The water deficit represents the most forbidding obstacle against the development of landscape gardening and new reclaimed agricultural areas. The high population growth, water scarcity, and potential impact of climate changes have raised the level of management and financial investments for enhancing water use efficiency of different sectors. The gardening and plant growing activities of landscape should focus on changing from a culture of water abundance to water scarcity that is expected in the future. With the current state of water scarcity, this chapter presents an assessment of Egypt's water system challenges and policies.

Assessment of current water status

Water resources

Egypt lies in a semi-arid to arid region, where most of its renewable fresh water is transported by the Nile River from the Ethiopian Highlands and the Equatorial Plateau. The available conventional fresh water supply is 59.8 billion cubic meters per year (BCM/y), comprising Egypt's Nile water quota of 55.5 BCM/y, non-renewable deep groundwater (2.4 BCM/y), and coastal winter rainfall and flash floods of about 1.6 BCM/y, in addition to the desalination of seawater and brackish water (0.3 BCM/y) (Omar and Moussa, 2016). Non-conventional resources include reuse of agricultural drainage water, wastewater and industrial wastewater, as well as the shallow aquifer in the Nile Valley and the Nile Delta.

Conventional Water Resources

Nile River: Its source is the Ethiopian Plateau representing 85% of the river's yield at Aswan, and the Great Lakes and the South of Sudan representing 15%. Due to its annual flow variance and the succession of droughts and floods, the Nile River is completely controlled by the Aswan High Dam and seven barrages between Aswan and the Mediterranean Sea.

Deep groundwater: Its total quantity is 2.4 BCM/y. In terms of groundwater hydrology, Egypt can be divided into four provinces; Western Desert, Eastern Desert, Sinai Peninsula, and Northern Coastal Zone. The Nubian Sandstone Aquifer in the Western Desert is the largest in North Africa. There are substantial quantities in this aquifer, including the oases of Al-Dakhla, Al-Kharga, Al-Farafra, Siwa, East Al-Owaynat, and Darb Al-Arbe'en. However, the quantity that can be readily economically viable is limited. Groundwater in this aquifer was formed during successive rainy ages, and its ability to replenish is limited. In the Western Desert, 1.75 BCM/y is being utilized, while additional potential for future development plans stands at 2 BCM/y (MWRI, 2010).

Rainfall and flashfloods. Rainfall is very scarce except in a narrow strip along the northern coastal areas. Annual precipitation rates in the northwestern coast range between 192 mm/y in Alexandria to 102 mm/y in Al-Saloum, and gradually decrease eastwards reaching 80 mm/y in Port Said. Then they increase to 100 mm/y in Al-Arish, and climb sharply to 300 mm/y in Rafah. Flash floods occur in the Red

Sea area and in southern Sinai. Flash floods are utilized by dams and ground reservoirs. Rainwater and flash floods on the coasts of the Red Sea, Sinai, and the Mediterranean Sea are the foremost sources for Bedouins and tribes in these areas. The aggregate quantities of rainwater currently utilized is estimated at 1.6 BCM/y.

Desalination: Seawater desalination will be one of the most significant water resources in Egypt, which is bordered by the Red Sea to the east and the Mediterranean Sea to the North allowing a successful implementation of desalination units. The only remaining element is the high cost. The total quantity of desalinated water is 0.3 BCM/y. If seawater desalination is compared to that of saline or brackish, where salinity ranges between 1,500 to 5,000 ppm, it has a higher economic feasibility.

Non-conventional Water Resources
There are other non-conventional water resources, including: a shallow aquifer in the Nile Valley and Delta; and the reuse of agricultural drainage water and domestic and industrial wastewater. The shallow aquifer is replenished leaked water from the irrigation networks and agricultural lands. The shallow one in the coastal area in Northern Sinai is replenished by precipitation and flash-floods. The aggregate quantity of shallow ground water is 6.5 BCM/y, which is still within the limits of safe yield (8.4 BCM/y) (MWRI, 2010). Drainage reuse has been adopted officially since the late seventies by pumping from main and branch drains to fresh water in main and branch canals. Current agricultural drainage reuse is 15 BCM/y including water taken by farmers directly from drains.

Water Demand
Agriculture, drinking, and industry are main water consumers. Water is also used for electricity generation, navigation and the preservation of environmental habitat, which are considered water users not consumers. Part of water resources is earmarked for the purposes of tourism, entertainment, and fisheries.

Water uses in agriculture: It is the largest water user and consumer in Egypt with an overall volume of 68.5 BCM/y (85% of total water requirements) (Omar and Moussa, 2016).

Municipal and industrial water uses: It includes water supply for major urban and rural villages. The main part of this water comes from the Nile via canals or direct intakes, while the other part comes from groundwater. The percentage of drinking water coverage nationwide has reached nearly 100%. Although desalination of seawater or brackish water represents a small fraction at the national level, it is considered a major source of drinking water in some tourist areas alongside the coasts of the Red Sea and the Sinai. The aggregate quantity of water released to the drinking water sector is 9.9 BCM/y and the industrial water requirements are 2.4 BCM/y, excluding water used for cooling power stations (Omar and Moussa, 2016).

Water uses for navigation: Navigation is considered a water user, rather than a consumer. The Nile River's main channel and part of irrigation network are being used for navigation. The construction of High Aswan Dam improved navigation conditions in the Nile and ensures an appropriate depth for navigation.

Water uses for power generation: The Nile flows over a distance of 1,200 km from the High Aswan Dam to the Mediterranean. The total annual hydroelectricity along the river is about 14,632 GW/hour generated through the power stations of the High Aswan Dam, Aswan Dam 1, Aswan Dam 2, New Isna Barrage, New Naga' Hammadi Barrage, and Al-Lahoun Regulator at Bahr Yousif. It represents about 8 % of total power generated in Egypt.

Water uses for fisheries: Fish farms have spread extensively in Egypt due to their high return in comparison to agriculture. Fish cages are distributed along water-ways. Fish farms exist in substantial numbers in agricultural lands. Currently, there are about 300,000 feddan of fish farms along canals, drains, and Northern Lakes (MWRI, 2010). About 50,000 feddan exist in Kafr Al-Sheikh, Port Said, North Sinai and Sharqiya Governorates and in the Northern Lakes. Aquaculture is currently the largest single source of fish supply in Egypt, accounting for almost 75 percent of total production, with over 99 % produced from privately owned farms. Aquaculture production in Egypt is the largest in Africa, with one million tons of annual production (Shaalan et al., 2017).

Water Balance

The current volume of conventional water resources in Egypt is 59.8 BCM/year from the Nile River, effective rainfall and non-renewable deep groundwater. However, the total current water requirements for different sectors is 81.3 BCM/year. The gap is about 21.5 BCM/year, which is compensated by reuse of drainage water, wastewater, and shallow groundwater.

Water Challenges in Egypt

The water system in Egypt has been facing many challenges, which might be concluded as following:

Limited water resources: Surface water from the Nile is fully exploited, and shallow groundwater is being brought into full production. Effective rainfall and non-renewable deep groundwater are very rare. The total water supply is 59.8 BCM/y, which cannot compensate required water demands with 81.3 BCM/y.

Obstacles against improving the water use efficiency: The MWRI has been executing a number of projects for reducing seepage losses from waterways and infiltration losses from agricultural lands. However, the majority of these projects require areas for implementation, which, accordingly, require negotiations with landowners, in addition to their high costs. In municipal sector, maintenance of the long distribution network also requires high costs.

Uncertainty of climate change impacts: In recent past years, evidence of rising temperatures and changing rainfall patterns has been observed. The impacts are projected to increase both in frequency and severity. Annual temperature increased by 2.1° C, and a warming trend was observed. A precipitation decrease of 7% less than normal was observed in the period 1975 – 2005. Extreme climate events have frequently occurred during the last decade and there are indications that their intensity is increasing due to climate change (Ahmed et al., 2017). High tides coupled with large storm surges flooded large areas and coastal erosion has affected near shore areas. The flood water has reached and threatened to damage the international coastal road located hundreds of meters inland. Regarding Nile flow variation, there have been disagreements. El-Shamy and Wheater (2009c) provided a range between -60% and +45% of the Blue Nile flow by the end of the century using 17 General Circulation Models (GCMs). Strzepek & McCluskey, (2007) estimated 20 scenarios for variations of Nile flows entering Lake Nasser in 2050 and 2100 using five GCMs. They provided 12 reduced flows and 8 increased flows. Kotb (2015) presented six scenarios using Regional Circulation Model (RCM), which showed a mean annual flow increase in range of +7.15% to +23.21%.

Construction of dams on the tributaries of the Nile River: Any construction will impact the downstream discharges during the reservoir filling process. The Great Ethiopian Renaissance Dam is currently being constructed with a storage volume corresponding to approximately 1.5 years of mean discharges of the Blue Nile. During a six-year filling period, there will be an adverse impact on irrigation management of the High Aswan Dam, since agricultural water demand will be much higher than the water supply (Liersch et al. 2017).

Population increase: High population growth urges the country to undertake horizontal agricultural projects overexploiting the water. The per capita share of fresh water resources has drastically declined to about 570 cubic meters in 2018, and is expected to fall to 390 cubic meters by 2050.

Inequitable water access: The evaluation of water equitability in Egypt mainly depends on water quantity, believed to be satisfactory for the needs of farmers, all urban and most rural households. A comprehensive evaluation should comprise the sufficiency, accessibility, acceptability, and affordability. Initial evaluations indicate positive results for affordability, because irrigation water is free of charge and domestic water remains cheap compared to global prices. Insufficiency of financial resources: Implementation of long-term policies needs financial resources. Economic risks are critical in light of high long-term investments for enhancing the overall water system.

Water resources management in Egypt
There are a number of stakeholders managing the water. The Ministry of Water Resources & Irrigation (MWRI) is the main player, in charge of development and management of water resources, and operating and maintaining dams, weirs, irrigation canals and drainage canals. It monitors water quality. The Ministry of Agriculture and Land Reclamation (MALR) is involved in improving agricultural activities and land reclamation, including water management at the on-farm level. The Holding Company for Water and Wastewater (HCWW) provides water supply and sanitation services. The Ministry of Health and Population (MoHP), the Ministry of State for Environmental Affairs (MSEA), and the Ministry of Local Development (MoLD), also have cooperative and consultative roles.

Management of Irrigation Water

MWRI distributes irrigation water via an irrigation network (35,000 km) in coordination with the MALR, based on the planned cropping pattern. MWRI has been implementing various activities for enhancing the irrigation efficiency, including maintenance and lining of irrigation canals and maintenance of irrigation infrastructures. One of the remarkable projects is the Irrigation Improvement Project (IIP), which started in 1984 with the aim of improving 3.5 million feddans in the Delta by 2017, as well as minimizing water losses in the irrigation networks. The program activities include developing irrigation basins and laser leveling, as well as crop rotation.

Management of Drainage Water

The drainage comes from canal ends, leakage from waterways, or removal of unused water from agricultural lands by flow over or through the soil. The drainage and municipal and industrial effluents are transported by an extensive drainage network comprising field drains (open drains or sub-surface drains), collector drains, and main drains into irrigation canals and the Nile River. The drainage system is largely operated by gravity, except for a number of pumping stations in the Northern Delta. Mixing drainage with fresh water at pump stations is called official reuse. Another type of official reuse is called intermediate reuse, where water can be mixed from smaller drains with lower order irrigation canals.

Management of Drinking Water and Wastewater

Egypt's policy for drinking water supply includes service delivery, introduction of modern technology in operations and maintenance, and increasing the private sector's participation. The total number of water plants is 2175 with a capacity of 25.3 MCM/y. The total length of drinking water network is 165,000 km with a coverage percentage of 96 %, while the total number of wastewater treatment plants is 400 with a capacity of 10.62 MCM/y. The safe drinking water is supplied to the entire population in 222 cities and the majority of 4617 villages. Sanitation services are less developed with a coverage of 95 % in urban areas and less than 15% in rural areas. Only 0.7 BCM/year of treated wastewater is being used in irrigation, of which 0.26 BCM (secondary treated) and 0.44 BCM (primary treated). Another 2.95 BCM/year is pumped to drains and canals in the Delta. The total allocated land for wastewater reuse projects is 88,000 feddans in different governorates (Abdel-Wahab, 2015). Industrial wastewater is particularly related to small and medium industries discharging into waterways and sewerage networks.

Mitigation and Adaptation Policies

In Egypt, there are several categories of mitigation and adaptation policies, including: policies for water resources development, for rationalization of water utilization, for infrastructure rehabilitation, for depollution, for climate change adaptation, and for institutional, legal, HR, media, and research frameworks.

تصميم لمواجهة
التحديات العالمية للمياه

Changde, Sponge City, China

Designing for Global Water Challenges

Antje Stokman

When thinking of "urban water landscapes", most people imagine urban water-fronts along clean rivers, lakes and water features within the privileged open spaces of beautifully designed urban parks, plazas and gardens. The systems of water infrastructure for the supply of freshwater, the disposal of waste and rain water and protection from dangerous floods are usually not included in our ideas about the design of urban landscapes because these are understood to be solved by engineers in a technical and preferably invisible way. Our modern cities' "clean urbanism" (de Meulder 2008) is based on centrally organized and mostly underground infrastructure systems that transport drinking, rain and wastewater for hundreds and thousands of miles. The designs of architects, landscape architects and urban designers are usually based on the assumption that clean water is available and dirty as well as rain water can be disposed of, without them having to understand and take care about it. Contemporary landscape and urban design look at urban landscapes with mainly aesthetic considerations, constrained by an attachment to the picturesque. The predominant methods and techniques are based around an architectural paradigm of "final form" or a static outcome which should be kept by maintenance and prevent nature to "invade" and destroy the design (Yu, 2006).

However, the increasing speed, intensity and unpredictability of urban development in many cities around the world seriously outpaces the provision of high-standard water infrastructure and intensive urban greening. As a consequence, most megacities suffer under extreme water pollution and hygienic problems due to unsolved water management. In many cases the provision of drinkable water and sewerage services (especially to the residents of informal settlements) has been abandoned. Low-cost engineering solutions in the form of open wastewater channels, open sewage and flood basins and concreted river channels, leading through unmanaged open spaces, become a common sight within the urban fabric, especially in the outskirts of growing cities. These infrastructural water landscapes appear as dirty and dangerous no-go-zones within cities that are hostile towards people and the environment (Fig. 1).

Fig. 1 Dirty Urban Water Landscapes are dangerous no-go-zones within cities that are hostile towards people and the environment. Photo: Antje Stokman

Appropriating nature-based Water Purification Systems as Part of the Urban Landscape

As Elisabeth Mossop and Kongjian Yu suggest in their claims for "affordable landscapes" (Mossop 2005) and "Recovering landscape architecture as the art of survival" (Yu 2006), we should shift away from our current focus on privileged and expensive landscapes towards nature-based solutions to solve landscape problems related to urbanisation. As described above, one of the key problems of the current urbanisation is related to conventional concepts of water engineering – and a lot of money needs to be invested into exploring new solutions in the future.

In the 21st century, new concepts of "water urbanisms" (Shannon et. al. 2008) and "water-sensitive urban design" (Hoyer et. al. 2011) are starting to emerge, forming a new basis for interdisciplinary cooperations. The need for less expensive and more flexible forms of urban water infrastructure systems can be seen as a strategic chance to generate new ideas about built and managed nature-based systems of blue and green infrastructure that provide multiple economic, ecological and cultural functions. This means that the designers who are not used to thinking beyond beautiful, controlled and clean water need to get involved in technical ideas of storing, purifying and conducting waste and flood water – and the engineers need to think beyond the efficiency and functionality aspects of technical systems by integrating them into their cultural, social, aesthetic and ecological context. In the following part, two case-studies from China (Changde) and Peru (Lima) will be introduced to illustrate how to integrate nature-based waste water purification systems in designed urban landscapes.

Design for Flood Prevention and Waste Water Purification: Case Study Sponge City, Changde (China)

The water city of Changde is located in the western plain of Lake Dongting on the shore of the Yuan River, which is one of the four major tributaries of the Yangtse River in Southern China. Due to Changde's fast rapid growth, the amount of sealed surfaces and uncontrolled wastewater disposal is increasing drastically. To protect the densely built-up city from floods, all rivers and canals have been engineered to pass around and under it, rather than through it. Most of the historic canals that used to crisscross the city were filled in and became part of a vast network of underground water pipes, pumps and sewer systems, which are neither visible nor accessible. The Chuanzi river, passing through the north of the city, was cut off from its natural inflow and turned into a stagnating water body. This situation results in severe problems of flooding as well as water pollution, caused by the overflow from seventeen combined rainwater-retention and sewage basins located along the Chuanzi river (Fig. 2).

The initial design proposals for developing the polluted river to become part of a new waterfront park with adjacent new city districts envisioned a costly centralized and underground solution to solve the problem. Based on combined research studies developed within the framework of an EU-funded Asia Pro Eco project from 2005 to 2008, two expert teams from Changde and Hanover developed an alternative solution: Rather than investing a huge sum of money into a purely technical solution and an expensive park design, it was proposed to create an urban river landscape that makes use of the obvious synergies between affordable engineering approaches and the need to improve the ecological and social functions of the river landscape. Recognizing the potential in the results of these studies, in 2008 the municipality commissioned an interdisciplinary group of firms and academics from Wasser Hannover to develop a Framework Masterplan on Sustainable and Ecological Water Resource Management in Changde as a model project.

This plan proposed concrete guidelines and projects for creating an urban water landscape with a clear connection between the underlying hydrological system and hydraulic engineering as the major structural foundation of urban planning, including the use of catchment areas as the basis for physical planning and regulation. At the same time, it proposed a series of measures for nature-based solutions to infiltrate rainwater, purify wastewater and restore the river ecology – all based on low-tech, ecological approaches to engineering and urban water management. Building up on these proposals, a series of pilot projects were implemented throughout Changde by Wasser Hannover and other design teams. These demonstrate how flood protection, drainage, and water purification systems – as hybrids of built infrastructure, ecological functions and public green space – can serve as

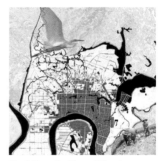

Fig. 2 Along the Chuanzi River in Changde, there used to be 17 open retention basins with heavily polluted water, situated adjacent to public and private open spaces in the middle of the city. Graphic: Antje Stokman

Fig. 3 Clean outflow from water treatment park with constructed wetland alongside Chuanzi River after implementation of the pilot project. Photo: Lothar Fuchs

fundamental components of change in the urban landscape. The upgrading of several water-retention basins along the Chuanzi River illustrates how the low-cost and nature-based improvement of their technical performance can be combined with affordable measures to improve the design and ecology of the waterfront park. Technically, the basins are subdivided into several chambers to assure that the water gets treated in different ways, according to the quantity and quality of the water. After a first pre-treatment, the mixed overflow (storm and sewage water) from the basins is cleaned in a series of constructed wetlands that become an essential part of the river park's landscape design (Fig. 3).

Based on their success in becoming one of the first Model Sponge Cities of the Chinese national government in 2013, Changde was able to secure further funding to implement even more projects. Embedded in a riparian waterfront design with multifunctional flood zones and levees, the upgraded water retention basins served as a starting point for the design of new public water landscapes by many interdisciplinary teams of hydraulic engineers and landscape architects. Making use of dynamic and self-correcting natural processes, the new river park performs as an artificial ecology that is characterized by a high degree of ecological resilience, requires little intervention and technical control while, at the same time, offering attractive landscape experiences and creating high urban biodiversity (Fig. 4). The park invites people to spend their time near the water and offers enough space for a large variety of recreational functions. As an expression of cooperation and friendship, the city of Changde built its own Hanover district, including German shops and coffee houses, right on the shore of the Chuanzi River, which was jointly opened by the two mayors in October 2016.

Fig. 4 The new riparian waterfront design alongside Chuanzi River integrated technical water treatment and improved river ecology to strengthen the self-cleansing capacity of the river. Photo: Lothar Fuchs

Design for Drought Prevention and Waste Water Purification: Case Study Lima Beyond the Park, Peru

The desert city Lima is located on a coast overlooking the Pacific Ocean. With its more than 9.5 million inhabitants, Lima is considered the second most extensive desert city in the world after Cairo. It has an average of only nine millimeters of rainfall per year. The glaciers feeding its three main rivers are melting, and the groundwater table has already reached critical levels. However, the majority of urban green areas are designed in a decorative manner, based on water-intensive lawns and artificial ponds, with little consideration for the desert environment. This results in a high demand for irrigation water, which is actually increased by the inhabitants' lack of awareness of water-saving and by inefficient technology. Only a small amount (only ten percent in 2011) of the total treated wastewater is officially reused for irrigation, while the use of drinking water for irrigation purposes puts even more stress on the expensive and scarce water resources.

At the same time, Lima is facing a vast expansion of informal settlements. Around twenty percent of Lima's population, mainly living in the hilly and peri-urban areas, lack many basic urban services including water supply and wastewater infrastructure, which has caused severe sanitary problems as well as environmental degradation. They receive drinking water, often of very bad quality, from private water vendors at high prices. To sustain farming and greening, in many informal settlements untreated wastewater is unofficially misused for irrigation purposes, with serious hygiene consequences (Fig. 5). Therefore, Lima's urban landscapes need radical rethinking to make water and landscape

systems perform in concert with one another and keep up with the increasing demand for water in a growing, more liveable and greener city.

From 2008 to 2014, a German-Peruvian research project on sustainable water management initiated developed strategies, tools and pilot projects for Lima's future water-sensitive urban development. A new approach combining infrastructure design with urban landscape design acted as a catalyst for urban transformation and assisted in developing an alternative water culture for Lima's future. Different strategies were developed to incorporate the water cycle into a multifunctional open-space system, which at the same time is designed to improve and protect the water cycle and act as a framework for urban development. Based on satellite imagery analyses and GIS-based tools, the project developed general planning principles and policy recommendations, a design manual as well as a simple design-testing and water-demand calculation tool.

In order to demonstrate water-sensitive urban development in practice, the lower Chillon River watershed to the north of Lima was chosen as a demonstration area to guide the implementation of a water-sensitive demonstration area (Fig. 6). It proposed several strategic pilot projects for communicating, testing, and promoting different low-tech and decentralized water-purification technologies as part of design strategies, such as reusing non-potable water for irrigation, catching fog to harvest water, and implementing less water-consuming planting design. By starting the process with a series of minimal temporary installations built within a series of interdisciplinary summerschools, the viability of various concepts was discussed with experts from a number of institutions as well as the local community (Fig. 7). Their implementation, inauguration and the resulting public exhibitions of results in the city center of Lima focused attention on the topics and the necessity of water-sensitive urban development in this zone.

Building on these experiences, a first pilot project was designed to demonstrate that a park can treat the contaminated water in existing irrigation channels to reuse it for irrigating urban green areas, thereby using less water than a conventional park, and at the same time creating an attractive public space for the community. The park was implemented in 2014 and is composed of three main parts, including a constructed wetland system with a reservoir for treated wastewater, a green recreational area with fruit trees, and a children's play area with dry surfaces and drought-resistant trees to provide shade (Fig. 8).

Fig. 5 Around 20 percent of the population in Lima, Peru, does not have access to public water supply, which leads to a practice of informally using wastewater to irrigate planted areas and thus create a minimum of green space in the desert. Photo: Antje Stokman

Fig. 7 During two interdisciplinary summer schools the students worked on site with local authorities and residents to design and build a series of minimal temporary installations, testing the viability of various concepts of redesigning the local water cycle. Photo: Maximilian Mehlhorn

Fig. 6: The lower Chillon River watershed in the north of Lima, Peru, was chosen as a demonstration area in order to develop a Strategic Landscape Framework Plan to integrate water management and landscape planning with social, cultural, and economic aspects, guiding the implementation of several pilot projects. Map: ILPOE, University of Stuttgart

Fig. 8 The Parque de los Niños in Lima, Peru was implemented as a pilot project in 2014. It is composed of three parts, a constructed wetland system with a reservoir for treated wastewater, a green recreational area with fruit trees, and a children's play area with dry surfaces and drought-resistant trees to provide shade. The section shows the constructed wetland which treats the contaminated water of existing irrigation channels and creates an attractive public space for the community at the same time. This water is then reused for the irrigation of urban green areas. Credits: ILPOE, University of Stuttgart

Fig. 9 Children playing in the Parque de los Niños in 2017, three years after project implementation, with the constructed wetland serving as a green element within the park. Despite some challenges in maintenance and operation by the district administration, the neighbors managed to secure the existence of the park based on community engagement.
Photos: Evelyn Merino-Reyna, Lima (top) Antje Stokman (bottom)

Based on a participatory approach, the park's design phase was used to re-establish a dialogue between neighbors, the irrigation commission and the local planning authorities. The park's performance, maintenance and use by the neighbors has been monitored since then by local universities and has proven to be successful despite some challenges (Fig. 9).

Another kind of beauty – water infrastructure as a spatial and aesthetic framework of the urban landscape

The modern ideal of "clean urbanism" with its invisible water infrastructure has disconnected the land-use from the logics of the watershed as well as people's experience from the water-related processes of the landscape. The potentials of modern water infrastructure systems for shaping urban form and meeting broader human, ecological and aesthetic objectives have almost been lost. Facing the simultaneous worldwide processes of extreme and unpredictable urban growth and decline coupled with the huge challenges concerning the affordability and functioning of present water infrastructure conceptions, new strategies are needed.

Within the presented projects, the different elements of water infrastructure no longer relate only to their own networks defined merely by functionality and efficiency, but to their context of cultural, social and ecological processes within the urban matrix. They shift the focus from the current practice of image-based landscape design to performance-based landscape design by applying nature-based solutions. They no longer consider urban open spaces an expensive luxury, but show that designed landscapes can purify polluted water and restore ecologies. The large investments necessary to build new cities and construct new infrastructure systems in the fast-growing urban areas around the world give opportunities to impose radically new spatial configurations at the level of infrastructural, landscape and urban planning. This opportunity can be considered a strategic chance to strengthen the cooperation between civil engineers, ecologists, urban designers, architects and landscape architects. By reuniting the built and the natural we may find new logics towards a more resilient development of infrastructural landscapes as a base of sustainable urban and regional form.

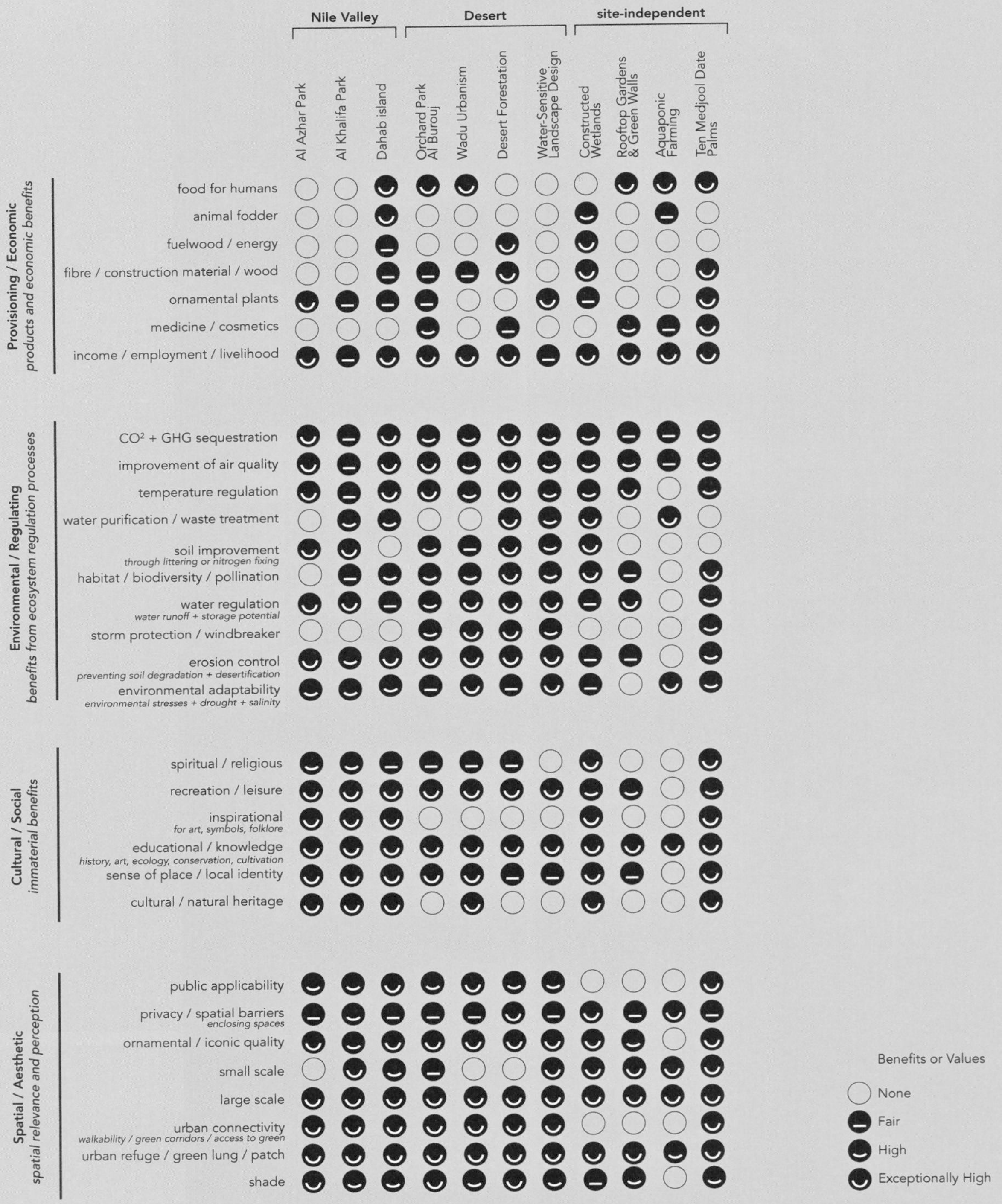

Columns (case studies):

Nile Valley:
- Al Azhar Park
- Al Khalifa Park
- Dahab island

Desert:
- Orchard Park Al Burouj
- Wadu Urbanism
- Desert Forestation
- Water-Sensitive Landscape Design

site-independent:
- Constructed Wetlands
- Rooftop Gardens & Green Walls
- Aquaponic Farming
- Ten Medjool Date Palms

Provisioning / Economic
products and economic benefits
- food for humans
- animal fodder
- fuelwood / energy
- fibre / construction material / wood
- ornamental plants
- medicine / cosmetics
- income / employment / livelihood

Environmental / Regulating
benefits from ecosystem regulation processes
- CO^2 + GHG sequestration
- improvement of air quality
- temperature regulation
- water purification / waste treatment
- soil improvement
  through littering or nitrogen fixing
- habitat / biodiversity / pollination
- water regulation
  water runoff + storage potential
- storm protection / windbreaker
- erosion control
  preventing soil degradation + desertification
- environmental adaptability
  environmental stresses + drought + salinity

Cultural / Social
immaterial benefits
- spiritual / religious
- recreation / leisure
- inspirational
  for art, symbols, folklore
- educational / knowledge
  history, art, ecology, conservation, cultivation
- sense of place / local identity
- cultural / natural heritage

Spatial / Aesthetic
spatial relevance and perception
- public applicability
- privacy / spatial barriers
  enclosing spaces
- ornamental / iconic quality
- small scale
- large scale
- urban connectivity
  walkability / green corridors / access to green
- urban refuge / green lung / patch
- shade

Benefits or Values
- None
- Fair
- High
- Exceptionally High

Productive Case Studies - Benefits and Values / Overview
inspired by: De Groot et al 2002, Viljoen&Wiskerke 2012, Millennium Ecosystem Assessment 2003

02 Learning From
التعلم من

The following projects offer integrated models for green spaces in the city and revolve around local food production and water conservation, as well as socio-economical approaches to make these possible. All of them are hybrid models that have multiple functions and benefits. While some have already been implemented, others are still waiting to be translated into an urban design context. All strategies may be combined and expanded and are waiting for further exploration in terms of their landscape design performance. LEARNING FROM looks at best practice examples to then build potential scenarios.

In parallel to urban growth, DESERT AFFORESTATION may generate urban forests with the use of domestic wastewater and the sun as given resources. WADI URBANISM proposes to capitalize on the given topography to create urban vistas and benefit from the productive landscapes in the dried river bed as an orchard park. Both produce distinctive landscapes paired with economic potential instead of only high maintenance costs. Building on first approaches to become more water-efficient in current arid open space design, WATER-SENSITIVE LANDSCAPE DESIGN works with a combination of different plant and water sources to create a variation of green areas that fulfill different needs and are therefore more resource-efficient. With ORCHARD PARK as the central green area in the new city of Al Burouj in Eastern Cairo, we are currently witnessing how a big international developer is implementing a park where food is cultivated. These new urbanization models generate green areas in arid environments that are not only visually and spatially pleasing. They become productive in a variety of ways – through food cultivation, by building on the given topography, through waste water as a resource for irrigation, and of course, using the sun. In the Nile Valley (and most impressively in the megapolis Cairo) we find GEZIRET EL DAHAB, one of the Nile's 144 rural islands which offer habitat to a number of species, most prominently migrating birds, while cultivating food for local consumption and providing a green lung for the city's inhabitants. Site-independent solutions that can be realized anywhere such as CONSTRUCTED WETLANDS, ROOFTOP FARMING or AQUAPONICS show us how, on a small to medium scale, urban micro-climates and the overall spatial quality may be improved while growing food or treating waste water. While the community scale demands a certain space availability and a societal consensus, the household scale enables users to implement these solutions individually. Incrementally applied, these may become an accumulative way of mitigating, for example, urban heat islands. Building on mounds made by centuries of accumulated waste, AL AZHAR PARK integrates three large-scale water tanks to create an artificial topography that hosts an Islamic Garden Park that has become a new international landmark for the city and a much-needed green lung for the local community. On a slightly smaller scale, KHALIFA HERITAGE AND ENVIRONMENT PARK transforms a derelict site within the dense urban fabric of Islamic Cairo into a neighbourhood park that will be irrigated with captured run-off water that is currently damaging the limestone foundations of neighbouring monuments. We are also learning from new socio-economical models to make these projects happen such as a new timber industry through desert forestation or the SINAI DATE PALM FOUNDATION. Ten Mejool Date Palm trees may provide a livelihood for an entire family, and the project therefore offers a valuable maintenance incentive by creating stewardship among the trees' caretakers on a private scale, while the trees provide a number of public benefits such as shade and orientation.

Photo: © Aga Khan Trust for Culture / Kareem Ibrahim

Al Azhar Park, Islamic Cairo

Al Azhar Park
Islamic Cairo

SITES International

In 1984, at the conclusion of the seminar on "The Expanding Metropolis: Coping with the Urban Growth of Cairo" funded by the Aga Khan Award for Architecture, His Highness the Aga Khan announced that the issue of the city's diminishing green spaces were to be addressed by financing the creation of a civic park.[1] The derelict Darassa site, a 30-hectare mound of rubble adjacent to the Islamic City, was the only available open space that met the scale. This site, with its Fatimid gates, Ayyubid walls, and Mamluk mosques, was not only rich in historical monuments, but posed several technical challenges.[2] Adjacent to Cairo's City of the Dead, it had been a debris dump for over 500 years. Construction required excavation, grading and replacement with appropriate fill. In addition, three 80-meter freshwater tanks for the city of Cairo were to be incorporated into the park design. On a larger scale, the project functioned as a catalyst for positive change. Beyond the Park, the program included the restoration of monuments and public spaces in neighbouring Darb al-Ahmar and socio-economic initiatives including housing rehabilitation, microfinance, apprenticeships and healthcare.[3]

After five years of design and construction, Al Azhar Park opened to the public in June 2004. The intent was to achieve sustainability by providing accessible green open spaces for the residents of the adjacent district, as for the Greater Cairo population, while working with local artisans and laborers on the construction of the park in an effort to improve their quality of life and economic status. The landscape architects were equally keen to protect and incorporate the historic Ayyubid wall within the park. The design theme derived from the contextual heritage of Old Cairo by adapting a distinctive interpretation of Islamic gardens design. It can be viewed as an "Islamic version of the Mixed Style or as a successful postmodern pastiche. Like a mid-nineteenth century German park, it has a rectilinear core and curvilinear surroundings, yet the core draws from a range of Islamic Paradise gardens, rather than from the Baroque Style."[4]

Landscape architecture considers plants as essential design elements with a functional, visual, and environmental role. Plants and other landscape elements must be integrated and considered in the early stage of a project to achieve a homogenous and integrated design.[5] The main pedestrian spine is the key feature of Al Azhar Park. It runs from north to south, from the high point of the restaurant to the pavilion with a chahar bagh, a quadrilateral garden layout based on the four gardens of Paradise mentioned in the Qur'an, and overlooking a lake fed by Nile water which serves as a water reservoir for irrigation. It is characterized by sophisticated geometric pavement patterns and incorporates a series of water features such as fountains, water basins, a chaddar and narrow water runnels, double rows of palms, aromatic plants and shady trees. On both sides of the main spine are secondary walkways with secluded seating areas, as well as sunken gardens and citrus orchards (bustan) to provide shade. The tops of the reservoir tanks translate into key design features. The series of geometric, sequential gardens blend meaningfully with the curvilinear and rolling topography of the site. Other key features of the park include a lookout plaza, observation points, children's play areas and the historic wall promenade and amphitheatre. There are over 325 different plant species – many native to Egypt and grown in a special nursery[6] on the western slope of the park as a testing ground.

Al Azhar Park under construction:
Building on the artificial topography
created by the integration of three
water storage tanks. Photo:
© Aga Khan Trust for Culture / Gary Otte

SCENARIO *The Al Azhar Park model is adapted to suit different scales and neighbourhoods and multiplied to provide civic parks and infrastructure where space can be made available. Governmental infrastructure projects are considered as potential sites. Funding, for example through corporate social responsibility projects by adjoining multinationals, is incentivised as they too would benefit from an upgrading of the neighbourhood.*

Urban Upgrading

A number of important historical monuments including the 14th Century Umm Sultan Shaban Mosque, the Khayrbek complex (encompassing a 13th century palace, a mosque and an Ottoman house), the Aslam mosque and Square and the Darb Shoughlan School were restored. In addition, local housing was renovated and returned to their owners.

Turning a Landfill into a Park

A total of 1.5 million cubic metres of rubble and soil equalling 80,000 truckloads, were moved.

Socio-Economics

Job training and employment opportunities were offered in different sectors such as shoemaking, furniture manufacturing and tourist goods production. Apprenticeships were made available for automobile electronics, mobile telephones, computers, and masonry, carpentry and office skills. Micro-credit loans enabled residents to open small businesses such as carpentry shops and drycleaners. Hundreds of young men and women in Darb Al-Ahmar found work in the park, in horticulture and on restoration projects.[7]

Econometrics

Total project cost USD 30,000,000. Today, the Park draws nearly two million visitors a year. Through gate receipts and revenues from the its restaurants, the Park has become self-sustaining[8].

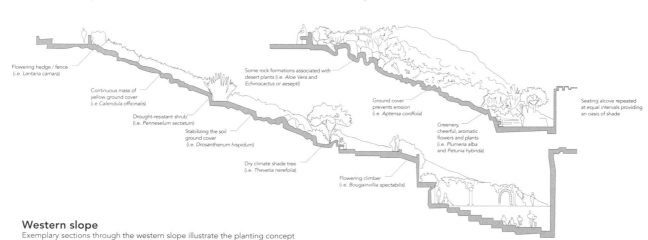

Flowering hedge / fence
(i.e. *Lantana camara*)

Continuous mass of yellow ground cover
(i.e *Calendula officinalis*)

Drought-resistant shrub
(i.e. *Penneselum sectatum*)

Stabilizing the soil ground cover
(i.e. *Drosanthenum hispidum*)

Dry climate shade tree
(i.e. *Thevetia nerefolia*)

Some rock formations associated with desert plants (i.e. *Aloe Vera* and *Echinocactus or aesepti*)

Ground cover prevents erosion
(i.e. *Aptensa cordfola*)

Flowering climber
(i.e. *Bougainvillia spectabilis*)

Greenery, cheerful, aromatic flowers and plants
(i.e. *Plumeria alba* and *Petunia hybrida*)

Seating alcove repeated at equal intervals providing an oasis of shade

Western slope

Exemplary sections through the western slope illustrate the planting concept

Al Azhar Park
From Landfill to Urban Infrastructure and Civic Park

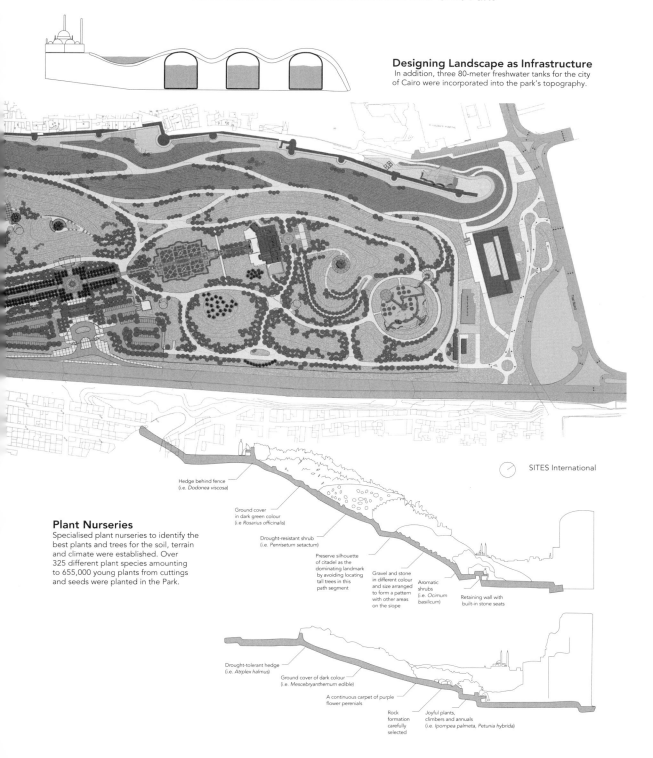

Designing Landscape as Infrastructure
In addition, three 80-meter freshwater tanks for the city of Cairo were incorporated into the park's topography.

SITES International

Plant Nurseries
Specialised plant nurseries to identify the best plants and trees for the soil, terrain and climate were established. Over 325 different plant species amounting to 655,000 young plants from cuttings and seeds were planted in the Park.

Hedge behind fence
(i.e. *Dodonea viscosa*)

Ground cover
in dark green colour
(i.e *Rosarius officinalis*)

Drought-resistant shrub
(i.e. *Pennisetum setactum*)

Preserve silhouette
of citadel as the
dominating landmark
by avoiding locating
tall trees in this
path segment

Gravel and stone
in different colour
and size arranged
to form a pattern
with other areas
on the slope

Aromatic
shrubs
(i.e. *Ocimum
basilicum*)

Retaining wall with
built-in stone seats

Drought-tolerant hedge
(i.e. *Atriplex halmus*)

Ground cover of dark colour
(i.e. *Mescebryanthemum edible*)

A continuous carpet of purple
flower perenials

Rock
formation
carefully
selected

Joyful plants,
climbers and annuals
(i.e. *Ipompea palmeta, Petunia hybrida*)

Park Site, Islamic Cairo

Khalifa Heritage and Environment Park
Islamic Cairo

Megawra Built Environment Collective

The Khalifa Heritage and Environment Park project converts a derelict 3000-sqm plot, partially used for solid waste dumping, into an urban garden with different amenities and improved circulation for persons of all abilities. It is a proposal by Athar Lina Initiative for a green space in Historic Cairo that extracts ground-water and reuses it for irrigation. It thus achieves two aims. It lowers the ground-water damaging the neighbouring Mamluk domes of Al-Ashraf Khalil and Fatima Khatun and provides the neighbourhood with a much-needed green space with recreational facilities for families including a kindergarten, play spaces for children, a women's sports and wellness space, an urban gardening and environment awareness center, shops and two waste collection points.

Based on the findings by Khalifa Groundwater Research Project, a proposal was developed for the collection of groundwater and water from leaking supply pipes that is currently damaging the monuments in the vicinity. While traditional de-watering approaches involve routing collected water to an already overloaded sewage system, this project will use it to irrigate a park. The project as intended will become a replicable model for aligning goals of quality public open space and improved environmental function, as well as serving as a model for government/civil society interdisciplinary collaboration.

- Enhancing public open spaces in an underprivileged inner-city neighborhood
- Empowering women, children and youth
- Fostering environmental sustainability and awareness
- Conserving heritage and historic building stock
- Creating jobs, alleviating poverty and enhancing economic vitality overall by providing spaces for shops and by celebrating important cultural heritage sites and thereby increasing tourism
- Improving accessibility to green open spaces for about 30,000 inhabitants of Al-Khalifa and the Zaynhum Housing Project, all within a 15-minute walking distance
- Dropping the water table at Al-Ashraf Khalil and Fatma Khatun Domes, and for the surrounding neighborhood without stressing the already-overloaded sewage system
- Reducing the urban heat island effect

The site before development: lower-lying monuments flooded by drainage water. Photos: Athar Lina

Khalifa Heritage and Environment Park is designed by Megawra – Built Environment Collective and A For Architecture in the context of Athar Lina Ground Water Research Project, organised by Megawra – Built Environment Collective in collaboration with Cairo Governorate and the Ministry of Antiquities and in partnership with Oregon, Cornell and TU Delft Universities and Takween Integrated Community Development. It is funded by the American Research Centre in Egypt, the US Embassy in Egypt and the Ford Foundation. The park is under construction and being implemented by Cairo governorate.

SCENARIO *Drainage water becomes a resource instead of a threat. Following the model of Khalifa Heritage and Environmental Park in Islamic Cairo, pocket parks are implemented to capture excess ground water. While contributing to the protection of lime stone building foundations, they offer much needed green areas for the adjoining communities.*

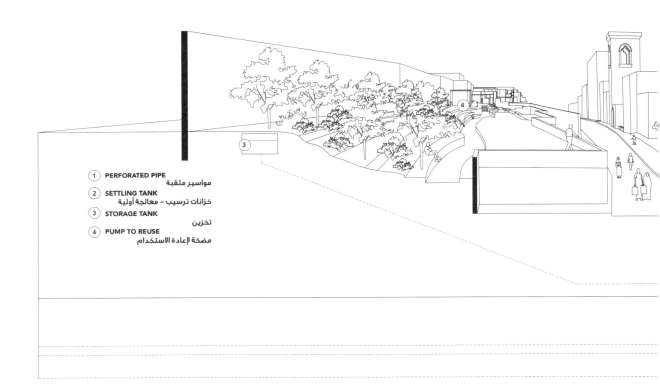

1. PERFORATED PIPE
   مواسير مثقبة
2. SETTLING TANK
   خزانات ترسيب – معالجة أولية
3. STORAGE TANK
   تخزين
4. PUMP TO REUSE
   مضخة لإعادة الاستخدام

Rising ground water tables and building damage

Because of leakages in sewer and supply networks the groundwater table rises. Foundations and buildings in the area thus suffer from rising damp and cracks as well as ground water overflow appearing in their surroundings. This causes damage and subsequently a risk of building collapse and a loss of valuable architectural heritage.

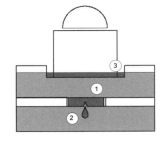

1. LACK OF MAIN-
   TANANCE + OVER-
   CAPACITY OF THE
   NETWORKS
2. SUPPLY + SEWER
   ARE LEAKING
3. FLOODING IS
   DEGRADING MONUMENTS

Khalifa Heritage and Environment Park
Conservation Through Irrigation

Concept drainage system

To lower the water table, a drainage system is needed: Perforated pipes are installed in the ground to collect excess water in a settling tank. Pumps transfer the water from the tank to the park. Stored in a tank, this captured water can be reused for the irrigation of neighbourhood parks or for flushing toilets.

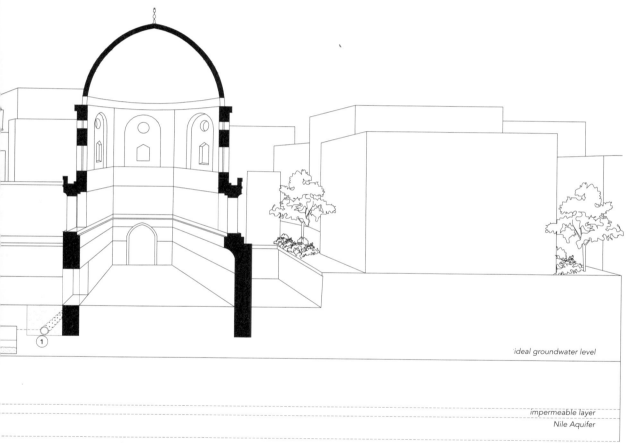

Water diversion and reuse

Diverting drainage water away from the monuments and capturing it produces an additional water source. When filtered, it can be used to create much needed green areas in dense urban environments.

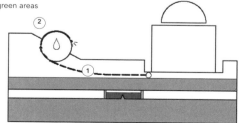

Dahab Island, Giza

Dahab Island - A green lung and site of local food
production for the megapolis, threatened by informal and
market-steered urban development.
Photo: Cornelia Redeker

Geziret El Dahab
Giza

Nil - Nile Islands Initiative

The Nile Islands make up one of Egypt's 30 protectorates. Formed by alluvial deposits and changing their shape and size according to currents and Nile water levels which still vary by around two meters, they are a remnant of the dynamic Nile landscape. Their soft embankments and dense fringe of swamp vegetation offer abundant habitat to birds, amphibians, fish and invertebrates and are one of the most important wintering grounds for water birds in Egypt today.[1] Intensive cultivation and increasing inhabitation are currently threatening the islands as habitat.[2]

Dahab Island in Giza provides a case study that is representative for the question of how to deal with the Nile Islands in the future. Geziret El Dahab is one of the six islands in Central Cairo. As yet practically car-free, it is a green haven that seems to have fallen out of time. The island is a site of local food production and an important green lung for the megapolis. With around 150 hectares, it is five times the size of Al Azhar Park. There is environmental degradation due to lacking sanitation and intensive cultivation and urbanization. The threat here is twofold: informal urban sprawl and market-steered recreational and residential development, possibly involving an eviction of current inhabitants, are threatening the island as habitat and green lung.[3]

What are prototypical design solutions for the island's diverse programs as eco-habitat, agricultural land, urban park and home to a grown rural community in the center of one of the world's densest cities with the lowest green area / inhabitant ratio?[4] On Geziret El Dahab we find many characteristics that cities all over the world are currently struggling to reinstall to reduce their ecological footprint. How to activate the island's qualities to protect this much needed public amenity, with its abundant ecosystemic services and home to a grown rural population? On the following page, we show how the needs for services and growth can be accommodated in the surrounding context of the city to avoid further urbanization of the island itself, while creating pedestrian and cycling connections from the island's felucca stops on the city sides to enable better access for islanders and visitors. For the island itself, we are anticipating a model of self-sufficiency that builds on the island's agro-community of 11,000 inhabitants[5] to further ensure the protection of one of Cairo's largest green lungs and popular urban escapes.

SCENARIO *Cairo brands itself with going green and Dahab becomes Egypt's first ecovillage island. Integrating vertical farming to provide livelihoods, vacant Nile towers in the direct vicinity provide housing for the growing island population. Switching to decentralized blue-green infrastructure to solve the sewage problem and to organic farming to cut costs for fertilizer, pesticides, and diesel for the water pumps, which can be replaced by using the Nile current and solar pumps, makes Dahab nearly self-sufficient. Pedestrian and cycling connections between ferries and public transport make the island a central park, while islanders have safe access to services nearby. Biodiversity increases.*

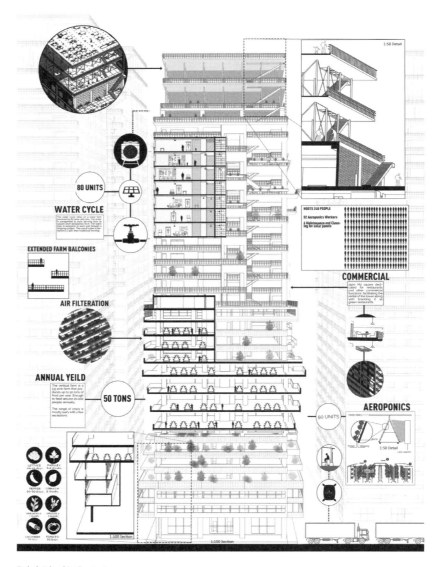

Dahab Island in Context
Vertical Vacancies to Accommodate Urban Growth and New Farming Models
Currently, around 12.8 million housing units in Greater Cairo are vacant.[6]
To avoid further encroachment of the island's agricultural land, the adjoining vacant Nile towers are revitalized to offer housing for the growing island population in combination with vertical farming in the direct neighbourhood of Geziret El Dahab

Geziret El Dahab
A Green Lung For The Megapolis

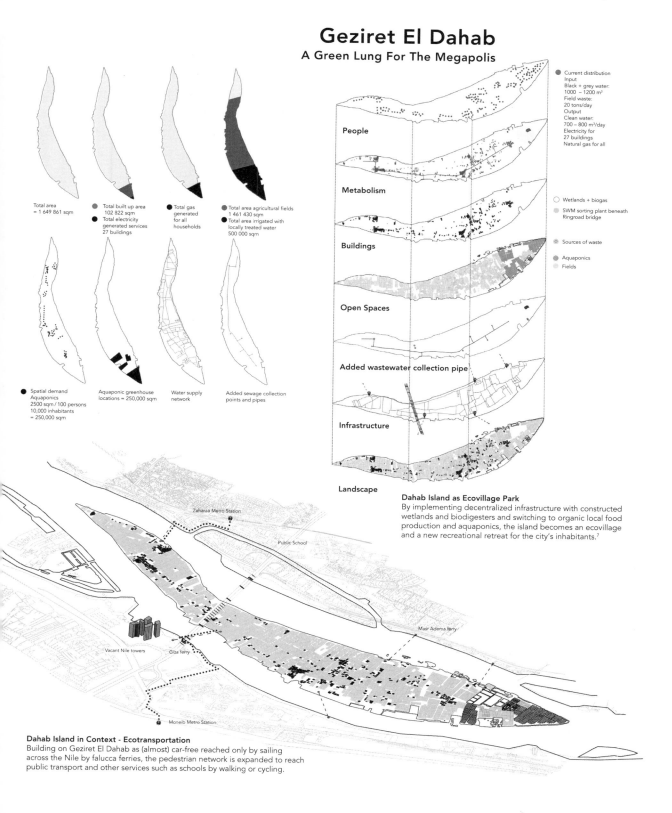

Total area
= 1 649 861 sqm

● Total built up area
102 822 sqm
● Total electricity
generated services
27 buildings

● Total gas
generated
for all
households

● Total area agricultural fields
1 461 430 sqm
● Total area irrigated with
locally treated water
500 000 sqm

● Spatial demand
Aquaponics
2500 sqm / 100 persons
10,000 inhabitants
= 250,000 sqm

Aquaponic greenhouse
locations = 250,000 sqm

Water supply
network

Added sewage collection
points and pipes

People

Metabolism

Buildings

Open Spaces

Added wastewater collection pipe

Infrastructure

Landscape

● Current distribution
Input
Black + grey water:
1000 – 1200 m³
Field waste:
20 tons/day
Output
Clean water:
700 – 800 m³/day
Electricity for
27 buildings
Natural gas for all

○ Wetlands + biogas
● SWM sorting plant beneath
Ringroad bridge

● Sources of waste
● Aquaponics
Fields

Dahab Island as Ecovillage Park
By implementing decentralized infrastructure with constructed wetlands and biodigesters and switching to organic local food production and aquaponics, the island becomes an ecovillage and a new recreational retreat for the city's inhabitants.[7]

Zaharaa Metro Station

Public School

Masr Adema ferry

Vacant Nile towers   Giza ferry

Moneib Metro Station

Dahab Island in Context - Ecotransportation
Building on Geziret El Dahab as (almost) car-free reached only by sailing across the Nile by falucca ferries, the pedestrian network is expanded to reach public transport and other services such as schools by walking or cycling.

Photo: Cornelia Redeker

Desert Forest, Luxor

Desert Afforestation

National Program for Afforestation

Afforestation is the planting of trees on land formerly used for purposes other than forestry. The availability of sun in the desert of Egypt enables trees to grow all-year round. Up to a certain extent, the more sunlight available for a tree, the higher the photosynthetic ability and thus tree production.

During the Fatimid era, a thousand years ago, Egypt was the first country in the world that established a national forest organization, mainly for the construction of ships.[2] Today, less than 0.07 % of the country's land area is covered with trees. For 2009, the FAO (2010) estimated a total area of 691 km[2] with nearly 74 million standing trees in Egypt. The country has almost no natural forests: Only relics of natural woodlands on the slopes of *Gebel Elba* (Mount Elba) in the south of the country and sparse, scattered mangroves along the red sea coast can be found. Artificial forests prevail and are planted as windbreakers with most common species being Casuarina and Eucalyptus.

Unutilized desert lands, sunlight, sewage water and its nutrients are resources with high potential that can be used for the establishment of plantation forests in arid lands and, subsequently, the production of renewable resources. Wastewater from municipal activities can be partially treated to be used in irrigating planted trees. Sewage water has a high content of the primary plant nutrients nitrogen and phosphorus, which are essential for tree growth. In addition, remnant sludge or solid waste from the primary wastewater treatment can be used to produce biogas and soil conditioner.

Apart from carbon sequestration, afforestation in arid regions can be established to combat desertification, sand dune fixation, erosion prevention, and coastal protection. As a windbreak and environmental buffer for human settlements, forests protect from wind, sand and pollution, create a favourable urban microclimate, improve air quality, enhance public health and contribute to reducing energy due to their cooling and warming effects on summer days and winter nights, respectively. Protecting arable and newly reclaimed lands using trees also contributes to food security. If cultivated areas are protected by a trees (greenbelt/windbreak), there will be a considerable reduction in environmental stresses (reducing plant damage, sand deposit and insects, improving the efficiency of irrigation and fertilization, conserving moisture in plants and soil) as well as an improvement of the microclimate, thus achieving a higher yield of the protected crops. Urban areas and agricultural lands can be protected according to the prevailing conditions by a series of windbreaks of trees of one row, three or six rows planted perpendicular to the prevailing wind direction. Economically, desert afforestation creates jobs and qualification opportunities through the establishment of new forest-based industries. From an urban perspective, desert afforestation offers an improved microclimate coupled with recreational opportunities for residents and even tourists due to the attraction of forests in arid regions. On a larger scale, their ecosystemic capacity to influence cloud formation and precipitation patterns is a further hypothesis to be explored.[3]

There are 35 desert afforestation projects in Egypt using sewage water today. Currently on hold, the "National Programme for the Safe Use of Treated Sewage Water for Afforestation", established in the early/mid 1990s, Egypt achieved a 3.3 % annual rate of change in forest cover between 1999 and 2000.[1]

> **SCENARIO** *Egypt develops a new timber industry from desert afforestation irrigated with treated waste water. Adjoining new urban communities benefit from a shaded leisure landscape and an improved microclimate. Wood is no longer imported and wood-related economies provide jobs in research, manufacturing, building and of course forestry. On a large scale, these desert forests combat desertification in a sustainable way and may even produce rain.*

Mixed Forests in the Desert
Precious hardwood species:
Gmeline or White Teak (*Gmelina arborea*),
African Mahogany (*Khaya senegalensis*),
Outeniqua yellowwood (*Podocarpus falcatus*),
Teak (*Tectona grandis*)
Hardwood species:
Mangium or Black Wattle (*Acacia mangium*),
Neem or Indian Lilac (*Azadirachta indica*),
Lemon-scented gum (*Corymbia citriodora*),
River Red Gum (*Eucalyptus camaldulensis*)
Softwood species:
Caribean Pine (*Pinus caribbea var. hondurensis*),
Canary Island pine (*Pinus canariensis C. Smith*)
Biofuel crops:
Jatropha (*Jatropha curcas*)
Jojoba (*Simmondsia chinensis*)
Windbreak species:
Orange Wattle (*Acacia saligna*)
Casuarina (*Casuarina equisetifolia*) [6]

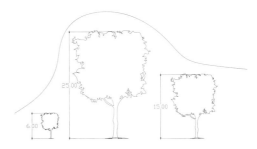

Environmental Buffer and Windbreaker
To cool prevailing winds from the North, desert forests, planted in rows of roughly 8-m-distance and at defined heights, can potentially improve the climate of adjoining neighbourhoods[7] and serve as windbreakers to avoid desertification, erosion and crop loss.

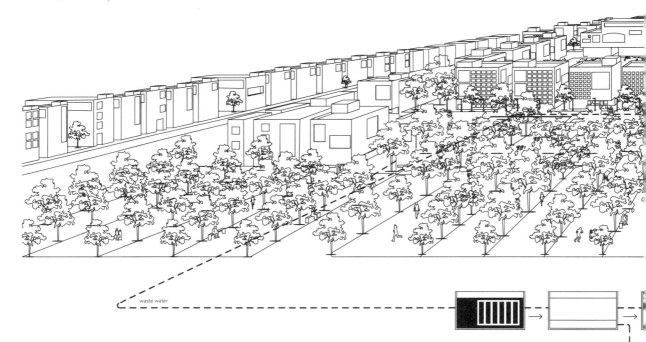

waste water

Internal Rate of Return
The Egyptian climate in combination with nutrient-rich wastewater allows trees to be harvested in as few as 15 years, at which point they produce about 350 m³ of wood per hectare. To give a comparison, in order to produce the same amount of wood in Germany, it would take about 60 years.[5] Estimated internal rate of return by afforsting 1,000 ha of desert lands using 14 tree species exceeds 12%.

Egyptian wood import
Between 2005 and 2015, Egypt imported a total of 12,300 tons of wood.[4]

Desert Afforestation
New Urban Forests

Desert Forestation, Urbanization and Carbon Sequestration

The average water consumption in Egypt per person is 230 l /day. Given the resources of 7 billion cubic meters of sewage water annually, of which only around 40% is treated, and nearly 1 million km² of desert land: with an average annual water requirement of 8,500 cubic meters/hectare, 5.5 billion cubic meters of Egypt's sewage water is sufficient to afforest over 650,000 hectares of desert lands and store over 25 million tons of CO_2 annually in new plantation forests. To the right, the Desert Forestation project in Luxor.

Econometrics

Kuwait Holding Company plan on creating a wood factory in Minya set to begin operating by around 2020. The project will plant trees using treated sewage water over 6,000 feddans (2520 hectares) of land. The projected cost of the project is at $168.5 million (EGP 3 billion), while the estimate of the annual production is at $50 million. Egyptian banks will be providing EGP 1 billion in funds to assist the project. With each tree farm that is built in Egypt, more jobs will be created while saving import costs. The Central Agency for Public Mobilization and Statistics (CAPMAS) released a report last year indicating that Egypt's imports of wood recorded LE 14.2 billion ($798 million) in 2016. The tree farm will boost the economy in terms of warehousing, refrigerating, sorting, packaging, wholesaling, and distributing included in a logistic zone which will produce 17,000 jobs.[11]

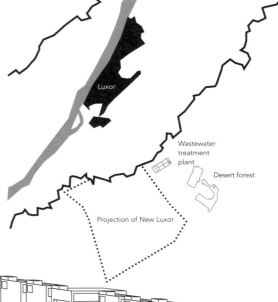

Luxor

Wastewater treatment plant

Desert forest

Projection of New Luxor

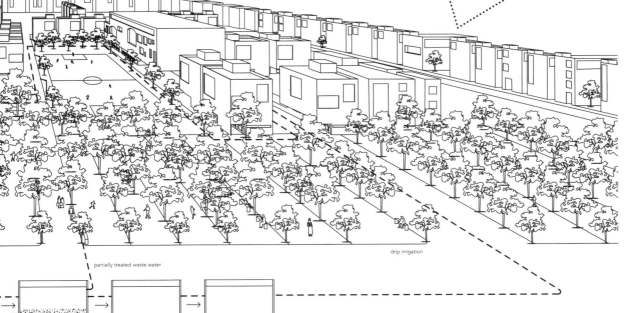

partially treated waste water

drip irrigation

Partially Treated Waste Water for Irrigation

The sewage water is freed from organic residues and pollutants.
The remaining high content of the primary plant nutrients nitrogen and phosphorus in the partially treated water (at this stage not fit for human consumption) are essential for tree growth. Remnant sludge or solid waste after the wastewater treatment can be used for the production of renewable energy (e.g. biogas) and soil conditioner.[8]

Climate

Large-scale afforestation may stimulate cloud formation and may result in rainfall that the country urgently needs to expand its agricultural production areas.[9] Large-scale plantations of Jatropha Curcas (10,000 km²) could lead to a reduction in mean surface temperature and an onset or increase in rain and dew fall at a regional level.[10]

Olive and fig plantations on the cascading bed of Wadi Kharouba

Wadi Kharouba, Marsa Matrouh

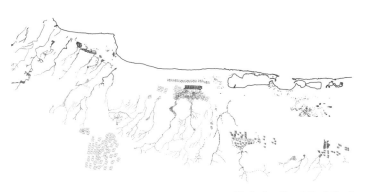

Wadis along Egypt's North Coast

Wadi Agriculture
Marsadev Project

Wadi Kharouba, Marsa Matrouh

National Desert Research Center Egypt
CIHEAM – Bari, Italy

Wadis have been cultivated since ancient times, irrigated by run-off from the rain that is also harvested and stored during the long periods without inundation. In Wadi Kharouba in Marsah Matrouh, the cultivated crops include fig and olive orchards, as well as watermelon. The Egyptian Desert Research Center together with the Mediterranean Agronomic Institute Bari teamed up with local Bedouin tribes for the Marsadev Project (completed in 2015) where a strip of 3 km of wadi cultivation now provides a livelihood for sixty Bedouin families. By merging valuable local knowledge with innovative technologies, the project managed to recover degraded lands, prevent erosion, enhance water saving and harvesting, enrich soil fertility, improve crop yields, provide appropriate conditions for livestock management, and finally alleviate poverty by boosting socio-economic conditions and gender issues inside local communities. Many rainwater harvesting practices are implemented in the area such as: in-stream bed water harvesting system in the bed of the wadis to grow olive and fig, macrocatchment water harvesting systems to store the water in cisterns (Roman cisterns are still in place and are currently being reactivated) and reservoir and micro-catchment water-harvesting systems such as semi-circular bunds for growing some forage shrubs. Of course, flash floods can also potentially cause damage. To mitigate the common risk of erosion and a loss of crops during flash floods, the wadi has been remodeled to function as a cascading system structured by retaining walls and culverts. It is terraced to slow down the current by creating basins. In addition, trees on the embankments may be protected by semi-circular bunds of stone to avoid erosion while holding the water for irrigation and creating magnificent cultural landscapes. Egypt has the second-biggest fig production globally.[1] And yet, currently figs are harvested from hand-to-mouth, too ripe and with lacking manufacturing channels to be marketed on a larger scale beyond the local.

Photos: Monique Jüttner

The building restriction within these natural features is similar to a water body, a golf course or any green area, as it ensures wide views and open spaces. The dynamic landscape and panoramic view of the opposite bank of these dry river beds show enormous potential for aligning urban development. As we can witness in New Tiba, wadis, as linear voids exempt from any building activity, offer much-needed open spaces within the urban fabric that are still waiting to be integrated in order to define its adjoining urban areas in a more meaningful way. They could easily accommodate sports fields, hiking paths and other two-dimensional features that are not at risk of being damaged by seasonal flash floods. As wadis that are also cultivated, they allow these voids to not only define spatial borders, but also to create vistas and to allow ventilation. As terraced orchards with sloped walls, they become urban parks with very distinct qualities that demand only small adaptations to become accessible and to create important green corridors for many of Egypt's New Urban Communities that are currently being realized in the desert.

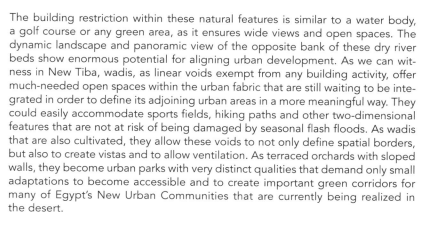

SCENARIO *New urban communities develop around cultivated wadis that serve as parks while enabling a vista as well as shade-spending productive landscapes that are irrigated with harvested rain water.*

Wadi Agriculture

is a traditional way of cultivation practiced by Bedouins in Sinai, and recently also along the Mediterranean North Coast. Currently, a governmental development program to cultivate wadis together with Bedouin communities aims at increasing efficiency in water usage, yield and manufacturing.

semi-circular bunds
made of earth or stone
bund tips facing upslope

cemented earthen dikes

Precipitation

Egypt is an arid region. Few areas along the northern and eastern coast as well as in the mountains in Sinai receive rainfall during a very short season. Harvesting and storing this water has a long tradition in Egypt.

How much agricultural area could be irrigated?

Macro-catchment run-off farming systems are referred to as «run-off rainwater harvesting from long slopes»
Size: 0.1 ha to 200 ha
Flow: Turbulent runoff, channel flow
CCR (Crop to Catchment Ratio): 10:1 - 100:1
Precipitation: 100 to 1000 mm/annum
Inclination of catchment: 5 - 60%
Cropping Area: Terraced or in flat terrain [6]

built area   buffer strip 1   slope   buffer strip 2   cultivation area

upper plain   terraced area   stream bed / main channel

Wadi Agriculture
Wadi Urbanism

Wadi Potential
In combination with agriculture, wadis may host water-efficient cultural landscapes. Their cascading terraces over the length of the river bed planted with olive and fig orchards and the semi-circular bunds to protect individual trees from erosion formulate a distinctive landscape and open space that has great potential to become the central productive spine and orchard park for new urban developments in the Egyptian desert.

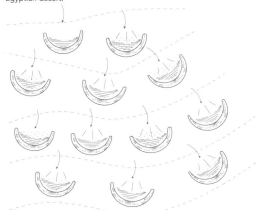

Catchment area
Wadis are natural catchment areas for rainwater. The slopes accumulate and collect water run-off that may be harvested in different ways, e.g. in cisterns. Water losses from evaporation, infiltration or retention diminish the amount of water collected. The efficiency of harvesting systems varies depending on soil types, land use and topography.

Water Lost
When wadis discharge into the Nile, the rain water is not lost. However, when flash floods discharge into the sea, costly desalination is required to make this water potable. During a recent flash flood in Wadi Bili west of El Gouna, an estimated 1 million cubic meters of water ran off into the Red Sea,[4] roughly enough to provide the city with drinking water for a year. Desalination also produces brine as a hypersaline biproduct at a ratio of 1.5 to the desalinated water that is extracted. This amount of brine is about 50% higher than previously estimated.[5]

Rainwater Harvesting
is a methodology to collect water from precipitation or mist, storing it or even purifying it further to be used for plant irrigation, livestock or household use depending on the water quality. As catchment areas, stone bunds or other tools as well as storage containers (e.g. cisterns) can be installed as practiced since ancient times to provide water supply.

Cisterns
Cisterns are subsurface water reservoirs or storage tanks. Their capacity ranges from 10 – 15,000 cubic meters while the shape and size of cisterns may vary. Old Roman cisterns can be as large as 1500 cubic meters (the larger ones were multiple cell cisterns with sub-surface side trenches). Cisterns built in recent years usually have a capacity of 100 – 300 cubic meters. The common chamber shapes are circular, elliptical and rectangular. Cisterns of larger capacity (> 300 cubic meters) generally have more than one cell, while single-cell cisterns are smaller, usually built where soil and rock conditions do not allow for large capacity.[2]

In many areas, small cisterns are dug in the rock. Larger cisterns are lined with compacted earth, clay, mortar coating, concrete or plastic sheets to avoid seepage. Runoff is collected from an adjacent catchment or channeled from a distant catchment. They are either dug below a solid rock layer or covered to reduce evaporation. In most cases, stilling basins (sedimentation traps) are attached in front of the inlet to reduce sedimentation: otherwise, regular cleaning of the cistern is required.
Large community cisterns can store up to 80,000 cubic meters of water.[3]

Al Burouj Orchard Park after one year of being planted. In the background:
the city centre under construction, October 2019
Photo: Peter Blodau

Al Burouj Orchard Park

Orchard Park
Al Burouj, Eastern Greater Cairo

Bustan Aquaponics

A programmed porosity of 60 percent in the urban tissue including large private, community or public green open spaces define New Urban Community (NUC) masterplans. The arid climate and water scarcity turn planting and maintenance of these, envisioned as housing embedded in lush green spaces, into an irrigation-intensive and costly undertaking. To maintain these green oases located on elevated desert plateaus, requires vast amounts of water and as of yet open spaces are limited to a recreational and aesthetic program. A majority of this is drinking water extracted from wells at great depths or delivered from the Nile via extensive pipe networks. Environmentally and economically, these are arguments for a different, more productive approach to landscape design. In the following example, irrigation water is used in a different way: to grow food.

Al Burouj, a new and, by NUC standards, small city for 180,000 inhabitants on 486 hectares, is currently under construction. Amidst one of the most dynamic urbanization corridors globally, heading east on Cairo-Ismailia Road towards the New Administrative Capital and around 30 km from Cairo's first desert extension at the beginning of the 20th century, Heliopolis, the international developer Capital Group Properties (CGP) has decided to do things differently. By teaming up with Bustan Aquaponics, the central green area of around 6 hectares is becoming productive. The design intent builds on the reintegration of food production within the landscape design. Fruit trees and herb fields in combination with a community centre and a farm-to-fork café will make up the new shared open space. The planting concept with 40 different varieties of trees builds on speaking to the five senses by including both evergreens and deciduous plants to create seasonal variety. Beyond their ornamental and sensual qualities, all plants are either edible, medicinal, and/or fragrant. Products will be sold to the residents through various outlets throughout the city, including a farm shop with post-harvest processing (juices, salads). The aim is to self-sufficiently finance the costs for water and labour as well as fertilizer and pest control. All areas will be designed barrier-free to create an inclusive public neighbourhood park for the inhabitants.

Al Burouj masterplan
Graphic: placedynamix.com

This community park concept offers much more diverse and educational activities than comparable green spaces. It also creates a different dynamic during the construction phase of 15 years. Amenities including a lake, wellness facilities and restaurants, an amphitheatre adjacent to the park for events, a planned petting zoo, combined with fitness and bike paths including a bike rental to connect the site to a vaster area, show how cultivation can enrich the park program. Compared to neighbourhoods which rely on vast lawn areas and ornamental plants only, Al Burouj Orchard Park offers seasonal distinction, a reconnection with local food production and a more diverse and rich landscape with a variety of canopy heights and building elements, but also scents and colours that together create a unique character and enhance biodiversity while making a more effective use of water.

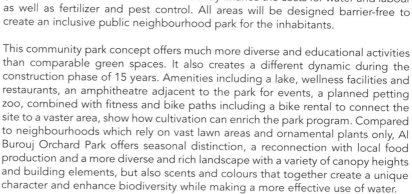

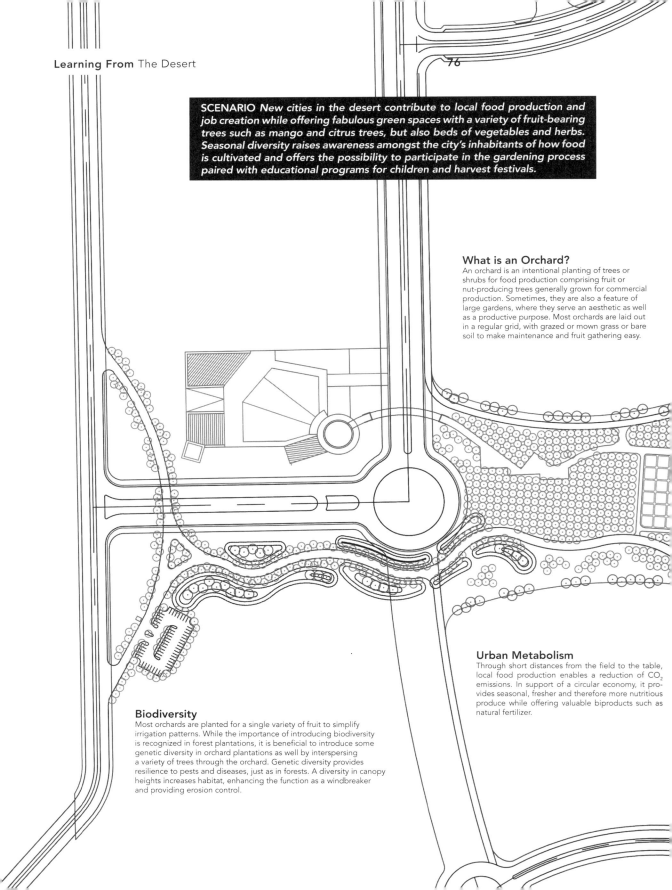

SCENARIO *New cities in the desert contribute to local food production and job creation while offering fabulous green spaces with a variety of fruit-bearing trees such as mango and citrus trees, but also beds of vegetables and herbs. Seasonal diversity raises awareness amongst the city's inhabitants of how food is cultivated and offers the possibility to participate in the gardening process paired with educational programs for children and harvest festivals.*

What is an Orchard?

An orchard is an intentional planting of trees or shrubs for food production comprising fruit or nut-producing trees generally grown for commercial production. Sometimes, they are also a feature of large gardens, where they serve an aesthetic as well as a productive purpose. Most orchards are laid out in a regular grid, with grazed or mown grass or bare soil to make maintenance and fruit gathering easy.

Urban Metabolism

Through short distances from the field to the table, local food production enables a reduction of CO_2 emissions. In support of a circular economy, it provides seasonal, fresher and therefore more nutritious produce while offering valuable biproducts such as natural fertilizer.

Biodiversity

Most orchards are planted for a single variety of fruit to simplify irrigation patterns. While the importance of introducing biodiversity is recognized in forest plantations, it is beneficial to introduce some genetic diversity in orchard plantations as well by interspersing a variety of trees through the orchard. Genetic diversity provides resilience to pests and diseases, just as in forests. A diversity in canopy heights increases habitat, enhancing the function as a windbreaker and providing erosion control.

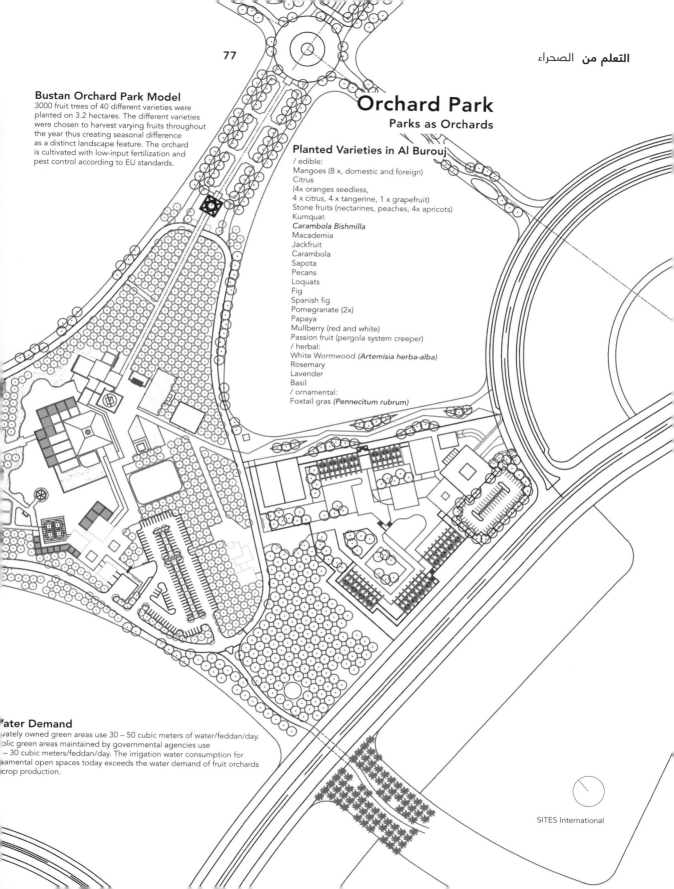

Orchard Park
Parks as Orchards

Bustan Orchard Park Model
3000 fruit trees of 40 different varieties were planted on 3.2 hectares. The different varieties were chosen to harvest varying fruits throughout the year thus creating seasonal difference as a distinct landscape feature. The orchard is cultivated with low-input fertilization and pest control according to EU standards.

Planted Varieties in Al Burouj

/ edible:
Mangoes (8 x, domestic and foreign)
Citrus
(4x oranges seedless,
4 x citrus, 4 x tangerine, 1 x grapefruit)
Stone fruits (nectarines, peaches, 4x apricots)
Kumquat
Carambola Bishmilla
Macademia
Jackfruit
Carambola
Sapota
Pecans
Loquats
Fig
Spanish fig
Pomegranate (2x)
Papaya
Mullberry (red and white)
Passion fruit (pergola system creeper)
/ herbal:
White Wormwood (*Artemisia herba-alba*)
Rosemary
Lavender
Basil
/ ornamental:
Foxtail gras (*Pennecitum rubrum*)

Water Demand
...vately owned green areas use 30 – 50 cubic meters of water/feddan/day.
...blic green areas maintained by governmental agencies use
...– 30 cubic meters/feddan/day. The irrigation water consumption for
...amental open spaces today exceeds the water demand of fruit orchards
...crop production.

SITES International

Madinaty, New Cairo, example of drip irrigation
Photo: Monique Jüttner

Al Rehab, New Cairo

Water-Sensitive
Open Space Design
Al Rehab, New Cairo

IUSD Ain Shams University

To secure their water supply, New Cities are fed by conventional water sources such as the Nile, ground or storm water. Large water infrastructures lift and transport Nile water to the desert cities. Highly or slightly saline groundwater from wells is extracted where the water table is not too low.[1] Rainwater occurs during spring as sudden events running off unused, either into the sewer or trickling into the ground. Treated wastewater, an unconventional source of water, could be supplied by waste water treatment plants (WWTP) located at some distance to the New Cities. Urban waste water is collected, treated in primary, secondary and tertiary stages and conveyed back as treated waste water (TWW) that can be used for irrigiation.[2] However, waste water treatment plants are currently not covering all urban areas. Where they are present, they do not yet use their full capacity. This is either because the population of New Cities does not deliver the calculated amount of waste water, or because treatment plants cannot yet deliver the required amount.[3] Considerable conveyance distances and frequent network leaks further limit distribution and availability. Various water sources thus show different quality levels suitable for irrigation or drinking. Until recently the prices did not substantially differ according to quality level, fostering the use of drinking water for the majority of open spaces. The following proposal for Al Rehab, a privately owned and managed residential compound in New Cairo housing 200,000 inhabitants with an area of 9,900,000 square meters and a total green area of 40%, proposes a restructuring of open spaces by applying a water-sensitive open design approach. Based on the understanding of "landscape as scenery", open spaces are currently not designed to be used by the inhabitants. There are no seating opportunities, shade is lacking and fences and hedges create barriers. The homogeneous design creates high maintenance and water demands. Large quantities of potable water in the new urban communities are used for irrigation. Infrastructure for the reuse of treated waste water (TWW) also exists in large parts of Al Rehab and makes up 60% of the water used. However, the quality is not reliable. It is also not enough to irrigate all areas, and there are some health concerns.

The study also shows that currently:
- it is assumed that the current water demand exceeds the water requirement by 60% due to losses caused by broken pipes and wasteful irrigation behaviour
- the landscape design prevailingly uses non-native plants not adapted to an arid climate
- plants with different water needs are frequently planted together, rendering a demand-based irrigation per plant impossible and inducing overwatering
- lawn as groundcover is found in most areas and a homogeneous repetition of plants and features was observed offering little diversity or even biodiversity
- open space was not intensively used possibly because of cultural preferences and the design which is rather oriented to provide a scenery instead of a use value
- open areas are largely designed without drainage systems, leading excess water to evaporate or to be lost into the depths of the desert
- Remaining in the soil are salts that slowly build up and impede plant growth

200 m

Private gardens
Greenery in the villa area
Courtyards
Greenery at the Food Court
Public Park
Roadside vegetation
Trees

Green open spaces in the focus area
Graphic: Lisa Deister

By varying water sources and reducing water consumption through the introduction of different hydrozones in combination with improved management and operation, the study highlights the potentials of water-sensitive open space design to create more interesting and diversified open spaces.

SCENARIO *The open spaces of new urban communities are designed in a water-sensitive way, including the active involvement of gardeners, plumbers and inhabitants. Different water sources and a restructuring of green open spaces according to function and plant-specific water demand reduce the overall water budget and use of drinking water in irrigation.*

Strategy Water-Sensitive Open Space Design

Support realization

Increase of areas irrigated with treated waste water (TWW)

PRECONDITION 1
Ensure water quality of TWW:
Implementation of quality control at WWTP
TWW polishing on site

Restructure green open spaces according to function + water demand

PRECONDITION 2
Efficient irrigation behavior:
Development of efficient management plan
for and with the gardeners
Creation of incentives program for the gardeners

Reduce water consumption

Reduce Demand:
Decrease in amount of green open spaces
Utilization of plants with low water demands

Reduce Losses:
Automation of irrigation system
Decentralized treatment of waste water to decrease losses during transportation and treatment process
Direct use of greywater for irrigation

Add other water sources

Reuse of condensate water from AC
Stormwater harvesting
Reuse of ablution water from mosques
Reuse of drainage water

Condensate water | Hydrozone L
The amount of condensate water reclaimed from A/C systems depends on the amount of exchanged air, its temperature and humidity content, the power of the A/C system and its operating hours. Temperature and humidity vary every day and, hence, also the amount of produced condensate water, which might not be sufficient to cover all water requirements. For this reason, the green open spaces selected to receive water from this source should be rather small and belong to hydrozone L in order to decrease the necessity for additional water sources.

Potable water | Hydrozone L
Due to health-related concerns relating to using TWW to irrigate villa areas, all green open spaces in these areas are currently irrigated with potable water. Options for changing this are limited due to a lack of awareness relating to the inhabitants. To decrease the consumption of potable water as much as possible, it is suggested that all green open spaces comprise plants with low water demands.

Current Water Use for Irrigation
Privately owned green areas use 30 – 50 cubic meters water / feddan / day (7.14 – 11.9 l / sqm / day) and public green areas maintained by governmental agencies use amounts of 20 – 30 cubic meters / feddan / day (4.76 – 7.14 l / sqm / day).

Hydrozones
Hydrozone H: plants with high water demand (approx. 5.73 l / sqm / day)
Hydrozone M: plants with moderate water demand (approx. 3.58 l / sqm / day)
Hydrozone L: plants with low water demand (approx. 1.42 l / sqm / day)

Water-Sensitive Open Space Design
Diversifying Water Sources, Plants and Uses

New Water Cycle

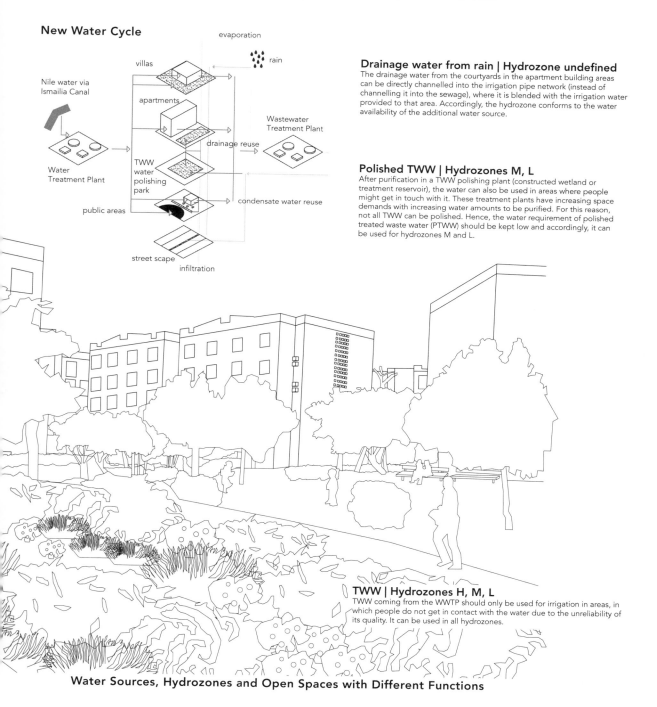

Drainage water from rain | Hydrozone undefined
The drainage water from the courtyards in the apartment building areas can be directly channelled into the irrigation pipe network (instead of channelling it into the sewage), where it is blended with the irrigation water provided to that area. Accordingly, the hydrozone conforms to the water availability of the additional water source.

Polished TWW | Hydrozones M, L
After purification in a TWW polishing plant (constructed wetland or treatment reservoir), the water can also be used in areas where people might get in touch with it. These treatment plants have increasing space demands with increasing water amounts to be purified. For this reason, not all TWW can be polished. Hence, the water requirement of polished treated waste water (PTWW) should be kept low and accordingly, it can be used for hydrozones M and L.

TWW | Hydrozones H, M, L
TWW coming from the WWTP should only be used for irrigation in areas, in which people do not get in contact with the water due to the unreliability of its quality. It can be used in all hydrozones.

Water Sources, Hydrozones and Open Spaces with Different Functions

Rooftop Farming in Maadi, Cairo

Rooftop Farm, Cairo

Urban Microfarms

Cairo

Schaduf Sustainable Living Solutions

As the Persian poet Nasir Khusraw attested in his travelogue entitled Safarnama almost 1000 years ago, kitchen and pleasure gardens were not exclusively for the urban poor, nor did structural concerns hinder their implementations. Rooftop gardens were already planted by residents in the well-off and densely-populated area of Fustat on high-rise buildings of up to 14 floors and irrigated via ox-drawn water wheels on the ground.[1] Rooftop farming has since become a global practice to contribute to local food production while compensating for the building footprint's lost green area. In combination with green walls, this is a low-tech, low-cost tool to transform the highly impermeable, heat-storing environment of Egypt's extremely dense informal areas, with its lack of green areas. They also offer alternative green surfaces for Egypt's urban desert expansions which are, although watering systems using treated waste water are in place, still reliant on more than half of their drinking water for irrigation. By greening building envelopes, dust and pollutants can be captured and temperatures lowered, providing urgently needed green and insulation to improve urban microclimates and thermal comfort inside of buildings.

With hydroponics, a soilless mode of agricultural production which saves up to 80% of water compared to conventional agricultural practices, green walls and rooftop farms offer private gardens where public green areas are extremely scarce. Schaduf has been implementing and exploring hydroponic rooftop farming systems and green walls in the Middle East since 2010. Hydroponics not only produce pesticide-free crops such as leafy greens and strawberries, but may also offer an additional income to its practitioners. Yet, this proves to be the biggest challenge. With a microcredit and training system in place to start the projects, Schaduf has developed an integrated business model to support rooftop farmers in low-income neighbourhoods in Cairo by marketing their products, thus theoretically enabling a return of investment from day one, spatial and social benefits being obvious. For rooftop farming to be successful on a larger scale, new, more creative economic models are needed: in this context, attaining a microcredit demands proof of eligibility (electricity bill in the owner's name, a national ID as well as a reference). Most inhabitants in informal areas are not able to deliver all three. In the meantime, Egypt's government has started a promising initiative to green the roofs of its institutional buildings (in 2015) with the aim of using them as training centers for university graduates and unemployed youth.

Tapas Restaurant, Cairo
Photos: Schaduf

As part of Egypt's Vision 2030 the governor of Cairo has announced the greening of all the rooftops on Cairo's buildings as part of the governorate's sustainable development plan. The inhabitants will not cover the plantation costs, but will be responsible for maintaining the gardens.[2] Also, in more affluent neighbourhoods private rooftop gardens and green walls are en vogue. Applied accumulatively on a larger scale, rooftop farms produce vast vertical parks and urgently-needed environmental buffers for Egypt's urban roofscapes.

SCENARIO *A national program to green existing building envelopes with rooftop gardens and green walls is launched. Innovative economic models turn inhabitants into successful urban farmers. Within 10 years, the lost agricultural land is compensated for, and livelihoods and appearances (especially of informal areas) improves drastically, making Egypt a frontrunner in combating desertification.**

Green Walls

Plants grow as hydroculture (see hydroponic techniques b, c) on various carriers (sponges, nets, pots) or on potting soil. Green walls can define spaces, are beautiful design objects and can produce food and provide sound insulation while rendering a space cool and pleasurable.

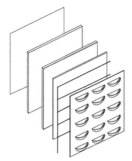

Roof Top Gardening

Crop types, growth cycle, costs and revenues
Ezbet El Nasr, microfarms project
(Schaduf, Cairo, 2015)

Mulukhya	1 Month	
Arugula	1 Month	
Lettuce	44 Days - 45 Days	
Parsley	3-4 Weeks	
Cucumber	70 Days	
Tomato	60-90 Days	
Pepper	6 Weeks	
Spinach	6 Weeks	

358$

Average Cost

42-70$

Monthly Revenue

Urban Microfarms
Rooftop Gardens and Green Walls

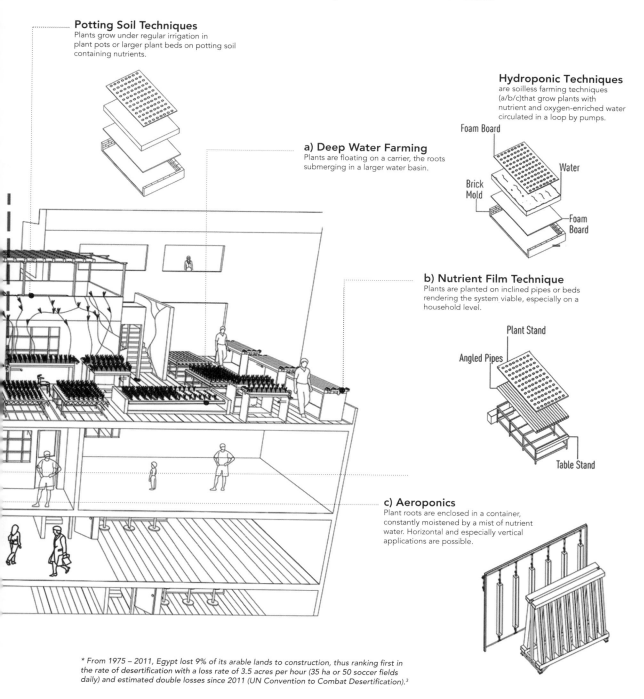

Potting Soil Techniques
Plants grow under regular irrigation in plant pots or larger plant beds on potting soil containing nutrients.

Hydroponic Techniques
are soilless farming techniques (a/b/c)that grow plants with nutrient and oxygen-enriched water circulated in a loop by pumps.

Foam Board

Water

Brick Mold

Foam Board

a) Deep Water Farming
Plants are floating on a carrier, the roots submerging in a larger water basin.

b) Nutrient Film Technique
Plants are planted on inclined pipes or beds rendering the system viable, especially on a household level.

Plant Stand

Angled Pipes

Table Stand

c) Aeroponics
Plant roots are enclosed in a container, constantly moistened by a mist of nutrient water. Horizontal and especially vertical applications are possible.

* From 1975 – 2011, Egypt lost 9% of its arable lands to construction, thus ranking first in the rate of desertification with a loss rate of 3.5 acres per hour (35 ha or 50 soccer fields daily) and estimated double losses since 2011 (UN Convention to Combat Desertification).[3]

Projected constructed wetlands
on the household scale integrated as
mastabas and property defining borders
for privacy in dense urban contexts
collage: Alshama Alfarraj, Rana Gharib

Constructed Wetlands on the household scale

Constructed Wetlands
Samaha Village, Dakhleya Governorate

National Water Research Centre Egypt

Constructed Wetlands (CWs) are treatment systems that use natural processes involving wetland vegetation, soils, and their associated microbial assemblages to improve water quality. CWs as low-cost, low-maintenance and low-tech solutions treat waste water that may otherwise discharge into surface waters or contaminate ground water and eventually the food cycle. CWs also increase our resilience to floods and droughts. They are flexible systems that can be applied on varying scales: from single households to entire communities. Also, the Egyptian government has realized the potential of decentralized wastewater treatment for the urgently-needed protection of public health and the environment for rural areas that accommodate 56% of the total population.

Samaha Village in Dakhleya Governorate offers a successful example. Built in 1995 for a population of 10,000 inhabitants, the constructed wetland can treat 1000 cubic meters of primary treated domestic wastewater per day. The existing *bayara* system of the village dwellings was adapted to provide settling tanks on a household scale for the horizontal subsurface-flow constructed wetland of around 4200 sqm that produces reusable water for irrigation[1] and papyrus, which is harvested to produce paper.[2]

The larger spatial demand of CWs, a main disadvantage in comparison to conventional sewage systems, may call for solutions on the household or building scale. As blue-green infrastructure, a constructed wetland to treat grey water can be combined with a sub-surface biodigester that transforms black water and organic waste. A segregated treatment of grey and black water raises social acceptance and allows the constructed wetland to become a garden feature.[3] This combined system is capable of reducing water consumption, recycling grey water for reuse, and providing propane gas and fertilizer as well as harvestable papyrus, reed or bamboo while contributing to the increase of green area as a landscape design element. To provide off-grid sanitation while enhancing the landscape quality of often densely built environments, constructed wetlands can be integrated in courtyards, as *mastabas*, as green elements on small squares, as floating islands, façade systems, or, if the structural capacity is given, on rooftops. They improve the microclimate, contribute to thermal insulation when integrated in the building, and offer diverse aesthetic and recreational qualities that architects are only beginning to explore, such as polishing treated wastewater for irrigation. For Landscaping Egypt, we projected a CW into the courtyard of a mosque.

Samaha Constructed Wetlands Dakhleya
Governorate
Photo: hcwm.com.eg

SCENARIO *Constructed wetlands to treat greywater are installed on a community or household scale wherever proper sewage treatment is missing. In combination with biodigesters for blackwater treatment and planted with papyrus, these constructed wetlands become a scenic garden feature that rebrands Egypt's most epic plant. Vocational training programs for ecoplumbers and papyrus manufacturing ensure proper installation and maintenance while offering new job opportunities.*

Sociocultural barrier to using CWs
Subsurface flow CWs where the waste water level is around 10 cm below the surface hinder the development of smells and breeding of mosquitos.

Plants
Papyrus, reeds, or bamboo (see plant atlas) grown in the sand serve as water-cleansing plants and also offer by-products such as papyrus paper, compost or biomass for energy production.

Status Quo
Egypt's rural areas make up 56% of the total population. They often lack proper sanitation, leading to diarrhoea and kidney failure.

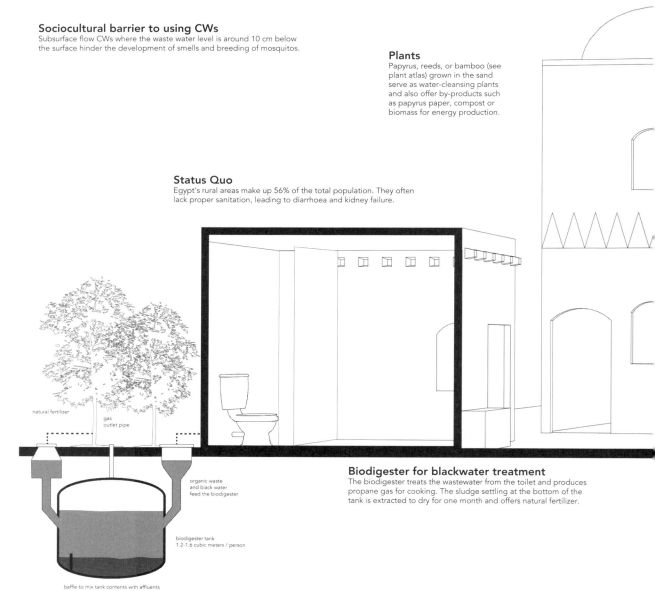

natural fertilizer

gas
outlet pipe

organic waste
and black water
feed the biodigester

biodigester tank
1.2-1.6 cubic meters / person

baffle to mix tank contents with affluents

Biodigester for blackwater treatment
The biodigester treats the wastewater from the toilet and produces propane gas for cooking. The sludge settling at the bottom of the tank is extracted to dry for one month and offers natural fertilizer.

Constructed Wetlands
Decentralized Ecosanitation

Community-Scale Constructed Wetlands
Description of main parameters and costs (in year of construction, 2001) for Samaha Subsurface Horizontal Flow CW is presented as follows[5]
· The design capacity is about 1000 cubic meter/day, while the actual discharge is about 1104 cubic meter/day
· Total construction cost is about 600 000 EGP compared to the cost of a conventional system for the same treatment size at 3 000 000 EGP for secondary treatment.
· Project area: 4 200 sqm vs. area of a conventional system of the same treatment size is 12 600 sqm for secondary treatment.
· Monthly operation and maintenance costs are less than 1000 EGP vs.16 000 EGP for a conventional wastewater treatment plant
· Manpower is only required for operation and maintenance, two full-time technicians and one part time engineer
· The plant produces bulrushes papers as a product

Household-Scale Constructed Wetlands
Depending on choice between horizontal and vertical flow systems, the spatial demand of sub-surface flow CWs in a warm climate with an average annual temperature > 20 °C between 1.2 – 3 sqm p.p.[4]

Water Reuse
the effluent can be used for
● irrigation
● aquaculture
● to flush

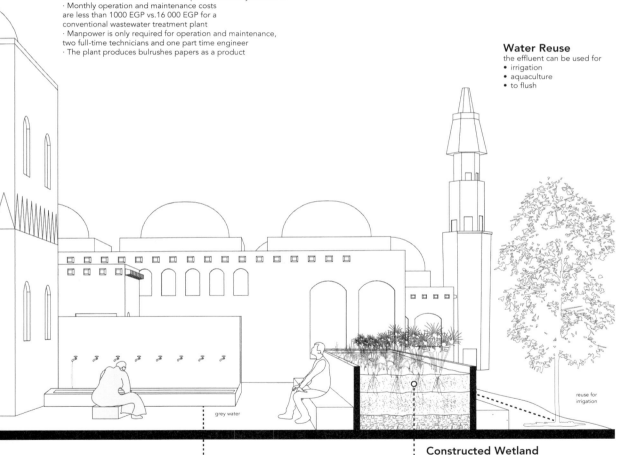

grey water

reuse for irrigation

Constructed Wetland
Primarily treated water slowly flows through the wetland, particles settle, pathogens are destroyed, and organisms and plants utilize the nutrients.

Sabil
The ablution water used for ritual cleansing is collected in a septic tank for solids to settle.

collecting tank

Green house with leafy greens production

Bustan Aquaponics, Giza

Aquaponic Farming
Giza

Bustan Aquaponics

Aquaponics is a recirculating farming system that combines hydroponics (soilless horticulture) and aquaculture. Fish generate waste that bacteria convert to fertilizer. Plants absorb the nutrients, and filter and oxygenate the water to then allow it to return to the fish. This symbiotic process of recycling wastes and recirculating water offers a site-independent system of food production and is over 1000 years old, dating back to Ancient Asia and the Aztecs.[1] It provides an ecological and affordable system to ensure food security and water conservation for a growing population.

Bustan Aquaponics is the first commercial aquaponic farm in Egypt. It was founded in 2011, and now has 12 employees. On 5,000 square meters, tilapia and leafy greens are grown in an aquaponic system. The aquaponic farm is embedded in an olive orchard of eight acres that complimentarily grows olives and root vegetables. With a total yield of 15,000 – 20,000 kg/year of vegetable production in addition to 5000 kg of tilapia production, the total vegetable basin surface of 300 sqm can produce at least the same quantity of vegetables and herbs as 1,200 to 1,500 sqm of land, including different types of lettuce, spring onion, endive, basil, pak choy and water cress, as well as fruit and herb crops of three types of heirloom tomatoes, borlotti beans, yellow string beans, chilli peppers, wild rocket and sweet basil.

Specifically, in the Egyptian context, framed by scarcity of water and agricultural land, large-scale aquaponics may become pivotal to ensure food security. Aquaponics is not yet established enough to respond to the economies of scale, therefore, small- to medium-scale systems on the building, household, business or community scale and catering to niche markets are defining current practice. They offer interesting possibilities for integration into the urban context, for example to tackle vacancy. As greenhouses within the urban fabric they may serve as light features at night. In Cairo, aquaponic farms could be accommodated in the largely abandoned Nile towers or vacant governmental buildings as ministries move to the New Administrative Capital.

When aquaponic farms are integrated within a host building, urban resources such as waste heat and CO_2 in exhaust air serve as an alternative to conventional CO_2 fertilization. Urban farms can further mitigate negative aspects of the urban heat island effect, as the additional vegetation, even if grown in greenhouses, helps to reduce the ambient temperature through increased evapotranspiration.[2]

(top to bottom):
Secondary structure for shading during the summer months /
Intercropping to diversify production /
Fish and filtration basins /
Floating plant holders in nutrient-rich water
Photos: Monique Jüttner

> **SCENARIO** *New urban communities develop neighbourhoods that incorporate aquaponic farms to facilitate their own consumption of fresh tilapia and leafy greens. Financial models and vocational training programs are provided to enable entrepreneurship and job creation. The site-independent farm offers a variety of adjoining business models and activities such as educational programs, farmers markets, or, as illustrated below, a farm-to fork-restaurant.*

Water Cycle

The water in the tanks is recirculated continuously. After leaving the fish tank, the water enters a clarifier that consists of a round fiberglass tank with several baffles placed at an angle that slows down the flow and causes particle sedimentation. Each day, the sludge accumulating at the bottom is drained and collected in a PE-lined pond beside the greenhouse. In this pond, the solid section of the waste water is filtered and collected in a burlap sack for further use as a high-quality compost; the water is used to irrigate the olives trees. The water then flows through a second particle trap consisting of two rectangular fiberglass basins filled with netting material.

While flowing through these basins to the outlet, most of the smaller particles attach to the nets. The nets are regularly removed and rinsed, the frequency depending on the amount of feeding. The water coming from the sediment traps comes together in an intensively-aerated square tank where the oxygen level is raised and carbon dioxide is removed. From here, the water flows to the horticulture unit by gravity.

The water in the long, shallow basins is aerated by air stones to provide the roots with oxygen and to enable conversion of ammonium to nitrate by bacteria. At the far end of the 30 m long basin the water is directed to an adjacent basin of similar proportions through which it slowly flows back to the fish unit, passing again through the roots of the vegetables. In the fish unit, the water collects in a sump; a 1.5 HP pump moves the water from the pit into the fish tanks. An automatic device with floater feeds the system with additional water when needed to maintain the overall water levels.[3]

Econometrics

Aquaponics demands for a relatively high initial investment (around 300,000 EGP in 2011) and intensive labour training. Fish feed makes up 60 – 70% of operating expenses. All building materials can be sourced from local markets.

Double Roof

A metal frame structure supports a mesh textile to shade the green house during the hot summer months.

Insulated fish basin tanks

4 round tanks of 8 cubic meters aerated with air stones, each accommodating 600 Nile tilapia grown to a weight of 800 – 1000 g

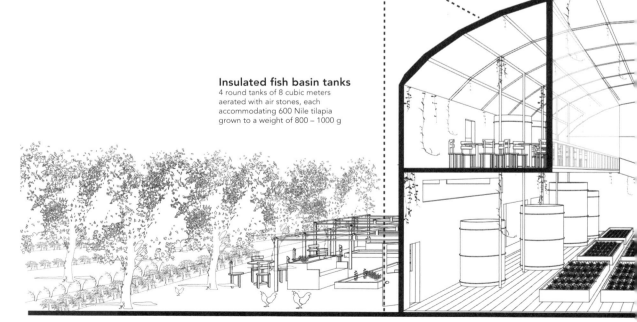

Adjoining land reclamation

Olive orchard with root vegetable beds as intercrop complement hydroponic produce. Off-cut from harvest is fed to chicken who lay eggs.

Biological pest control before entering and insect traps inside needed.

Aquaponic Farming
Food Production in the City

Settling tank
Sludge from fish basin can be extracted and dried to produce compost.

Nitrogen Cycle
Fish waste contains ammonia NH_3.
Bacteria turn ammonia to the plant nutrient nitrate No_3

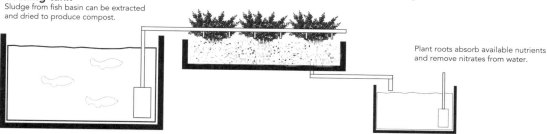

Plant roots absorb available nutrients and remove nitrates from water.

Tilapia Fry is available in Egypt and sustainable

Pump returns water to fish.

Footprint
Aquaponics uses up to 1/10 of water used in traditional soil-based agriculture, and produces four times the amount of leafy greens in addition to the fish production.

Water/Ambient Temperature Control
Suitable ambient temperature range for most vegetables is 18 – 30 °C
Water temperature for tilapia 22–32 °C
The optimal temperature for aquaponics is
Root zone temperature = around 22 °C
Bacteria and Nitrication = 25 – 30 °C

A fan and pad controlled environment cooling green house is ideal in extremely hot and cold environments to optimize production.

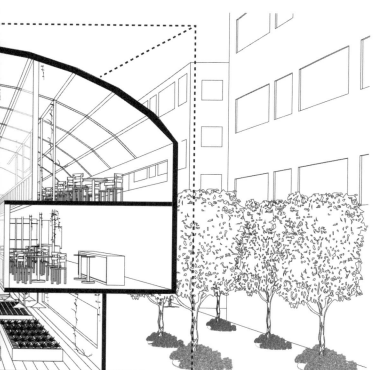

Duckweed
can also be fed to fish. It is ideal for aquaponics as it thrives on the waste fish leave behind, filtering the water so that it is again fit for fish. Duckweed is grown in the external sludge ponds, then harvested and dried. Added to the fish feed it provides a high vegetable protein supplement covering approx. 40% of protein demand.

Date Palm Pollination in Spring

Photo: Cornelia Redeker

Ten Medjool Date Palms
Nuweiba, South Sinai

Sinai Date Palm Foundation, Habiba Organic Farms

Egypt is rich in a diverse set of cultural landscapes expressing a genuine understanding and intense interaction with the natural environment in terms of climate, water and vegetation. For centuries, communities were based on a deeply rooted connection with the specific landscape and organized space corresponding to their social structures. Some have managed to persist until today. In the last century, pressing problems of urbanization and food production have been countered by large-scale megaprojects that are significantly reshaping the territory. Beyond that trend, recent approaches tactically build on vernacular landscape traditions by expressing a new valuation of historical and evolving cultural landscapes. These projects aim to make local communities, currently fully reliant on the tourism sector, more resilient to its extreme economic fluctuations.

Established and operated by Habiba Organic Farm, the Sinai Palm Date Foundation is bringing new means of sustainable income to the local Bedouin community. With a pilot project already underway, the focus of expanding date palm agriculture in the city of Nuweiba promises to be an exciting development in the years to come. By encouraging the funding of Medjool date palm trees, Habiba organizes and coordinates the planting and care of organic, fruit-producing trees that can provide a steady stream of income for the Habiba Learning Center that offer after-school education programs for local children. Date palms can also ensure a livelihood. According to the Sinai Date Palm Foundation, ten Medjool date palm trees can provide an income for one Bedouin family. With the support of the foundation hindrances, such as initial costs and maintenance for the time until the first harvest, are bridged. Through the project's unique focus, the Sinai Date Palm Foundation is connecting a wide range of people from varying cultures in the pursuit of organic, sustainable agriculture, as well as promoting education for the Nuweiba community. Partners from around the world have the opportunity to sponsor a palm tree, helping the local community while encouraging cultural enrichment and the collaboration of ideas in the process.

The palm tree, also considered the "tree of life" is a holy tree both in Islam and Christianity. Beyond its delicious dates, it offers an abundance of resources that must not be wasted. Pits are oil suppliers; the trunk and panicles can be used as building material. All other remnants can be used for composting or as animal feed. When fertilizing the soil with biological compost, it can store 20 percent more water. As a typical cultural landscape of Egypt along the Nile and in the oases of the Western Desert, the date palm trees are planted as orchards offering just enough shade for the complementary planting of vegetables and other plants on the ground. Spatially, the date palm is a very emblematic tree that, when planted in rows, may provide orientation and shade for pedestrians. On the following pages, we are projecting the Medjool date palm as a shade-giving tree on the Alley of the Sphinx in Luxor, making this epic connection between the temples of Karnak and Luxor more walkable and enhancing Luxor's role as the world's largest open-air museum.

Learning From Site-Independence

> **SCENARIO** *Based on the assumption that ten Medjool date palms are able to support one family and that all Egyptians would cultivate date palms: with the population of Egypt being around 100 million inhabitants and families consisting of five members on average, this would equal 20 million families and 200 million trees, placing Egypt before Saudi Arabia with around 25 million trees with an average annual yield of 15,000,000 tons of dates while adding to spatial quality and ecosystemic services.*

Grey Water Recycling

No. of aligning households
84 buildings x 10 appartments
(840 households/4 inhabitants)

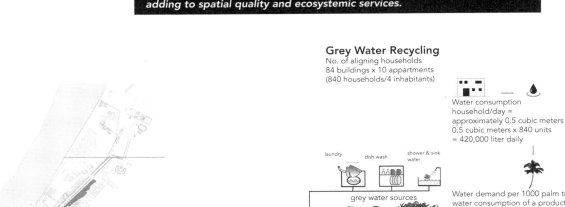

Water consumption household/day =
approximately 0.5 cubic meters
0.5 cubic meters x 840 units
= 420,000 liter daily

Water demand per 1000 palm trees
water consumption of a productive palm
tree approx. 290 liters/day
290 x 1,000 trees =290,000 liters/day

laundry   dish wash   shower & sink water

grey water sources

pre-treatment

soil-box planter

dispersion

irrigation

1000 Palm Trees for the Alley of the Sphinxes

Alley of the Sphinxes: around 400 palm trees. City Entrance Axis: 74 palm trees plus palm nurseries and additional open space plantations. Palm trees are arranged on a 10*10m grid.

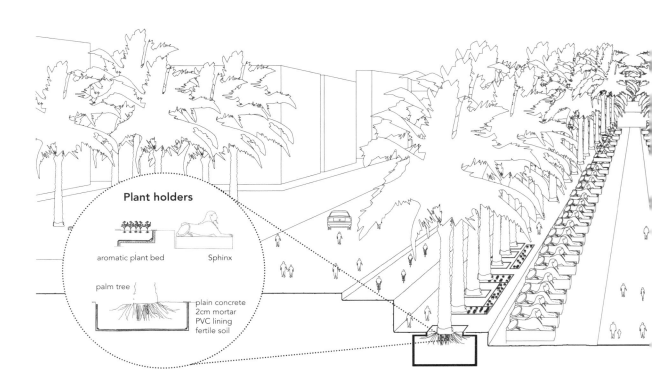

Plant holders

aromatic plant bed   Sphinx

palm tree

plain concrete
2cm mortar
PVC lining
fertile soil

Ten Medjool
Date Palms
Shade, Food and Livelihood

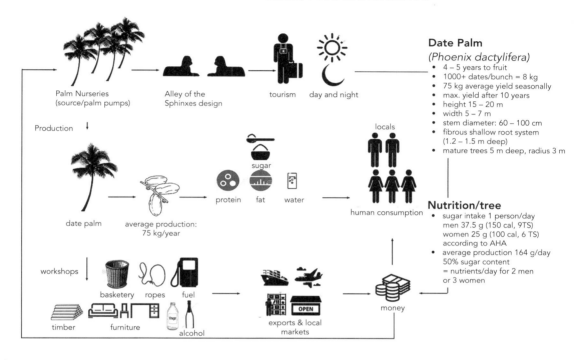

Palm Nurseries
(source/palm pumps)

Alley of the
Sphinxes design

tourism   day and night

Production

date palm

average production:
75 kg/year

sugar

protein   fat   water

human consumption

locals

workshops

basketery   ropes   fuel

timber   furniture   alcohol

exports & local
markets

money

Date Palm
(Phoenix dactylifera)
- 4 – 5 years to fruit
- 1000+ dates/bunch = 8 kg
- 75 kg average yield seasonally
- max. yield after 10 years
- height 15 – 20 m
- width 5 – 7 m
- stem diameter: 60 – 100 cm
- fibrous shallow root system
  (1.2 – 1.5 m deep)
- mature trees 5 m deep, radius 3 m

Nutrition/tree
- sugar intake 1 person/day
  men 37.5 g (150 cal, 9TS)
  women 25 g (100 cal, 6 TS)
  according to AHA
- average production 164 g/day
  50% sugar content
  = nutrients/day for 2 men
  or 3 women

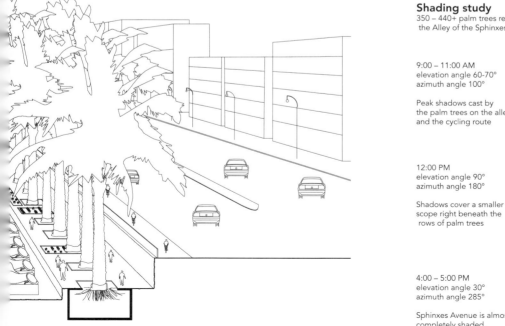

Shading study
350 – 440+ palm trees required to shade
the Alley of the Sphinxes

9:00 – 11:00 AM
elevation angle 60-70°
azimuth angle 100°

Peak shadows cast by
the palm trees on the alley
and the cycling route

12:00 PM
elevation angle 90°
azimuth angle 180°

Shadows cover a smaller
scope right beneath the
rows of palm trees

4:00 – 5:00 PM
elevation angle 30°
azimuth angle 285°

Sphinxes Avenue is almost
completely shaded.

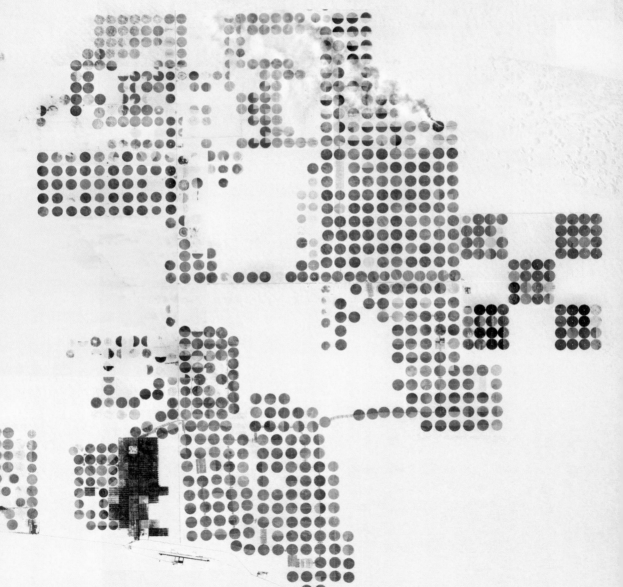

Pivotal Irrigation Agriculture, Toshka Land Reclamation, Western Desert

The Larger Scale
Urbanization, Agriculture, Land Reclamation

Kareem Ibrahim, Deena Khalil, Salwa Salman

Introduction

Egypt's rapid urbanization has contributed to a massive agricultural land loss that could threaten its food security. Rapid urbanization, population pressure and the accompanying housing and infrastructural development have stretched agricultural lands, which serve as a main source of livelihood in Egypt, to a point of major erosion due to urban encroachment. Despite these facts, the relationship between urbanization and agriculture in Egypt is not so straightforward, as urban encroachment is only one side of the story.

In this paper, we explore three characteristics of the relationship between urbanization and agricultural land in Egypt. Firstly, as hinted above, for decades Egypt has adopted land pricing and urban policies that have led to the erosion of existing agricultural lands in the Nile Valley. Secondly, in the wake of existing fertile agricultural land erosion in the Nile Valley, state policies have relied on land reclamation projects on desert land, in the hope that newly constructed agricultural communities would in turn create an economic base for urban and industrial communities, creating a New Valley. These attempts have seen little success. Thirdly, the volume of government investment in land reclamation policies far exceeds state investment to maintain existing land, thereby paralleling the official urban planning policy of pouring resources into new urban communities while neglecting existing cities. In the remainder of this article, we delve into each of these themes in more detail.

The Erosion of Agricultural Land through Urban Policies

The imbalanced concentration of nearly 95% of the Egyptian population around the Nile River Valley and the Delta has been one of the main demographic challenges to the Egyptian government for, to say the least, the last 60 years. One of the key impacts of this unbalanced distribution is the fast-growing urban, formal and informal, encroachment upon land of different uses, especially agricultural land. Cartographic data collected between 1992 and 2015 shows a loss of about 177,619 feddans[1] of old fertile agricultural land to urban expansion in the Nile Valley at an annual rate of 7,400 feddans.[2] This exponential urban growth, deemed to be inevitable, has driven the Egyptian government to follow various policy-tracks and strategies to contain it.

The redistribution of land under the banner of liberating Egyptian farmers from feudalism became a key development approach and gained political weight as a part of the revolutionary narrative[3]. This was coupled with an expansion in the industrial sector leading to the establishment of large industrial and manufacturing complexes near existing cities. Dorman (2013) notes that former Egyptian President Gamal Abdel Nasser "(...) preferred to locate industrial development closer to the existing agglomeration, usually on arable land, ironically putting in place the infrastructure and employment opportunities which would later support the growth of informal settlements."

In the wake of the 1967 war, which hindered formal urban expansion despite the introduction of state-subsidized housing and urban master planning by Nasser, informal encroachment over agricultural land increased.[4] The fragmentation of landholdings coupled with urban and residential expansion over agricultural land set the basis for the loss of agricultural land to urbanism. With the liberalization of Egypt's economy under the Open-Door Policy in 1974 and after implementing the Structural Adjustment Policies in 1991, land values and land-use for real-estate purposes increased significantly. By 1993, Egypt had lost 16% of its total agricultural land.[5] During this period, the deliberate sterilization of arable land for construction purposes became a prominent practice. To combat such practices, three main laws were enacted to stop the sterilization (Law no. 2 of year 1985) and building on agricultural land (Law no. 116 of year 1983). Furthermore, in 1996 a martial law criminalizing building on agricultural land was enacted.[6] Nevertheless, all attempts to combat urban expansion over agricultural land were short-lived.

Between 2011 and 2016, Egypt lost around fifty thousand feddans of arable agricultural land to urban infringement.[7] The long-awaited execution of the Unified Building Law 119 of 2008 is believed to facilitate the containment of informal urban expansion over agricultural land. Meanwhile, the Egyptian government has made notable success in compensating for the erosion of old agricultural land through mega land reclamation projects. Such landscape transformations remain, however, highly dependent on costly water infrastructural projects and have reportedly failed to reach the desired outcomes in the past. J. Barnes (2012) depicts that:

"Rather than try to improve agricultural production in the old lands, many government and business leaders think that it is better to invest in the new lands of the desert margins where profits will be greater."

Agriculture as a Driver of Urbanization
Successive Egyptian governments have for decades struggled with population pressure with the concentration of people and cities (and, in turn, economies and job opportunities) in the Nile Valley. In the face of these economic and demographic pressures, the Egyptian state has reacted by implementing land reclamation and desert development projects, with the aim of greening the desert and redistributing Egypt's population. In the early days after the Free Officers revolution in 1952, the Egyptian state adopted a policy of ensuring livelihood opportunities for the rural population, the fellahin – a policy that relied not only on agricultural land redistribution but also on trying to substantially increase the cultivated area (Voll, 1980). However, early definitions of land reclamation were limited to making virgin desert land arable, and setting up the accompanying social and administrative structures necessary to make it inhabitable. Eventually this definition expanded to include the creation of new industrial communities based on the reclaimed land. One of the earliest projects was the Liberation Province (Mudiriyyat Al-Tahrir) which was envisioned as more than a project to

merely reclaim agricultural land, but rather as a project to establish a new Egyptian rural society (ibid). As described by Voll (1980), "the project was to include 1.2 million feddans, divided into 12 districts each with 11 villages. Land would be farmed cooperatively in large units with highly mechanized techniques. Settlers were chosen only after intensive social, medical and psychological tests, and underwent a six-month training period to inculcate modern ideas. The concept of the project expanded to include an industrial center which would manufacture the construction components and process the harvest. … The program encompassed the reclamation of land, the design of model villages including houses of concrete and brick and all necessary public services, and the creation of agricultural cooperatives which would provide technical services as well as inputs and marketing."

By the late 1950s, a new idea began to surface that added to the existing ideas on expanding Egypt's agricultural land. This idea was based on the redistribution of the population away from the Nile Valley to a New Valley in the Western Desert. Millions of feddans were made available for distribution and cultivation along the oases of Kharga, Dakhla, Siwa, Farafra, and Bahriya, among other areas. Both the Mudiriyyat Al-Tahrir and New Valley projects saw very limited achievements in terms of making the land arable and inhabitable, and both struggled to attract inhabitants.

When the Nile floods of 1998 caused the Lake Nasser reservoir to risk overflowing rather than allowing the excess water to be wasted, the Egyptian government announced a project to construct a new city in the Western desert that would be greened via these excess waters. Located near Lake Nasser in Egypt's south-western desert, the Toshka mega-project was planned to house millions of Egyptians and to host a new city built upon a newly budding agricultural and industrial economy. With agriculture as the main driver, the project was planned to include, at later stages, *"mining, alternative energy production, and possibly oil and gas production and tourism".[8] The project was hailed as Egypt's "project of the Millenium" and was "part of an on-going state-led hydraulic mission, a drive for 'horizontal expansion' of living space started in the 1950s".[9]*

The project was initially planned to be carried out in two phases that would be completed by 2017. However, in 2005, the government announced the cancellation of Phase 2, and extended the completion date of Phase 1 to 2022.[10] Many reasons underlie this decision, including the many technical difficulties faced by the project, such as the high salinity levels and the presence of underground aquifers.[11] Government authorities have not made public any feasibility studies, progress reports, or budgetary information about the project, but what little data is available shows an outcome very different from the planned vision. Despite this, the project is still ongoing today, and President Sisi visited the area in March 2019 to inspect the farms and plantations.[12] Ultimately, it is clear that the plan to increase Egypt's arable land while also relying on agriculture to drive the creation of new urban centres and industrial economies around it has been much more difficult than initially foreseen.

The Paradigm of "Investing In The New"

Egypt's two main development policies that have remained consistent since 1952 until today are: constructing new urban communities in the desert and implementing large-scale land reclamation projects as showcased in the previous section. The overpopulation of the Nile Valley has become the dominant trope in the rhetoric around national development. Resources have been channeled to serve these policies. Billions of pounds from successive national budgets have been directed towards such projects, including "six mega land reclamation projects and 22 so-called New Cities over the last sixty years".[13]

Out of the 22 new urban communities, "not a single new urban community has reached its target population and the vast majority have not even surpassed the 50% mark".[14] This trend is also true for the Desert Hinterland Villages Project, lying at a sort of midway between desert development and rural development. The project aims to set up new villages in the desert hinterlands of the Nile Valley to then motivate residents of existing rural areas to relocate to these new villages. It appears that 21 desert hinterland villages have already been constructed in eight governorates across Egypt, and another 16 are under development.[15] According to a scan of satellite imagery from 2012, much progress has taken place in regard to construction, but not a single inhabitant has been recorded in any of the constructed villages.[16]

Despite the hurdles faced by new city projects, the agricultural land reclamation projects, and the Desert Hinterland Villages Project, all schemes continue to consume a substantial portion of the national budget. An analysis of the 2015/2016 national budget – focused on components related to the built environment – found that 30% of the built environment budget was spent on the new cities, serving only 2% of the population, while 48% is spent on the existing cities and villages which host 98% of the population.[17] Shawkat and Hendawy (2016) draw on this analysis and find that the gross spatial inequality in regards to access to the built environment – such as safe shelter, secure tenure, adequate water and sanitation – is "less to do with population density, and more to do with the formal drive to expand into the desert".

Conclusion

The Egyptian state's drive to lead an exodus from the Nile Valley proves challenging, although it has certainly been persistent. Whether greening it or urbanizing it, the desert seems to have an almost mythical hold on the public – and official – imagination in Egypt.

With the urgencies of climate change, water scarcity, pollution and an increasing population which is for the most part very young and on a low income, Egypt's agriculture-urbanization nexus can greatly benefit from new, more integrated and adaptable models to ensure resilience. Moving away from large-scale industrial solutions and conventional master planning demands in favour of a multi-scalar approach that could largely benefit from the tactical capacity of the small scale. Making existing and new developments in the Nile Valley and in the desert more capable of coping with environmental, economic and social stresses demands new more integrated landscape planning strategies to make our urban environment more liveable – also in terms of well-being. For the existing developments, this implies a retroactive approach in order to benefit from the given densities and short distances while increasing open areas and urban green to ensure ventilation, accessibility, and a healthy environment. For the new cities, a more resource-efficient and walkable approach to urban design that is capable of providing a livelihood for all income levels is needed. An incremental approach relying on efficient, moderated monitoring and evaluation processes to enable learning and adaptability both socio-economically and environmentally may be a fruitful approach for all three spheres: the development corridor of the Nile Valley, the existing desert expansions and the new generation of cities in the making.

Public Green, New Cairo

03 Revisited and Projected
اعادة النظر والعرض

Typologically, one aspect that we find in all historical, but also in contemporary open space design in Egypt is the *hortus conclusus*, the enclosed garden. On the quest for more water-sensitive and productive garden typologies that are rooted in the local, we of course come across the ANCIENT EGYPTIAN GARDEN with its diversity and richness in productive plants, inclusion of animals and the specific rectangular spatial quality that define these enclosed spaces. Given the abundance of Islamic monuments, the ISLAMIC GARDEN, surprisingly enough, has not found too many prominent applications in the contemporary Egyptian context until recently with Al Azhar Park and the AUC Campus in New Cairo. With its combined formats of garden types of the urban courtyard, the bustan (orchard) and the kitchen garden, we only begin to explore its richness and potential when it comes to productive open space design. The DESERT/CACTUS GARDEN was added to the list as a model which is of course the most water-sensitive. We find the most stunning Bedouin desert garden examples in Sinai with ancient olive orchards and a vast variety of medicinal plants. In contemporary garden design, cacti are often found as one of many themes within a larger garden complex. Although 94% of the country is desert, we have not been able to find entire gardens that follow this theme and feel that succulents in combination with drought-resistant native trees offer a third garden typology that deserves to be explored in a more extensive way.

With the projection of the three native garden design models onto a typical shared open space plot of a multiple-apartment villa neighbourhood in New Cairo ,we aim to show how culturally and geographically rooted garden typologies in their productive essence may produce a thematic design brief, that builds on a long local history of garden design which is both productive, water-sensitive and beautiful. Different canopy heights and complimentary planting are inherent to all of these typologies. They are also all lawn-free. In combination with the decentral reuse of waste water and composting of organic waste, these garden models advocate stewardship for the land.

Pharaonic Inspired Garden, Sakkara

Photo: Hala N. Barakat

Ancient Gardens
الحدائق العتيقة

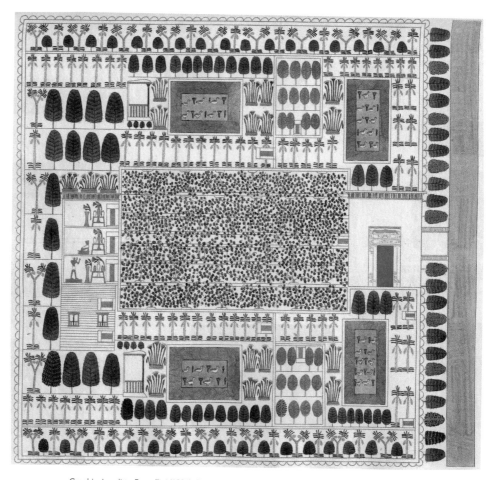

Graphic: Ippolitto Rossellini (1834). Di monumenti dell' Egitto e della Nubia. Pisa
https://digi.ub.uni-heidelberg.de/diglit/rosellini1834bd4_2/0072

Amun Temple Garden in Karnak – Depiction in the Grave of Sennefer, Thebes-West, Egypt, grave no. 96, 1400 BC

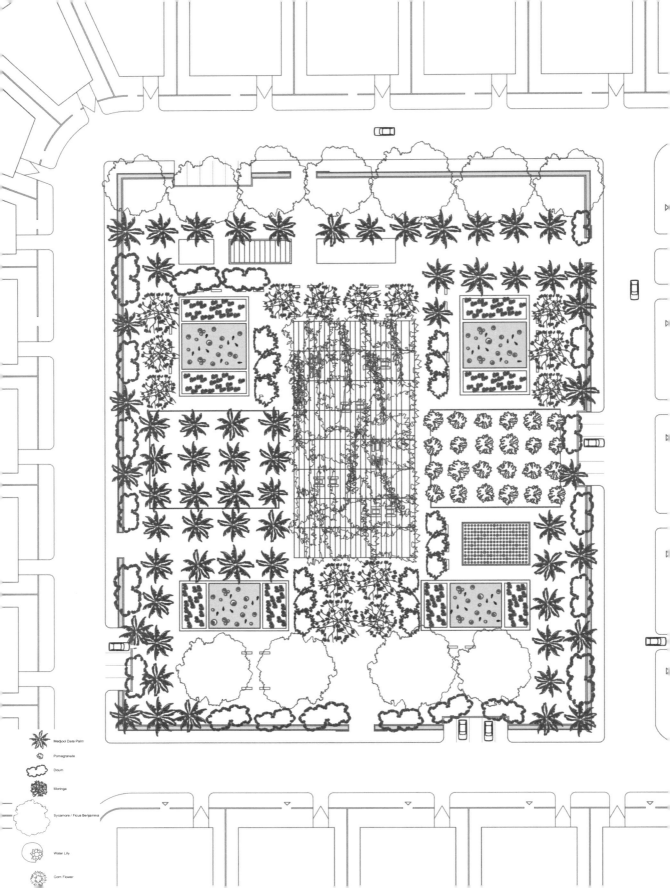

Medjool Date Palm

Pomegranate

Doum

Moringa

Sycamore / Ficus Benjamina

Water Lily

Corn Flower

Ancient Gardens
الحدائق العتيقة

Ancient Egyptian gardens, such as the one depicted in the Amun temple, were places of worship, contemplation and productivity. Temples, tombs (including the pyramids) and private houses had gardens. Detailed descriptions of their layout and quantifications of the planted trees give us a very precise understanding of how these gardens were designed.

Rectangular and close to symmetrical in their geometric pattern, water bodies were framed by parcels and the organization of plants was defined by their height, their religious symbolism as well as their water needs. The gardens were enclosed spaces. High plastered walls, sometimes painted and tiled, served to protect them and to hide them from the vulgar. Gates were and still are important architectural features in Egyptian landscape design. Gate posts were elaborately decorated to mark the entrance. Inside of the gardens, we find smaller buildings for shade and as hideaways.

Central and prominent in the design are walled water bodies which also give the pharaonic gardens their name. *Scha'* means lake or pond as well as garden.[1] Rectangular or t-shaped pools and lakes were supplied with Nile water by canals. The water was used to irrigate, but also to drink, to refresh and to breed fish and birds. Fish were not only eaten, but also served as offerings as well as for aesthetic pleasure. Birds included pigeons, doves, duck and geese. Also, lions, antelopes, oryx and ibex were found in ancient garden depictions. The gardens were further decorated with sculptures and statues which were mostly religious in tomb gardens representing the owner engaged in activities related to the gods.

Plants were chosen for their productivity. Their ornamental qualities played a secondary role. Trees were usually planted in rows or as borders. The inventory of the tomb of Ineni, the mayor of Thebes in the time around 1490 BC, includes a precise inventory of around 500 trees that were planted: 73 sycamore figs, 31 mimosas, 170 date palms, 120 doum palms, 5 figs, 12 vines, 5 pomagranates, and 1 argun palm, 9 willows and 10 tamarisk.

This shows the focus on productive trees, and possibly also the difficulty of cultivating the argoun palm, already recognised in ancient times. Another feature of the ancient garden that we still find in the Egyptian countryside today is the pergola planted with grapevines, providing not only shade, but fruits and leaves and serving as one of the pharaonic gardens central and most prominent features.[2]

In many of the depictions of ancient gardens we find tree goddesses such as Isis, the mother of Horus as a sycamore fig tree representing the provision of eternal water and nourishment.

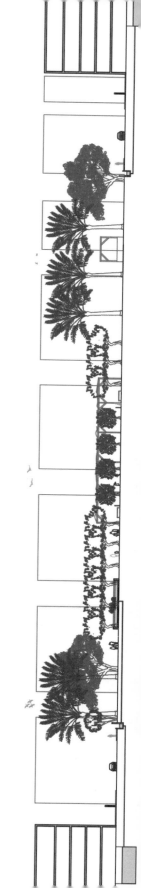

Al Azhar Park, Islamic Cairo

Islamic Gardens
الحدائق الإسلامية

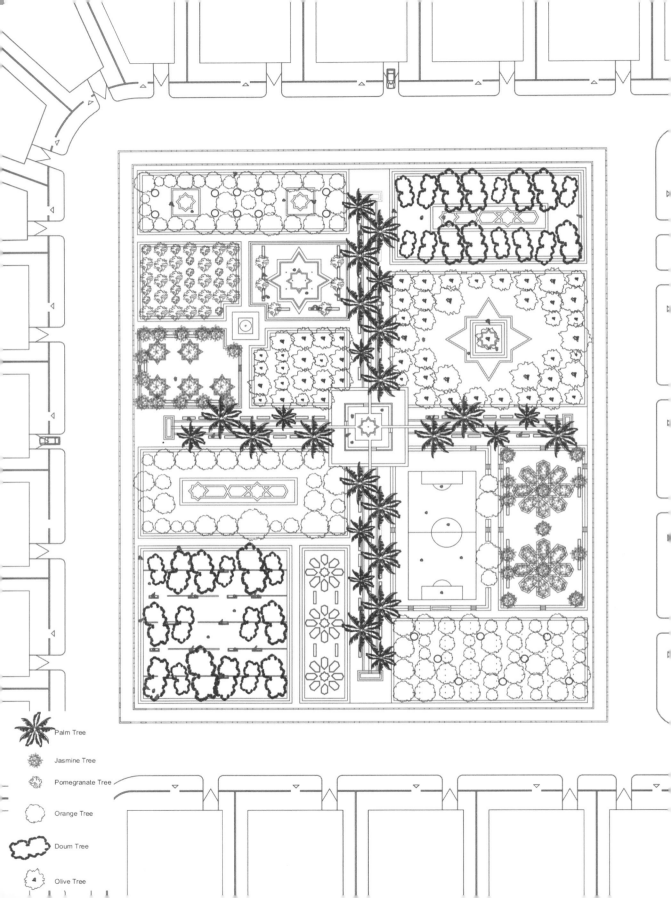

Palm Tree

Jasmine Tree

Pomegranate Tree

Orange Tree

Doum Tree

Olive Tree

Islamic Gardens
الحدائق الإسلامية

Islamic gardens are defined by grids of different scales and proportions with a variety of geometric systems and repetitive elements. Complex symmetries and patterns define structures and masonry, and the tiling of surfaces show the architectural, man-made quality inherent to Islamic gardens.

Although it is a landscape design practice that has brought forth a myriad of variations, when imagining ourselves in an Islamic garden we tend to immediately visualize the four-partite quadrant layout. Known as the chadar bagh, four often submerged plant beds are clearly defined by tiled paths and a central water feature. Sunken gardens for planting enable the experience of a tree canopy at eye level.

The Islamic garden tradition includes multiple typologies. Only where plants become productive beyond the singular ornamental plant or tree do we find extensive soft scapes. Beyond the enclosed, contemplative hard scape of the courtyard, the ensemble is further made up of the bustan or orchard with date, citrus and olive trees and a kitchen garden with vegetables and herbs. Together, they create an ensemble.

Whereas in western garden traditions, continuous green areas where the majority is lawn expand into the landscape, Islamic gardens are created in stark contrast to nature. Often enclosed by walls, arcades, or as a courtyard, they are introverted spaces for contemplation and sensual pleasure involving limited movement rather than a vast space that anticipates walking. Sometimes plants are completely abandoned. Instead, arcades or a portico frame views of distant orchards or landscapes. The primarily hard scape of the courtyard design, as well as the focus on shade and water features, reflect the water-scarce environments of Islamic garden culture. Narrow water runnels and the chaddar, a cascading, ruffled element that engages the sonic senses, are carefully positioned along paths towards a central fountain, while water-aligned paths represent the rivers of paradise of water, milk, honey and wine.

Evolving in cultures rooted in agricultural practice, the rectangular layout and orientation benefit from the sun, with southwest-facing designs and axial relationships, generally oriented in a north-south direction, reflecting the celestial relationship of garden designs.[1]

Bedouin Garden, South Sinai

Desert Gardens
الحدائق الصحراوية

Photo: Monique Jüttner

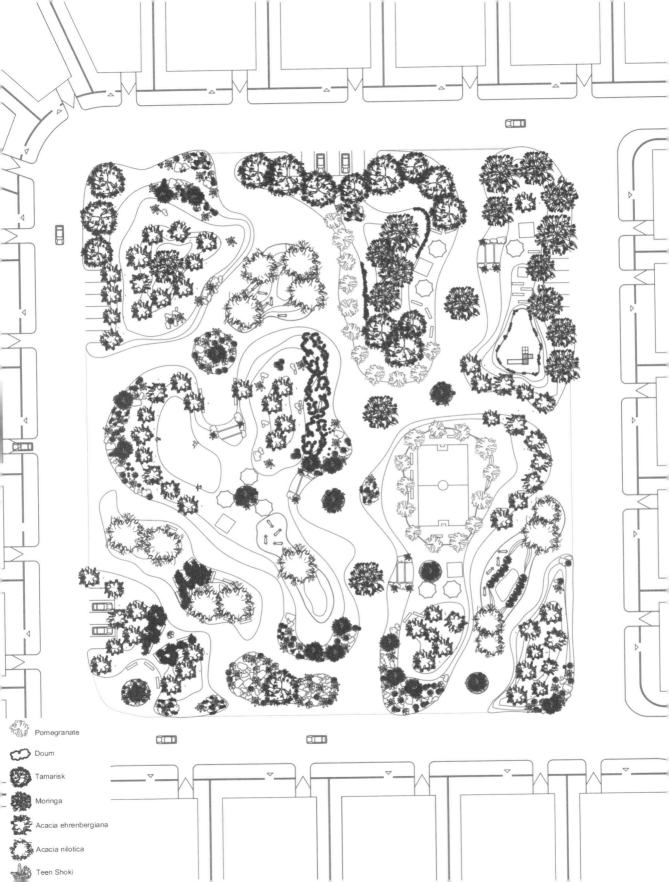

Pomegranate

Doum

Tamarisk

Moringa

Acacia ehrenbergiana

Acacia nilotica

Teen Shoki

Desert Gardens
الحدائق الصحراوية

Desert Gardens, also known as xeriscapes or dry landscapes, reduce or eliminate the need for supplemental water for irrigation by planting a completely different, much more diverse repertoire of plants than the typical association with cacti would cause us to assume. We find a highly drought-tolerant selection of certain palms, like the argoun, acacias and bushes to provide shade and break the wind, certain shrubs and grasses and ground covers, as well as a selection of succulents. The repertoire of desert plants also hosts highly productive plants such as olive trees, pomegranates or caper bushes, edible cacti such as prickly pear, and aloe vera as a medicinal succulent.

With little maintenance effort and water requirement, desert, stone and cactus gardens answer to an emerging need for economic landscapes, but also reflect a global trend towards sparse design termed as zero scaping.[1] These are qualities that we find in the diverse Bedouin cultivations: in their mountain gardens in Sinai and palm orchards in the oases of the Western desert, as well as in their fig and olive plantations in the wadis along the North coast. All are arid cultural landscapes of stunning beauty that capture and evolve from the given topography.

Although a recent discovery of the desert shows an emergent appreciation of arid landscapes as places of contemplation, withdrawal and nature experience, they are per se considered hostile environments and, in the Egyptian culture of inhabiting the lush and fertile Nile Valley, often not recognized at all. Yet, with 94% of the Egyptian landscape being arid, choosing plants that need little or no water offers a valid approach to open space design that is only beginning to be explored[2], until now usually as a themed segment within a larger garden conception.

Desert gardens grow on a rocky or sandy terrain. In our perception, they are often reduced to cacti; these create a unique aesthetic with their rare blossoms in vibrant colors and sculptural silhouettes comparable to the sensual richness of underwater gardens of coral reefs. The cactus can be planted against the backdrop of a straight wall in a very orthogonal hardscape context. Their thorns provide natural borders. The variations in shape and height and absence of lawn make cactus gardens perfect for more organic layouts that are enhanced by variations in the topography. For example, small hills and swales can be used as a tool to create privacy, as they block views and physical access. High temperatures and overall water scarcity make shade and water features elements that make people wish to linger, physically by lowering the temperature, but also visually through the cooling association. Singular trees, such as the Acacia Tortillis with its umbrella canopy celebrate the provision of much sought after shade, while very selective water features additionally produce habitat gardens that attract wildlife, especially birds.

Bedouin orchards master the convergence of architectural elements (majestic stone walls, a fire place, a spring, or single stones) with the scarce, natural landscape such as a solitary tree articulated by the setting of captivating valley and mountain landscapes. Desert gardens could draw aesthetic strength in a similar way. The desert has manifold faces. Its topography is a sculpture of environmental forces with few but strong natural elements; an interplay of structure and color of rocks, dynamically forming dunes and hillocks evolving around enduring pioneer plants of striking shape or color (Acacia ehrenbergiana / Teen Shoki).

التخطيط لنظام الغذاء
والتراث المصري

Foodmiles from Producer to Consumer: Bananas traveling on the Ringroad, Cairo

Photo: Monique Jüttner

Planning for Egypt's Food System and Heritage

Monique Jüttner, Hala N. Barakat, Undine Giseke

Over the course of thousands of years, different regions of the world developed very divergent ways of agricultural cultivation that were deeply rooted in local geography, climate and culture. Cultural landscapes are the result of this intensive, long-term interaction of humans with nature, marked by a physical transformation of the surface of the earth and by the evolution of differing food systems and heritage reflecting the local givens. Intensified urbanization since the 19th century has disturbed this close relation of humans and their environment, blurring the clear divide of urban and rural spheres. Worldwide agricultural production underwent massive transformations and intensification to feed a growing population, significantly changing how food is produced, processed, distributed and consumed. Most regions today are heavily entangled in a globally active food regime that is marked by large scale mass-production, impacting local agriculture and city regional food systems.

The Roots of Egyptian Food Heritage[1]
Prehistory – the transition from roaming to sedentary living and farming
Egypt looks back on a particularly ancient food heritage originating in prehistoric times around 10,000 years ago, when desert dwellers lived around water bodies formed in the depressions after rainfall and relied on wild grasses[2] as nourishing staples, as well as fruits, rhizomes, legumes and other herbaceous plants for food and fodder[3]. Marking the beginning of the Predynastic period,[4] the onset of arid conditions forced dwellers to move to the Nile valley, where better conditions allowed the cultivation of grains (wheat and barley) and of various beans and peas, inducing a major change of lifestyle. As wheat and barley do not grow wild in Egypt, they were presumably introduced from the Fertile Crescent and became staple foods. Excavations from ancient settlement sites and tombs along the Nile and in the Delta retrieved charred grains, seeds and fruits[5] of which some were cultivated and others were growing wild.[6] We can assume that grains, seeds, as well as the rhizomes of tiger nut were ground and made into bread and cake. Pulses (beans, peas and vetches) were cooked and appreciated for their high protein content, and green leafy plants were added for flavor and to make soup, while fruits were eaten raw, cooked or dried.

Pharaonic rule and state led agriculture
Kings and Queens of the Dynastic period[7] ran expeditions, conquered new lands, established trade routes and migration, and introduced many new plants to the region. Plant remains indicate an abundancy of plant varieties present at that time, but tell us little about their precise use. Pharaonic depictions vividly describe a well-organized cultivation and processing of beer, wine and grains. Some vegetables[8] could have been consumed solely raw or accompanying bread and cheese, while others[9] must have been cooked to make green soups and sauces. It is likely that the tradition of mixing bread with vegetables into a fatta (Nubian cuisine) and combining pulses with leafy greens has persisted since then[10]. Pulses such as lentils and sprouted beans (nabet) presumably were used as a base for broth and broad beans (green or dry) to make Bessara paste. Before the arrival of

rice, a variety of grain products complemented the diets of humans. Grains were milled into fine flour for bread making, leaving a variety of by-products such as desheish, possibly freek and keshk.[11] Fruits were consumed raw and used in cakes.

Souvenirs of Foreign Rulers and International Trade
With the arrival of the Greeks and Romans,[12] aromatic herbs (bay leaves, sweet marjoram, rosemary) and various tasty fruits (apple, apricot, mulberry, lemon) as well as cabbage and carob were introduced from the Mediterranean and culti-vated, whilst pepper and nuts (pine nut, walnut, hazelnut) were imported.
The long period of Arab rule during medieval times[13] spread Islam in Asia and Africa and brought active exchange of food items between Egypt, India and the Far East. Chicken, for example, arrived from Persia by the 8th century, leading to a surge in animal consumption. After the discovery of the Americas in 1492, Portuguese traders brought an array of vegetables, fruits, nuts, grains and tubers first to the Mediterranean and later to other parts of the world[14] establishing tomato, zucchini, guava, strawberry and prickly pear as indispensable parts of the Egyptian cuisine. During the 18th century, the spice trade routes passing through the Red Sea flourished. Rice and especially spices[15] originating from regions bordering the Indian Ocean enriched the local cuisine with new flavors. Ginger and galangan were imported from China, saffron from India, mastic from Greece and salt, olive oil, raisins, flour and fruits from Europe, while Egypt was famous for its sugar.[16]
Just as international trade considerably influenced Egyptian food heritage, so did foreign occupations such as the long periods of Ottoman rule in Egypt during the 16th – 19th century, the French invasion at the turn of the 19th century or the period of British Protectorate in the 20th century. A popular cookbook[17] from the 1940s presents the modern Egyptian cuisine as a mixture of traditional and foreign dishes of African, Mediterranean, Arab, French, English, Italian, Greek and Turkish cuisine vividly illustrating the culinary effects of international trade and foreign rule in Egypt.

Food, Agriculture and Water Engineering in Modern Egypt
Radical modernization, Nile regulation and a transforming agriculture
Since pharaonic times, agriculture in Egypt has relied on the annual Nile flood and its fertilizing silt sedimentation in the Nile Valley and Delta using basin ir-rigation. A system of dykes and basins distributed the flood water that arrived regularly between August and October[18] in the farmed Nile plane. During non-flood periods water was lifted and directed to farmlands using the shaduf and tanbour, and later also the saquia and motor-driven pumps allowing the irrigation of one summer crop per year. This well-managed cultural landscape basically remained in place till the early 19th century, when Muhammad Ali and subsequent rulers of his dynasty induced a radical modernization process by establishing a modern administration, modern education and an early in-dustrial production system for world markets. Triggering major technological, social and economic change Egypt's food production, consumption and distri-bution significantly transformed. The storage and controlled release of the Nile flood became a key measure to increase agricultural productivity and to allow an industrialized production of cotton, rice and sugarcane for export.[19] In the 1830s, the first dams and canals were constructed. Water infrastructure steadily

increased, releasing agriculture from the constraints of seasonal flooding and establishing perennial irrigation with double or triple harvests. Cultivation patterns transformed, and were soon dominated by cash crops. The suspension of natural flooding led to unforeseen consequences in the form of salt water logging and a decline in soil fertility, creating a need for complex drainage networks and pumping stations and increased animal husbandry for manure.[20] With the construction of the Aswan High dam in 1968, energy provision, full flood control and water storage was achieved, allowing water to be distributed over long distances and to expand agricultural lands. Early agricultural reclamation projects in the 1950s aimed to augment arable lands for feeding a growing population. Despite these efforts, with continuous population growth in the 1970s and 1980s and large parts of agricultural production for export markets, Egypt increasingly had to cover its food needs with food imports. The containment of informal urbanization on valuable arable lands and the expansion of agricultural lands into the desert became paramount objectives of official development policies, pushing forward large scale desert reclamation schemes using industrialized farming techniques since the 1990s.

Development Policies, Economy and Diets
During harsh wartime in 1941, a comprehensive system of food subsidies on basic food commodities had been put into place as a response to food emergency. Social change, induced by an agricultural reform following the 1952 revolution,[21] strengthened the spatial pattern of smallholder farming in the 'old lands'. Aiming for social welfare, the Nasserist regime established a subsidized and protected economy consolidating the system of food subsidies (ration cards and subsidized foot items) as social currency consequently exposing the nation to food price fluctuations on world markets, and climbing public expenditures for food subsidies.[22]

Food shop on wheels, New Cairo

With a fundamental restructuring towards market liberalization in the early 1970s (the Infittah Policy of Sadat), Egypt's economy faced modernization, industrial development and the opening of the country to foreign investments.[23] Attempts to remove the food subsidies led to bread riots in 1977, revealing the crucial connection between food and political stability. Food subsidies persist to this day as a primary mechanism for food security in Egypt,[24] but render the nation vulnerable to import shortages and price hikes. The global food crisis of 2007/08 hit the nation severely, triggering uprisings in 2007 that presumably initiated the chain of events that led to the Arab Spring in 2011.[25] Compared to the world average, the Egyptian population shows an outstanding prevalence for obesity[26] and diabetes. The prominence of wheat in the Egyptian diet[27] is rooted in local food culture to some extent, but is also an effect of the availability of subsidized baladi bread at almost no cost. Sugar and vegetable oil[28] are also available at nominal prices, and consumers prefer subsidized food items over other staple foods. This induces over-consumption and waste. The appearance of multinational food and beverage chains on the Egyptian market or the striking numbers of western style coffee shops in Cairo[29] since the 1990s can be understood as ambassadors of a globalizing food system. It is expected that consumers will diversify their diets,[30] with an increasing GDP per capita tending to lead them to prefer more Western-style products and increasingly neglecting local food culture.

Biodiversity and Food Heritage Protection
Agricultural production in developed countries builds on a well-established formal seed market that is dominated by a limited number of globally acting seed producers organized in an international Union (L'union internationale pour la protection des obtentions végétales (UPOV)).[31] It is assumed that in countries of the NENA[32] region, only 10 percent of farmers' seed needs are covered by the formal seed supply.[33] In Egypt, the majority of seeds are imported, with only a small portion locally produced. In 2002 Egypt adopted a law[34] that gives breeders of new plant varieties derived from inside or outside Egypt exclusive rights for the commercial exploitation of the variety. The law reflects the will to adhere to international agreements,[35] to attract foreign investments and to engage the private sector for seed breeding, but at the same time compromises biodiversity and the independence of local farmers to breed and trade seeds. As a response, Article 79 was incorporated into the Egyptian constitution in 2014, enshrining the right to food, the safeguarding of sustainable food sovereignty and the protection of local plants and agricultural biological diversity, thus de facto empowering local producers, fostering biodiversity and highly valuing Egypt's food and plant heritage. To balance both, economic interests and values of local agricultural and food heritage is challenging but will be a key measure for a rapidly transforming food system in Egypt.

Food and the City
For a long time, urban planning has been blind in terms of urban food supply.[36] Not only a rising number of research activities, but also several international initiatives and policies are dealing with the topic of urban growth, food planning, and urban food systems. To give one example: From 2015 to 2019, 203 cities signed the Milan Urban Food Policy Pact,[37] among others Algiers, Bobo-Dioulasso, Cape Town, Dakar, Nairobi, and Tunis from the African continent. They all acknowledge that cities have a strategic role to play in developing sustainable food systems and promoting healthy diets, and agree that current food systems are being challenged to provide permanent and reliable access to adequate, safe, local, diversified, fair, healthy and nutrient-rich food for all. Evidently, cities do exercise substantial influence on landscape and agriculture worldwide through their food systems. For an urbanizing society such as Egypt, this is equally true.
The food system can be described as a phenomenon of local interactions between cities and their surrounding landscapes as well as other parts of the country or the planet, called the global hinterland. In recent science this aspect is given the name telecoupling,[38] which describes flows between globally distant places. In parallel, the public as well as the scientific focus shifted to the cities' role within the food system. An important step is to better understand the urban food systems (UFS) or the city regional food system (CRFS) and its vital links, not only between cities and rural communities but also within the city itself. In terms of our research, the very first step is to understand and describe UFSs in an integrated, trans-sectoral way in order to overcome traditional sectoral approaches. We consider an urban food system as a major urban infrastructure integrated into the urban landscape that can be tracked down to the five components of production, processing, distribution, access/

consumption and reuse through their spatial manifestations. Within our research, urban agriculture served as a starting point towards analyzing the urban food system. In the urban region of Greater Casablanca, we focused on conceptualizing and operationalizing urban agriculture as part of the urban food system and as a new type of green infrastructure. Conceptualizing urban food systems becomes even more fruitful by linking urban food production to other major urban services such as water, waste, and energy as part of the urban metabolism.

It is challenging to investigate the different components of an urban regional food system in their multiple dimensions (economic, social, cultural, ecological and/or spatial) without neglecting the context-specific variations. Conceptualizing the UFS and its components spatially – all along its components from production to disposal/valorization - serves to help us understand and assess very different processes, actors, scales and flows within the UFS. The systemic view of food serves as a lens to analyze food as part of the urban metabolism, with flows between components and interfaces with other relevant thematic fields of urban planning in growth centers. The spatialization of the Urban Food Systems enables one to structure and localize resource flows within an urban system and to make linkages and interfaces more visible, address and localize actors and stakeholders' roles within the food system, identify and generate possible synergies and linkages between related sectors, to address the administrative and governance needs of territorial urban planning and discuss the question of appropriate scale for food system components in the context of urban growth centres.

A major task will be the question of how to provide urban systems with adequate infrastructure services and how to establish a rapid trans-sectoral urban planning methodology. The Rapid Planning Project conducted in Kigali, Ruanda and DaNang, Vietnam,[39] for example, exercised just such an integrated approach by creating a model and simulating scenarios of the urban metabolism trying to generate synergies between different flows of the urban metabolism such as urban agriculture / food, water, waste, and energy.

Implications for the Future

Spatializing food infrastructure as a trans-sectoral and interactive infrastructure has the potential to foster new ways of thinking towards methods and concepts. This kind of infrastructure is not necessarily technology-orientated but has a strong focus on (civil) actors and their social practices, trans-sectoral planning and metabolic flows and processes related to spatial entities. Interactive infrastructure indicates a general endeavor for networking and exchanging in different dimensions – between people on a cultural and economic level, between physical infrastructure and social actors, between the urban and natural system and between other infrastructures – actively enabling an urban metabolism by seeking trans-sectoral linkages. New ways of thinking towards methods and concepts on multiple spatial scales are to be developed. Building on the local food and landscape heritage can be a valid point of departure for an emerging Egyptian landscape practice responsive towards local social, economic, food, water and environmental urgencies.

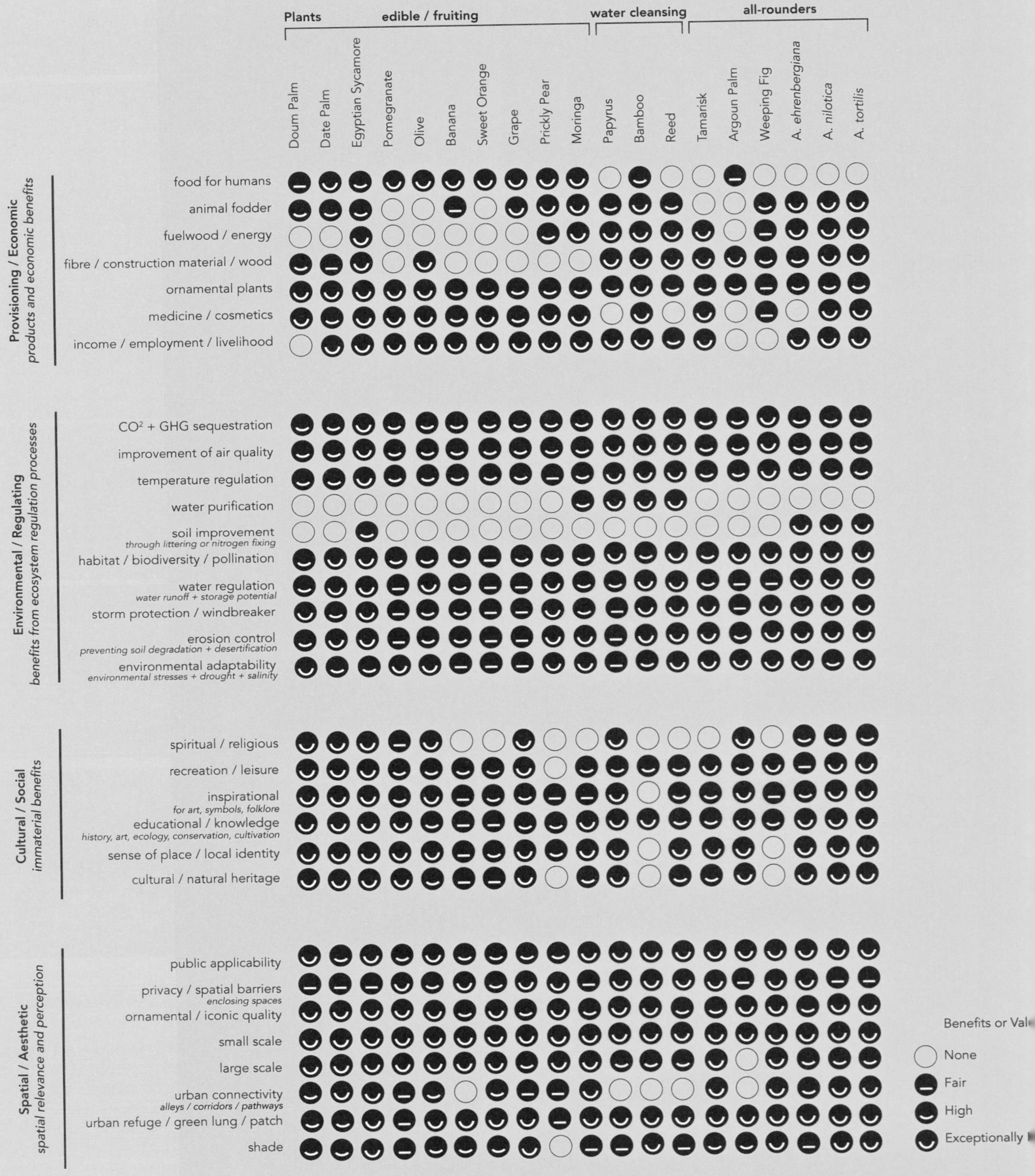

Plants

edible / fruiting — water cleansing — all-rounders

Column headers:
Doum Palm, Date Palm, Egyptian Sycamore, Pomegranate, Olive, Banana, Sweet Orange, Grape, Prickly Pear, Moringa, Papyrus, Bamboo, Reed, Tamarisk, Argoun Palm, Weeping Fig, A. ehrenbergiana, A. nilotica, A. tortilis

Provisioning / Economic
products and economic benefits
- food for humans
- animal fodder
- fuelwood / energy
- fibre / construction material / wood
- ornamental plants
- medicine / cosmetics
- income / employment / livelihood

Environmental / Regulating
benefits from ecosystem regulation processes
- CO_2 + GHG sequestration
- improvement of air quality
- temperature regulation
- water purification
- soil improvement
  through littering or nitrogen fixing
- habitat / biodiversity / pollination
- water regulation
  water runoff + storage potential
- storm protection / windbreaker
- erosion control
  preventing soil degradation + desertification
- environmental adaptability
  environmental stresses + drought + salinity

Cultural / Social
immaterial benefits
- spiritual / religious
- recreation / leisure
- inspirational
  for art, symbols, folklore
- educational / knowledge
  history, art, ecology, conservation, cultivation
- sense of place / local identity
- cultural / natural heritage

Spatial / Aesthetic
spatial relevance and perception
- public applicability
- privacy / spatial barriers
  enclosing spaces
- ornamental / iconic quality
- small scale
- large scale
- urban connectivity
  alleys / corridors / pathways
- urban refuge / green lung / patch
- shade

Legend — Benefits or Value:
- None
- Fair
- High
- Exceptionally High

Productive Plants - Benefits and Values / Overview
inspired by: De Groot et al 2002, Viljoen&Wiskerke 2012, Millennium Ecosystem Assessment 2003

04   Productive Plants
النباتات المنتجة

Our work on productive plants began with an inspiring visit to Orman gardens and its herbarium in Cairo, where we were introduced to the rich archival heritage of botany. The following work builds on the comprehensive body of existing botanical knowledge[1] in Egypt over the last decades.

Plants are the subject of many different disciplines,[2] each one using a different lens. Biology, for example, looks into physiological and chemical processes of plants, while forestry and agriculture focus on their economic value based on the plant's ability to produce food, wood or fodder. Architecture, landscape and urban design, on the other hand, traditionally address the aesthetic and spatial qualities of plants as design elements or ornament, while the plants' productive values are often neglected. Ecology, which evolved as a branch of biology relatively late in the 20th century, acknowledges interconnected processes between organisms – including plants and animals – and their environment, and consequently crosses disciplinary boundaries to explore these processes. Understanding the environment as a complex, holistic system that includes humans led to the concept of ecosystem services. As a human-centered perspective, it describes the "capacity of natural processes and components to provide goods and services that satisfy human needs, directly or indirectly"[3] and invites design and planning disciplines to integrate the multiple dimensions of landscape and plants. Interdisciplinary research over the last decades distilled various frameworks to capture the multiple dimensions of values arising from ecosystem services.[4]

With the given overview, we apply ecosystemic values to our plant selection. The selection reflects upon the described multiplicity of values inherent within one species to reach beyond a classical botanical atlas. An integrated approach aims to overcome sectorial knowledge to embrace the multiple values of plants. Exemplarily chosen and portrayed with in-detail descriptions, drawings and a potential spatial design, the selection includes typical species from the fields of forestry, agriculture and horticulture, as well as species popular in landscape architecture and urban design. Our set of examples collects fruiting trees, water cleansing plants, soil-improving plants and plants that prevent erosion. Belonging to varying habitats, they are not applicable in all urban environments. Some may be of interest for water-scarce urban contexts and harsh desert climates or marshes, while others perform well only in the Nile Valley and Delta. Without aiming for completeness and hoping to inspire further exploration, the following set of selected plants reflect on the multiple values and resulting potentials of each plant beyond the either/or to being productive and beautiful.

Doum Palm as specimen tree, Giza, Cairo
Photo: Farah Sarwat

water requirement	sun requirement	drought resistance	wind resistance	salinity tolerance	growth rate	shade
low	high	moderate	high	moderate	slow	medium

Width up to 8 m **Height** 10 – 17 m

Habitat Coastal North and East Africa, widespread throughout Sahel from Senegal to Egypt, Egypt: Upper Egypt

Soil poor to moderately fertile, well drained, tolerant of a wide variety of soils, on silty and sandy soil as well as wadi beds, tolerates high temperatures

Form a deciduous palm with a Y-shaped trunk, forming up to 16 large crowns (diameter of up to 1.2 m) with long fan-shaped leaves

Foliage large, dark green, waxed fan leaves

Flowers 1m long panicles

Bloom October – December

Fruits edible, oval fruit (diameter 6 – 10 cm) with a red outer skin covering the sweet, fibrous fruit pulp and a large kernel, fruits are produced after 5 – 6 years of growth

Trunk forking, producing 2 or more stems, Y-shaped trunk with dark grey bark

Roots principal deep root and fibrous side roots (1.2 – 1.5 m deep)

Aroma gingerbread taste of the fruit pulp

Propagation difficult, seeds in spring

Maintenance low

Ecosystem Services

Provisioning – Economic nutritious fruits, a drink made from the fruits is a known health tonic, medicine, timber, ropes, baskets, animal fodder

Regulating – Environmental CO_2 sequestration, climate and water regulation, biodiversity, habitat

Cultural – Social local culture and nature heritage

Aesthetic – Spatial an iconic specimen tree of impressive habit for private small gardens and larger public parks providing fair shade

Doum Palm
نخيل الدوم

com. name Doum Palm, Ginger Bread Palm
gen. sp. *Hyphaene thebaica*[1]
arab. name Nakheel Aldoum

a infructescence / b cross-section of a fruit with kernel and pulp

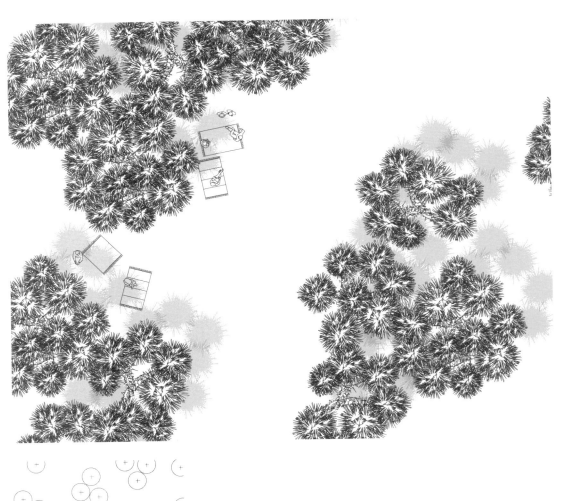

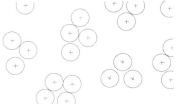

Doum Palm
نخيل الدوم

Native to Egypt, the doum palm grows along the Nile, and is frequently cultivated in Upper Egypt. Ancient depictions of pharaonic gardens found on tomb walls or papyrus documents show the doum as a recurring element, often with baboons. Doum fruits were found amongst the offerings in Tutankhamun's tomb. Its presence in ancient documents proves the palm's particular relevance at the time as a source of nutrition, and as a shade-giving, ornamental tree associated with religious beliefs or sacred meaning.

The mesocarp (outer layer) of the doum fruit has a delicious sweet taste. It is rich in carbohydrates, proteins and potassium, and offers a source of fibres and antioxidants. A cold drink made by infusing dried crushed doum fruits in hot water is very popular in Egypt as a refreshing beverage and health tonic. It shows antioxidant, anticancer and antifungal properties,[2] and helps to control blood pressure and to treat bilharziasis as well as haematuria. The wood of the tree is valuable timber resistant to insects.[3] The leaves are used to make ropes or baskets; the seeds have been used to produce buttons.

The doum palm, with its highly branching stem and its dark green leaves is an imposing plant. As a single specimen tree or as a cluster, the doum palm can appear in a grand manner, offering a large shade canopy. Once a crucial food plant ranking second after the date, the doum today is rarely found in Egypt. As it is an expensive plant that is hard to transplant, it is also not excessively used in landscape design. In rural areas the plant is often stressed by heavily browsing livestock and is considered a threatened species. Recent studies explore the commercial potenital of new products partially replacing wheat in baked goods[4] or developing syrup or jelly[5] building on the plant's high nutritional value and health benefits.

The rediscovery of this plant's various health benefits, its long cultural tradition and beauty as well as its ability to grow in hot arid desert climate makes it a perfect plant for gardens in the New Urban Communities or for historic sites.[6]

20 years   12 years   8 years   2-3 years

Shady date palm forest, farm, Siwa Oases
Photo: Monique Jüttner

water requirement	sun requirement	drought resistance	wind resistance	salinity tolerance	growth rate	shade
moderate	high	moderate	high	moderate	fast	medium

Width 5 – 7 m   **Height** 15 – 20 m, up to 30 m
Habitat North Africa, Southwest Asia, India, extensively cultivated in hot, dry climates; Egypt: the most commonly cultivated tree, especially in the oases of the Western Desert, Nile Valley, Mediterranean Coast of Sinai, Al-Arish
Soil different types of soil from silt to sand, including newly reclaimed lands, can survive inundation and saline soils
Form an evergreen, long lived, imposing, tall palm with a slender, straight column-like trunk
Foliage large 2 – 5 m long leaves, composed of many linear, greyish green leaflets, arranged in various planes, tree grows new leaves each year, each leaf lasts about five years
Flowers long stalked panicles 1.2 – 2 m, dioecious plant (males and females on different trees), requires wind pollination or artificial pollination for optimum yields

Bloom April
Fruits dates[2] are ellipsoid to cylindrical (2.5 – 8 cm long), edible, sweet, varying in taste, fleshy, yellow to reddish brown, only female trees produce fruits
Trunk rough trunk formed by sections of old leaf bases, wildly growing palms have many trunks, single trunk when cultivated
Roots fibrous shallow side roots (1.2 – 1.5 m deep), mature trees 5 m deep tap roots, radius 3 m, shallow roots need
Aroma -
Propagation seeds and suckers, easily transplanted
Maintenance high when cultivated for fruit production, date palms require artificial pollination by skilled workers climbing the tree, annual cut of old leaves, requires proper irrigation regime[3] or underground water close to the surface, tolerance of short drought periods of 2 – 3 months only, high salinity decreases yields

Ecosystem Services

Provisioning – Economic fruits, date juice, liquid sugar, protein yeast, vinegar, marmalade, liquor, unripe or young dates as fodder, leaf petioles used for making cages, fences, furniture and fuel; fibres of leaves for making ropes, baskets, trunks for building construction

Regulating – Environmental erosion control, wind protection, water, climate and air regulation, a habitat for animals

Cultural – Social a tree that embodies local identity and cultural heritage and provides spiritual and educational values

Aesthetic – Spatial an impressive palm, suitable for public and private spaces of multiple scales, providing an imposing gesture as well as shade

Date Palm
نخيل البلح

com. name   Date Palm
gen. sp.   *Phoenix dactylifera*[1]
arab. name   Nakheel Albalah

a fruit / b fruit with seed, mesocarp and epicarp / c dates on spikelet / d leaf with base and leaflets

Date Palm
نخيل البلح

Date palm as alley, Sekem farm, Belbeis
Photo: Monique Jüttner

Persisting in the harshest desert environments and tolerating water salinity, the date palm is the symbol of life, deeply rooted in the culture of the arid MENA region. Known in Egypt since predynastic times and cultivated since ancient pharaonic times,[4] the date palm was by far the most important source of nutrition for people and animals in desert environments. To this day, Bedouins find it culturally unacceptable to let a date palm die. Rich in minerals, fibres and vitamin A and containing more carbohydrates than other fruits, dates are beneficial to health[5] and an affordable and delicious source of energy.[6] The leaves and stems are used for building, basketry, ropes or thatching. Trees provide shade and help to control desertification, especially in the oases.

Egypt is the largest producer of dates worldwide.[7] Available in different ripening stages,[8] various cultivars are grown to produce dry,[9] half dry[10] and high moisture[11] content dates mainly for local consumption. While half dry and high moisture dates dominate the production in Egypt, the commercially more valuable ripe dry dates[12] occur in a few regions only. Largely encompassing small holder farms,[13] date farming sustains rural families[14] or agropastoralists and helps to reduce rural unemployment and poverty (see Chapter 03 Learning from – Ten Medjool Date Palms).

Cultivated in groves,[15] as intercrop or as field margins,[16] date palms need considerable amounts of water, but tolerate drought periods up to 2-3 months. Basin irrigation persists in the old lands,[17] but water scarcity calls for more sensitive irrigation techniques. As a dioecious plant, date palms require artificial insemination, which also involves elaborate pruning and cleaning of the trees. Bats feed from the date's sap and can cause unattractive stains on façades and floors. Covering the fruit stands and positioning palm trees at some distance to buildings will mitigate this effect without impeding the bats' role as pollinator and seed disseminator.

The presence of the date palm as a single tree or a cluster is imposing. Dense groves form a light permeable shadow crown, allowing for other crops to be grown complementarily below their canopy. As an alley, they emphasize a path, charging the meaning of the building or place to which it leads. Placed in rows, they enclose a space, in the typical manner of ancient pharaonic gardens. Combining beauty and productivity, the date palm is a key species for multifaceted landscape design. Planting fruit trees in public spaces and organizing the care and fruit harvest without conflicts arising either from visiting bats or individuals appropriating the fruits is a challenge calling for unconventional management concepts that still have to be developed.

+30 years   15 years   7-8 years   1-2 years

Arching canopy of a Sycomore Alley, Maadi, Cairo
Photo: Monique Jüttner

water requirement	sun requirement	drought resistance	wind resistance	salinity tolerance	growth rate	shade
moderate	high	moderate	high	moderate	moderate - slow	good

Width 12 - 20 m **Height** 15 - 20 m

Habitat Africa and Arabian Peninsula, not indigenous to Egypt, grows in warm climates

Soil humus-rich, leafy, moist, well-drained, only with high groundwater levels, moderate tolerance towards salinity

Form an evergreen tree with a wide, large and dense canopy

Foliage ovate, dark-green, leathery and long leaves (15 cm)

Flowers petal-less flowers borne in the leaf axis, enlarge to form the fig

Bloom July - August

Fruits small (4 cm) edible yellow-red figs, up to three fruit bearing cycles per year

Trunk yellowish-green bark

Roots extensive stabilizing root system, 70 - 90 cm deep

Aroma -

Propagation cuttings, not producing seeds in Egypt, hard to transplant

Maintenance cultivation for fruit can be complex, requires pruning, gashing and climbing the tree

Ecosystem Services

Provisioning – Economic food (fruit, jam), fodder, wood, charcoal, medicine, beauty (sap, bark, roots)

Regulating – Environmental air and soil improvement, habitat for animals, erosion control, water and temperature regulation

Cultural – Social a cultural heritage tree symbolizing local identity, offering recreation

Aesthetic – Spatial a tree with a broad and dense crown throwing deep shade, impressive grandeur, enhances connectivity and makes a place

Egyptian Sycamore
الجميز

com. name	Mulberry Fig, Egyptian Sycamore
gen. sp.	*Ficus sycomorus*[1]
arab. name	Algemeez

a fruit / b twig with leaves / c twig with cluster of figs

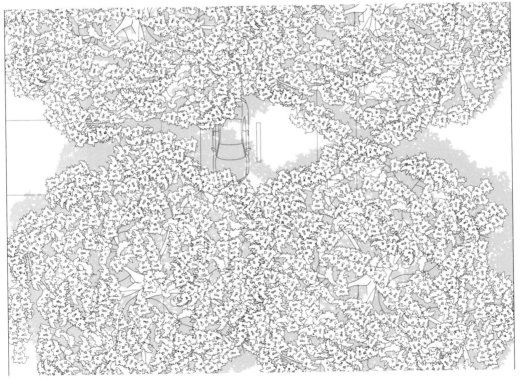

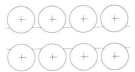

Egyptian Sycamore
الجميز

Sycomore tree, Fayoum Oasis
Photo: Monique Jüttner

Since its introduction 5000 years ago,[2] the sycamore has a long history of cultivation in Egypt. Ancient pharaonic temple or house gardens[3] included considerable numbers of sycamore trees as a source of nutrition and shade. Depictions of sycamores in ancient scripts or tombs often show the tree as a goddess[4] with hands reaching out offering water and fruits epitomizing how it was appreciated and its importance and sacred meaning during that time. In desert regions the decay-resistant, hard wood was useful for well construction, sarkophagi[5] making, building construction, furniture and as fuel or charcoal.

Considerable amounts of sycamore figs are produced and consumed regularly by local communities[6] in Egypt today. Rich in vitamins, minerals, fibres and calcium, the juicy and sweet fruit contributes to a healthy diet. In traditional medicine, treatments[7] with the plants sap, bark, leaves or roots are common. In Egypt, the tree's fruiting cycle can repeat up to three times. The fruit ripening process is closely related to the life cycle of the sycamore wasp that inhabits the fruit and renders it inedible. Gashing the figs – a practice that is known since ancient times – induces and accelerates the ripening process before the wasps finish their cycle and preserve the fruit.[8]

Their relevance as source of food declined with the introduction of other fruit trees that are easier to farm. It persisted because of its ornamental value based on its impressively large and dense canopy and the peculiarly sculptural form of its trunk. Its strong roots stabilize dunes or riverbanks, extensive leaf littering improves soils and helps other species to grow. The exploration of possibilities for using the fruit in jams or other agro-industry products is a recent trend in Egypt. Planted as a single specimen tree on a square, in a courtyard or along a street, it defines a place, providing welcoming shade to a congregating family or neighbourhood. As a row or alley, it forms a dense arching canopy, dispensing shade and giving a monumental atmosphere to the street. The sycamore's ornamental, productive and nutritional values are equally fascinating, and call for it to be brought back to the tableau of contemporary landscape and garden design, agro-forestry and industry.

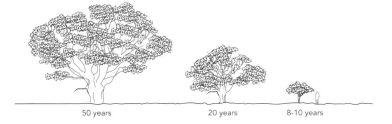

50 years   20 years   8-10 years

Pomegranate, St. Catherine, Sinai
Photo: Monique Jüttner

water requirement	sun requirement	drought resistance	wind resistance	salinity tolerance	growth rate	shade
moderate	high	moderate	high	low	fast	medium

Width 1 - 3.5 m **Height** 1.5 - 3.5 m up to 9 m
Habitat native to Persia, Southwest Asia, Mediterranean region
Soil prefers heavy, moist soils, heavy loams; can adapt to different types of soil, some cultivars show good tolerance[2] towards salinity
Form a deciduous shrub or small tree with ornamental value as specimen plant
Foliage attractive foliage, with glossy-green, oblong leaves
Flowers flaming orange-red, 4 - 6 cm flowers with petals growing solitary or in small clusters
Bloom May - July

Fruits spherical (diameter 5-12 cm) yellowish-pink fruits, with a leathery skin and calyx of 1 - 6 cm, inside compartments with pink juicy arils of bitter-sweet taste, fruit production starts after 3 - 4 years, fruits cannot ripen off the tree, but can be stored for several months, fruit harvest 18 - 30 t/ha[3], 30kg/tree[4]
Trunk multiple, twisted trunks, trained to multi- or single stem when cultivated
Roots fibrous root system, 30 - 50 cm deep
Aroma -
Propagation hardwood cuttings or from seeds
Maintenance moderate, irrigation regime is necessary for fruit production

Ecosystem Services

Provisioning – Economic juice / juice blends, fresh fruit (arils), jams, jellies, syrup (grenadine), decoration, medicine, dye, grains, extracts for cosmetics and health products

Regulating - Environmental water, climate and air regulation, drought resistance

Cultural - Social a cornerstone of local food heritage, a source of inspiration

Aesthetic - Spatial an iconic (flowers and fruits) specimen, for spatial enclosure, private and public spaces

Pomegranate
الرمان

com. name　Pomegranate
gen. sp.　*Punica granatum*[1]
arab. name　Rumman

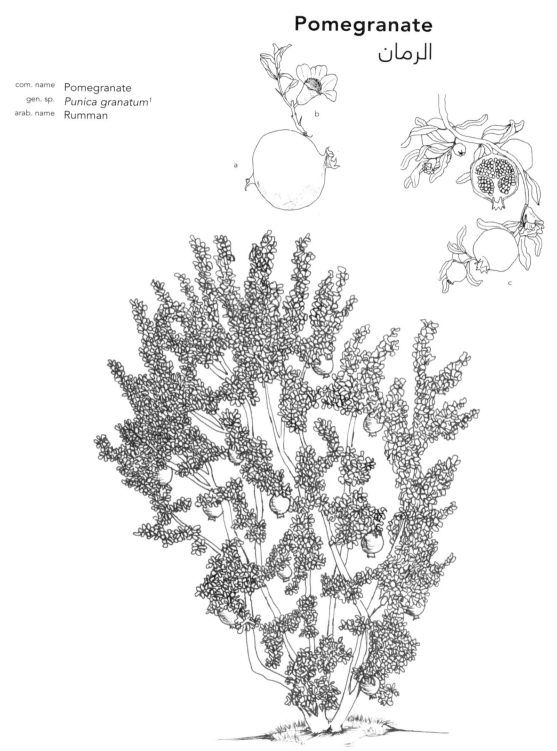

a fruit / b flower / c branch with fruits

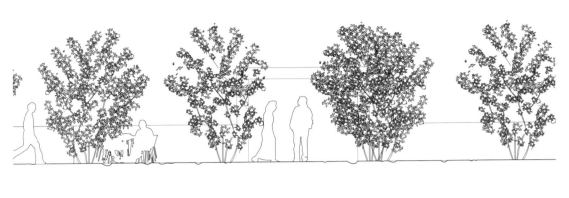

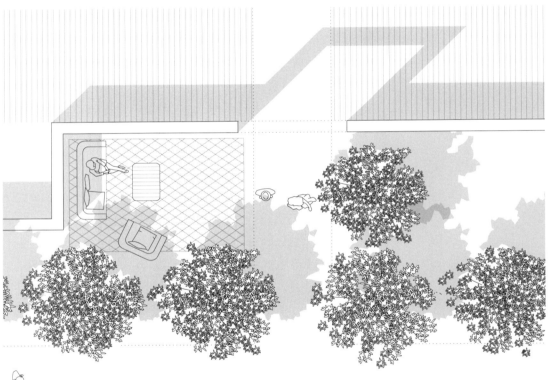

0   1   1.5

Pomegranate
الرمان

Pomegranate, Sinai
Photo: Hala Barakat

Native to Persia and Southwest Asia, the pomegranate spread across the Mediterranean and has a long history of cultivation in this region. Introduced to Egypt during the New Kingdom,[5] pomegranate became a relevant element of ancient gardens.[6] Flowers were worn as floral decorations and were a symbol of love referred to in ancient literature. Fruits represented fertility and were offered to gods and the deceased. The appearance of pomegranate in the texts of the Bible and the Koran prove its longstanding cultural relevance.

As a small tree or shrub, pomegranate is popular for its delicious fruits and beautiful red trumpet flowers that are a special ornament of every garden. The bark was (and still is) used to dye leather a yellow color. As a cornerstone of Middle Eastern food cultures, pomegranate trees are a frequent feature of private gardens and a typical element of Bedouin orchards around St. Katherine in Sinai. Commercial fruit production for export and local markets is concentrated in the area of Assiut.[7]

For the cultivation as a fruit orchard, a spacing of 2 m x 6 m is recommended for young trees and 4 m x 6 m for mature trees not exceeding 3.5 - 4 m in height to allow enough light for every tree, easy pruning and harvesting. Successful fruit production needs fertilization and training of the trunk to a single or multi-stem of 3 - 4 main branches. Although it is a drought tolerant plant, a proper irrigation regime is indispensable. As it prefers heat and tolerates some soil salinity, it is an interesting plant for arid climates, slightly saline soils or irrigation with recycled water.[8]

As the fruit[9] contains high amounts of antioxidants and further active substances contributing to good health, pomegranate has not only become more popular amongst Egyptians in recent years, but also amongst the scientific community and various economic sectors. Emerging are new markets for health and beauty products[10] and medicine.[11]

Planted as a single tree or as a dense hedge, the pomegranate can be a highlight of every private garden, providing the household with delicious and healthy as well as decorative fruit. Extending the planting of this drought-tolerant tree to include the public sphere may be a valuable pilot project for exploring models of urban productivity.

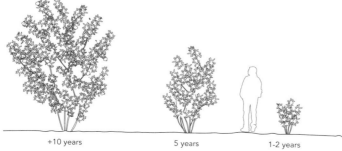

+10 years   5 years   1-2 years

Impressive old olive tree, orchard, Sinai
Photo: Monique Jüttner

water requirement	sun requirement	drought resistance	wind resistance	salinity tolerance	growth rate	shade
low - moderate	high	high	high	moderate	fast	medium

Width 4 - 6 m   **Height** 5 - 10 m

Habitat Mediterranean basin and Africa, Egypt: Oases, Nile Delta, Northwestern coastal regions, Wadi El Natroun, North Sinai

Soil all kinds of soil, preference for calcareous, sharply drained soils, poor to moderately fertile, vulnerable to inundation

Form an evergreen, long-living, single-stemmed tree or multi-stemmed shrub with spreading crown that becomes irregular with age

Foliage leathery leaves (grey-green above, silvery beneath) oblong 4 - 10 cm by 1 - 3 cm, new leaves are produced every 2 years

Flowers small, white, fragrant flowers arranged as racemes

Bloom June - July

Fruits oval green fruits (olives)2, 4 cm long, green colour ripening to red/black, first fruits after 3 - 4 years of planting, full production after 6 - 7 years, fruits contain 7 - 8% oil

Trunk usually single stem, also occurs as a multi-stem tree; irregular, twisted trunk, old trees with impressive thick twisted trunk

Roots fibrous root system, 50 - 70 cm deep

Aroma flower, fruit

Propagation from seeds or semi-ripe cuttings

Maintenance moderate, commercial fruit production requires proper irrigation, pruning, pest and nutrient management, weed control

Ecosystem Services

Provisioning – Economic fresh and pickled olives, olive oil, fuel for cooking or lamps, hair oil, soap, wood, medicine

Regulating - Environmental soil fixation, air purification, erosion control, tolerance to environmental stresses

Cultural - Social a tree rooted in local culture, providing knowledge and educational value

Aesthetic - Spatial a specimen tree in public space, suitable to create connectivity or a refuge, an aging tree provides strong character and good shade

Olive
الزيتون

com. name   Olive Tree
gen. sp.   *Olea europaea*[1]
arab. name   Shagerit Alzaiton

a flowers in clusters / b fruits on a branch / c fruits

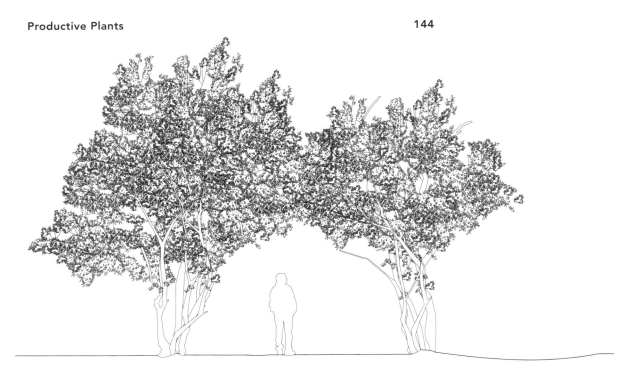

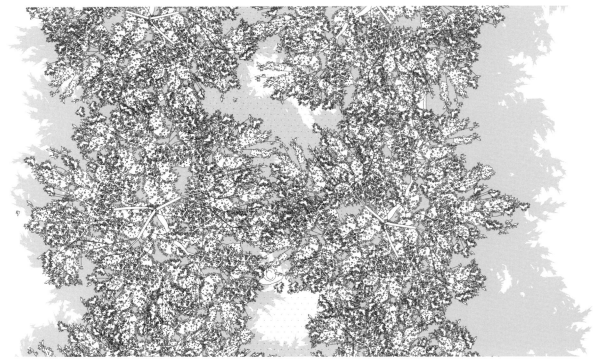

Olive
الزيتون

Young olive orchard, Sinai
Photo: Monique Jüttner

The cultivation of olives to harvest table olives and extract olive oil has a long tradition, deeply rooted in the culture of the Mediterranean. Ancient Egyptians cultivated olive trees as a garden feature since the New Kingdom. Leaves were used in garlands and bouquets,[3] while olive oil was used for ointments and for lighting. Impressive old olive trees are emblematic for Bedouin and monastery orchards in Sinai.[4] Valued as a medicinal, ornamental and fruit-bearing plant, in the oases it is favored for its strong wood ideal for window or chest making. Virgin olive oil contains essential fatty acids and anti-oxidative compounds that provide high oxidative stability, an appealing taste and smell as well as health-promoting properties.[5] An increased awareness of consumers for healthy diets worldwide triggers the demand for virgin olive oil[6] - representing a great potential for the Egyptian context.

In the past decades, Egypt has become an important commercial olive production site in the MedAgri region.[7] The olive tree is well adapted to harsh climates, poor soils and even saline irrigation water and thus suitable[8] for marginal land such as slopes, watersheds or newly reclaimed land[9] where most of the current production in Egypt concentrates. Primarily, table olives for local consumption are cultivated, while olive oil production has less significance[10] at present. Typical yield fluctuations are mitigated by mechanical or chemical thinning. Planting patterns and orchard densities[11] are to be aligned with cultivar, optimal sun exposure, irrigation type, harvesting and pruning methods.

Singular olive trees are an eye-catcher especially when they are old. Providing food and shade, they are habitat for people and animals. Integrated into small-holder mixed-farming systems, olive orchards support rural livelihoods. Recent efforts to develop rainwater harvesting methods in the watersheds along the north coast[12] are promising to intensify productive ago-industries, to boost local communities and to halt land degradation (see Chapter 03 Learning from – Wadi Urbanism). Olive orchards are not typically used as landscape design elements yet. They may offer an interesting plant for public spaces as fruits are not directly edible. Introducing valid management models, olive orchards could become a beautiful feature of edible public landscapes.

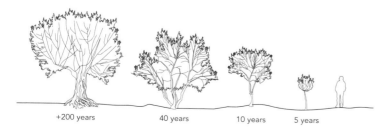

+200 years   40 years   10 years   5 years

Banana trees along the Nile banks, Garden City, Cairo
Photo: Monique Jüttner

water requirement	sun requirement	drought resistance	wind resistance	salinity tolerance	growth rate	shade
high	high	very low	high	low	fast	medium

Width 3 - 3.5 m **Height** 5 - 7.5 m

Habitat not native to Egypt, imported from Malaysia, Indonesia, India

Soil well drained, prefers alluvial soils of river valleys, acidic soil and adequate fertility, saline soil decreases plant growth and fruit production

Form a tall, perennial plant with pseudo-stem formed by overlapping leaf sheaths and an underground corm growing suckers to reproduce

Foliage large light green leaves forming the pseudo-stem

Flowers a single inflorescence emerging on a peduncle from the pseudo-stem comprises male and female flowers with large purple-violet bracts and develops the yellow banana fruits

Bloom November - February

Fruits Bananas in a bunch, fruits for commercial use are picked when green and artificially ripened with ethylene gas in storage rooms

Trunk core formed by overlapping leaves

Roots shallow network roots

Aroma -

Propagation from suckers

Maintenance high, if commercially cultivated proper irrigation regime is required

Ecosystem Services

Provisioning – Economic dried and fresh banana fruit[2], juice, fodder, fibre for paper, packaging and textiles, cosmetics

Regulating - Environmental stabilizing soils, windbreak (depending on cultivar), temperature regulating, air purification

Cultural - Social a recreational and educational plant

Aesthetic - Spatial a specimen or cluster in private spaces providing soft shade

Banana
الموز

com. name Banana Tree
gen. sp. *Musa L.*[1]
arab. name Shagarit Almooz

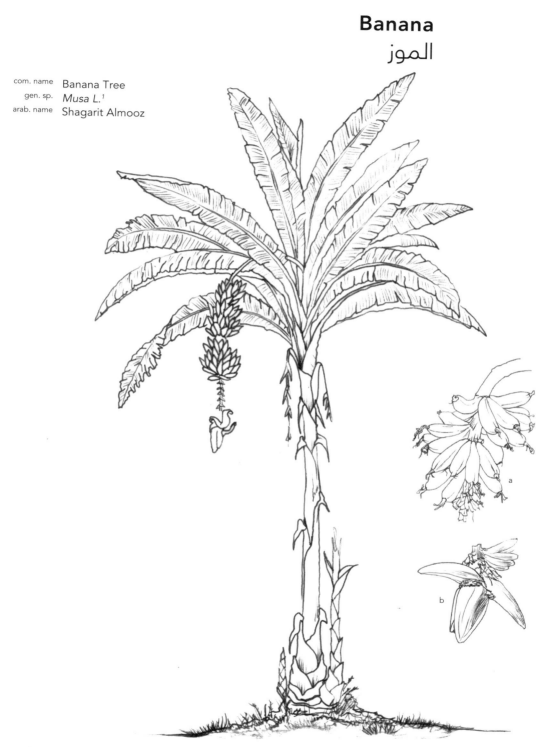

a infructescence / b inflorescence

Banana
الموز

Banana trees along a canal, Ismailia
Photo: Monique Jüttner

The banana originates from humid tropics but has been imported to Egypt alongside the intensifying spice trade between the east and the west[3] during medieval times. Grown in Egypt since then, cultivation intensified during the last century[4] establishing a variety of common cultivars.[5] The Dwarf Cavendish 'Hindi' – referred to as 'moz baladi' – is most frequent with a small, sweet banana fruit. For this water-intensive plant, the Nile valley and delta are the more suitable habitats, while reclaimed land in the desert requires considerable irrigation efforts.

Compared to other fruits, bananas have a high nutritional value.[6] Containing potassium and Vitamin C, they provide for a healthy diet. Being a valuable food crop (coming after rice, wheat and maize) their cultivation for self-consumption and livestock fodder is popular. Commercial, small-scale farming or cultivation for local markets can generate income models for low-income families.

The leaves of the plant are fibrous and a good raw material for building construction, rope or paper production, as well as for natural packaging or decorative wrapping (as recent experiments show). Antibiotic properties[7] have been found in banana peel, and in some cultures the sap and peel are applied to the skin for medicinal purposes. The dense root system stabilizes and improves soils. Planted as a field or bigger cluster, bananas noticeably improve the microclimate.[8] Some particularly robust cultivars[9] are frequently used as a windbreak alongside plantations. Planting patterns[10] are to be chosen depending on cultivar, irrigation type and intercrop.

With its giant leaves, the banana is a very impressive plant, even more so when the extraordinary flower appears and ripens to a bunch of yellow fruits. A bigger cluster or group provides good shade whereas a hedge frames open areas and protects from wind, also preventing people looking in. Beyond its agro-economic relevance the plant deserves more recognition as a source of shade, food, subsistence and as an ornamental plant on a household level and as an element of productive orchards integrated into ornamental landscape design. Due to its water demand, it should, however, only be planted in the Valley and Delta.

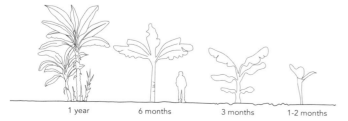

1 year   6 months   3 months   1-2 months

Orange tree in a private kitchen garden, Fayoum
Photo: Monique Jüttner

water requirement	sun requirement	drought resistance	wind resistance	salinity tolerance	growth rate	shade
moderate	high	moderate	moderate	moderate	moderate	medium

Width up to 4.5 m **Height** 5 - 7 m

Habitat Southeast Asia, the Mediterranean

Soil prefers moist fertile soils, neutral to slightly acidic, well drained soils

Form a small evergreen tree with a rounded crown or large shrub with fragrant flowers

Foliage fragrant, glossy dark green, elliptical to ovate compound leaves

Flowers sweet-scented white blossoms

Bloom February - March - April

Fruits edible orange-yellow fruits[2] with sweet-sour taste, od 6 - 10 cm diameter, the pulp is structured in wedge-shaped compartments, fruit remains on the tree across the winter

Trunk short, single-stemmed trunk with irregular branches

Roots fibrous roots, 50 - 70 cm deep

Aroma scent of flower, leaf and fruit

Propagation semi-ripe cuttings, propagated from seeds. Trees need more time to bear fruits

Maintenance high, optimal fruit production requires proper nutrition, irrigation, pest control, pruning and harvesting management

Ecosystem Services

Provisioning – Economic fresh fruit, juice, jams, gelatines, desserts, all parts of the fruit as cooking ingredient, dried and pulverized as food and soft-drink flavouring, candy, confections, pectin (thickener), finisher pulp (by-product), essential oils from flowers and leaves for cosmetics and perfumes, medicine

Regulating - Environmental water regulation, air purification

Cultural - Social inspirational tree giving a sense of place

Aesthetic - Spatial a tree suitable for small or larger patches in private and public spaces offering soft shade

Sweet Orange
البرتقال

com. name Sweet Orange, Navel Orange
gen. sp. *Citrus sinensis*[1]
arab. name Bortokal

a fruit / b branch wih flower

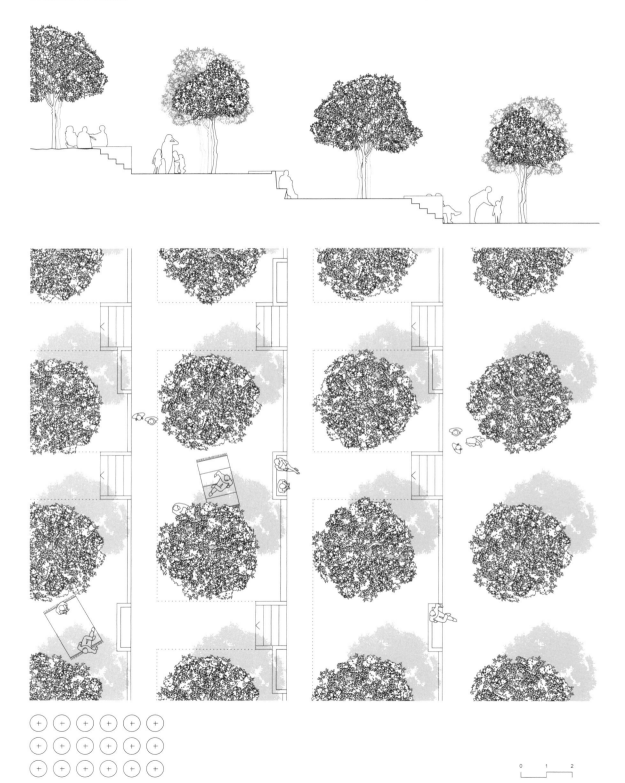

Sweet Orange
البرتقال

Orange as specimen in a private courtyard,
Dahab Island Palace, Giza
Photo: Monique Jüttner

Citrus sinensis belongs to a genus of 16 species. Citrus cultivation was presumably introduced to Egypt[3] and to the Nile Valley in the 2nd/3rd Century AD. In ancient times, citrus was a luxury product valued for its rind, which was used in medicine, cooking and perfumery; today, its value lies more in the edible fruit. Throughout the last decades Egypt considerably increased its cultivation area and yields advancing to the 7th-largest producer of oranges worldwide in 2016.[4] Navel and Valencia varieties represent half of the annual production grown for export, while other varieties are cultivated for local consumption.[5] Farming concentrates on the 'Old lands' in the delta but increasingly also on reclaimed 'New lands'[6] in the desert. About half of the orange-producing acreage is run by small-scale producers.[7]

Although oranges are a major fruit crop with considerable economic value,[8] orange yields in Egypt are low by world standards due to challenges such as pests, inadequate desert soils with increasing salinity, ageing trees[9] as well as unsuitable pruning, harvesting and irrigation techniques.[10]

Being nutritious and rich in vitamin A, oranges are health-promoting and thus valuable on world markets, rendering them a preferred permanent crop. Large-scale corporate production applying capital-intensive, automated farming techniques requires only a few permanent jobs[11] while small producers provide diverse jobs and livelihoods, proving to be more sustainable from a socio-economic and ecological perspective. Organic farming products are gaining in importance and increasingly offer opportunities for small-scale farmers. Mixing crops is a strategy of organic farming which is economically viable for small producers as it allows them to diversify their produce to integrally manage their farms and to raise crops for subsistence supply at the same time.[12] Planting patterns[13] are customized depending on various parameters. Intercropping[14] with other fruit trees, field crops, herbs or flowers provides wind protection, creates biodiversity, and allows good aeration and sun exposure, lowering the risk of pests.

The tree's white blossoms, orange fruits and striking fragrance are a delight in every garden. Integrating orange orchards into private or public open spaces and finding new ways of managing them as an integral part of open space design is promising for urban landscapes to become more productive.

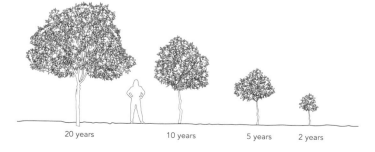

20 years   10 years   5 years   2 years

Grape vine on a gazebo, Fayoum
Photo: Hala Barakat

water requirement	sun requirement	drought resistance	wind resistance	salinity tolerance	growth rate	shade
moderate	high	very low	moderate	moderate	fast	good

Width 1.5 – 9 m (climbing along trellis)

Height 1.5 – 10 m (climbing up to 16 m if unpruned)

Habitat native to Mediterranean, Turkey, Western Asia, stretching from the Black Sea to Afghanistan

Soil deep, well-drained soil (loamy or sandy)

Form a perennial, deciduous climber, can grow in many forms along a support structure[2]

Foliage palmate lobed leaves (9 – 28 cm wide), attractive foliage with changing color[3]

Flowers white or pale green flower clusters, mostly dioecious, few varieties are monoecious requiring cross pollination

Bloom May

Fruits berries in clusters, with seeds or seedless, with a waxy peel, ripe by July until September

Trunk a strain with bark that easily detaches, becomes more woody with age

Roots 30 – 80 cm deep

Aroma sweet scent during inflorescence

Propagation hardwood cuttings, grafting

Maintenance high, labour-intensive, pruning, pest control, irrigation and nutrient management, some varieties can be invasive requiring management, high water rquirement in the beginning of the year

Ecosystem Services

Provisioning – Economic table grapes (fresh, dried)[4], juice, wine, wine leaves, jam, jelly, vinegar, seed oil, fodder

Regulating – Environmental habitat, air purification

Cultural – Social a cultural heritage plant, representing inspiration and knowledge

Aesthetic – Spatial valid as dense shade canopy in private and public space, to form an urban micro refuge

Grape
العنب

com. name Common Grape
gen. sp. *Vitis vinifera L.*[1]
arab. name 'anab

a cluster of fruits

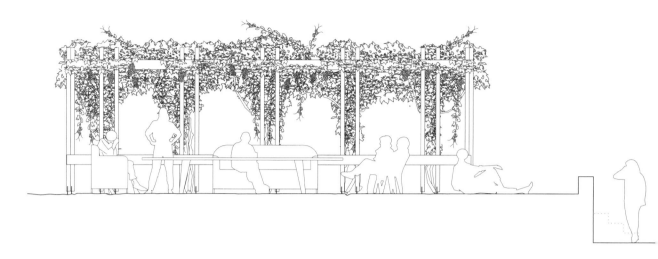

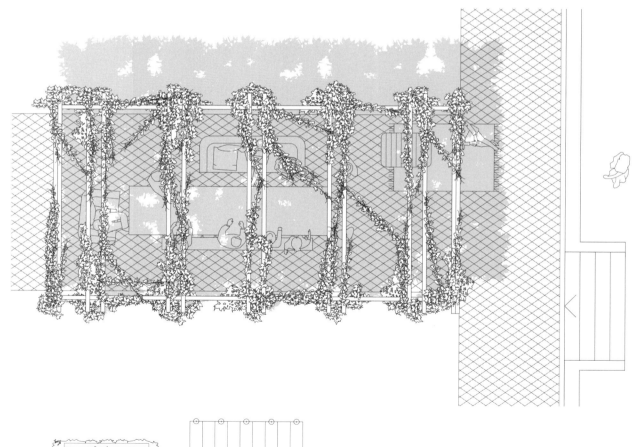

0   0.5   1

Grape
العنب

Vitis vinifera L. has a long history of cultivation in various places of the world. Cultivars for table fruit, dried fruit or wine production emerged from wild grapevine and are grown on root stocks, which have proved to be most pest resistant and to adapt well to local conditions. First cultivated in the region between the Black Sea and Iran,[5] the grapevine was introduced to Egypt and developed into a thriving royal winemaking industry by the beginning of the old kingdom.[6] A wide range of pharaonic depictions and artifacts vividly present the cultivation of grapes harvesting and the process of wine making during that period. With the advent of Muslim religion abolishing alcohol consumption, the relevance shifted to fresh or dried table grapes. To this day, they are essential for both local consumption and export. Mashi, or vine leaves filled with rice and beef, are a cornerstone of Egyptian culture. Leaves and seeds are also good animal fodder and medicine[7]. Beyond vitamins and high biologically active flavonoids content,[8] grapes are rich in various health-benefitting components and show a high nutritional value.[9]

Advancing to be the fourth-largest table grapes producer worldwide in 2014,[10] grapes became the second most valuable export crop after oranges[11] in Egypt. Among different white and coloured varieties with early or late maturity, a part is grown as table grapes[12] and another part for wine production.[13]

To determine the optimal yard layout, support structure[14] and plant density,[15] various parameters have to be considered: cultivar, local climate, orientation, soil conditions, soil fertility, irrigation type and the applied harvesting and pruning methods.[16] Grape production is labor-intensive and requires sophisticated knowledge, skills and extensive care to reach high yields. Vines start bearing fruits after 4 years. They do live for many years,[17] but productivity decreases after 20-30 years.

Vitis vinifera L. is a perfect climber. It can be grown in many forms on pergolas, arches or follies as a central decorative space in the garden, a shading roof for a gathering or an attractive screen to ensure privacy. Plant material regularly left over from pruning is good for composting. An inviting habitat for birds or other plants that need shade to grow, vines are a beautiful, versatile and productive

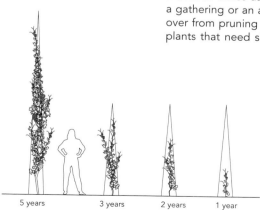

5 years   3 years   2 years   1 year

Cactus garden with prickly pear, Sekem farm, Bilbeis
Photo: Monique Jüttner

water requirement	sun requirement	drought resistance	wind resistance	salinity tolerance	growth rate	shade
very low	high	very high	high	moderate	slow	in-significant

Width up to 3 m **Height** 2 – 3 m

Habitat Mexico, Spain, Egypt

Soil moderately fertile to humus-rich soil, well drained, gritty to sandy and sandy loam texture

Form a long-lived, bushy cactus composed of fleshy rounded segments (cladodes)

Foliage succulent, oblong, greyish-green cladodes show areoles with glochids and spines, waxy skin

Flowers bowl-shaped, yellow or pink flowers

Bloom April – May

Fruits edible ovoid, spiny fruits of yellow-orange-red color

Trunk woody, thick stem

Roots shallow, fleshy root system, 30 cm deep, spreading outwards 4 – 8 m

Aroma -

Propagation easily by stem cuttings

Maintenance moderate, for good yields appropriate management is required

Ecosystem Services

Provisioning – Economic fruits[2], fodder, juices jams, syrups, candies, medicine, cosmetics, bioenergy

Regulating – Environmental soil fixation, erosion control, water regulation, air improvement[3]

Cultural – Social an inspirational plant of educational value

Aesthetic – Spatial an effective security barrier or fence, a specimen of sculptural impression, good for grading terrain and modelling slopes, not a good source of shade

Prickly Pear
التين الشوكي

com. name   Indian Fig, Prickly Pear
gen. sp.   *Opuntia ficus-indica Syn. O. engelmannii*[1]
arab. name   Alteen Alshoki

a fruit / b cladode with flower

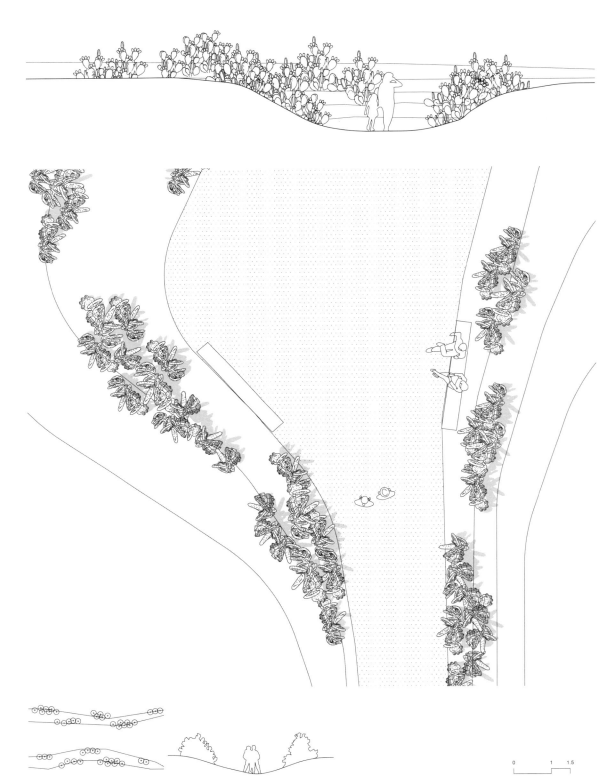

Prickly Pear
التين الشوكي

Prickly pear, Sekem farm, Bilbeis
Photo: Monique Jüttner

Originating in Central Mexico, *Opuntia ficus-indica* was brought to Spain in the 15th century.[4] From Spain, it spread throughout the Mediterranean, Africa, the US and Australia. The plant is thriving in arid and semi-arid climates as it adapts well to water scarcity and drought, with thick cladodes that store water and limit evaporation. Cacti have been used by ancient Mesoamerican civilizations for their medicinal properties[5] and in the human diet.[6] Juicy fruit contains sugar in high amounts and fiber, as well as proteins, amino acids, vitamins and minerals. Cladodes contain carbohydrates and proteins. Good nutritional values and a high water content[7] in all plant parts also render it a good source of drinking water and forage complement for animals.

Withstanding drought and thriving on marginal soils, the prickly pear is perfect to stabilize soils and mitigate erosion. On lands with a fast rainwater run-off, cacti delay the outflow and allow for better rainwater use, thus considerably improving land in the long term. With a high WEU[8] factor, plants can survive on an annual rainfall of 200 mm only, but need more for fruit production.[9]

In Egypt,[10] prickly pear is grown for local consumption in small amounts only,[11] although commercial fruit production building on food and non-food uses[12] for agro-industries and export markets shows considerable potential.[13] Commercial orchards are organized either free-standing trees, in rows, as hedges or as intercrop. Plant densities range from 500 – 1250 plants to high densities of 2000 plants per hectare.[14] Fully productive at five years, they reach a lifespan of 100 years if well managed. Yields are highly irregular, and the glochids and spines call for skin protection and skilled harvesters.

Prickly pear considerably improves land prone to erosion like watersheds or coastal rangelands of the north and west with the seasonal rainfall. As a drought-resistant and unpretentious plant, it is a suitable crop for reclaimed lands. As an effective windbreak, biological fence or ornamental feature, it can grow in various urban and rural contexts, in which it offers food, economic opportunities, environmental benefit and ornamental value.

With an extraordinary morphology, colorful flowers and fruits, prickly pear is an impressive specimen plant. Thinking of it as an edible landscape element that structures and models public or private open spaces, it offers fascinating approaches to desert garden design.

+15 years   6 years   4 years   2 years   1 year

Moringa tree, Fayoum
Photo: Cornelia Redeker

water requirement	sun requirement	drought resistance	wind resistance	salinity tolerance	growth rate	shade
moderate	high	high	moderate	moderate	fast	medium

Width 7 – 9 m **Height** 7 – 15 m

Habitat NE. Africa, Arabian Peninsula, N. Syria, Red Sea region, Turkey, E. Europe, E. India

Soil poor to moderate fertile, sharply drained, sandy or clay soil

Form a deciduous xerophyte[2], a semi-evergreen tree or shrub with a loose crown

Foliage small glossy green compound leaves on young branches only in spring, leafless for the rest of the year to avoid water losses

Flowers pink or white panicles, sweetly-scented

Bloom April – May

Fruits 15 – 30 cm long, narrow ribbed pods of green color, containing 8 – 15 seeds (behen-nuts[3])

Trunk greyish-green bark

Roots fibrous, 50 – 70 cm deep

Aroma flower

Propagation seeds and cut stems

Maintenance low, commercial farming requires proper irrigation and maintenance

Ecosystem Services

Provisioning – Economic ben oil (fine machine lubrication, cosmetic and medicinal use, for cooking or as food), leaves[4] and pods[5] as food and fodder, bio-diesel, fuel, traditional medicine, powder, dietary supplements

Regulating – Environmental environmental adaptability, habitat, soil fixation, water and air purification

Cultural – Social a cultural heritage plant linking local traditional knowledge, inspiration and recreation

Aesthetic – Spatial an attractive tree for private and public open spaces, a loose crown provides filtered shade

Moringa
المورنجا

com. name Moringa, Ben Oil Tree, Horseradish Tree
gen. sp. *Moringa peregrina Syn. M. forssk, fiori*[1]
arab. name Alhaba, Alghaliah, Alyassar

a twig with flowers / b pods

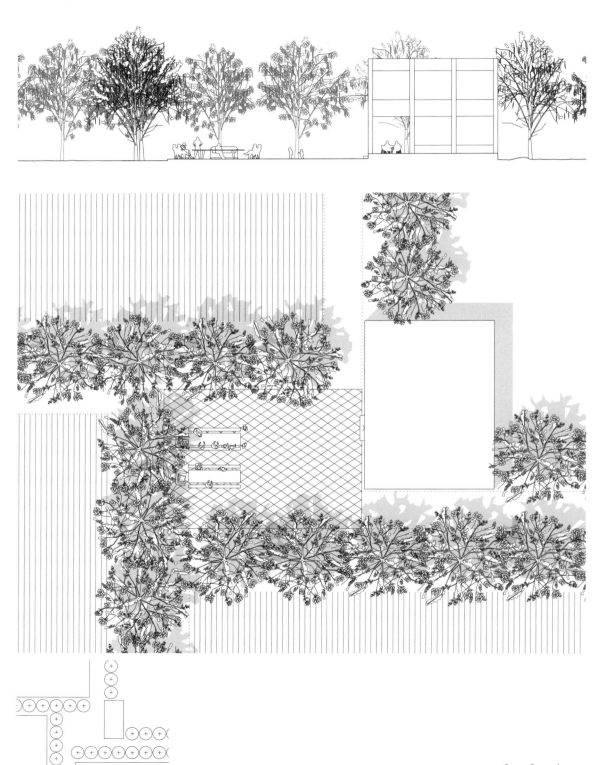

Moringa
المورنجا

Out of the family of *Moringaceae*,[6] *M. oleifera* is common in tropical Asia and Africa and appears deeply rooted in local history, tradition and culture, while *M. peregrina* is native to Egypt, spreading from the Dead Sea to the Arabian Peninsula. Ancient Egyptian artefacts and writings indicate that Moringa was cultivated in gardens for its ornamental value[7] and that ben oil was extracted from its seeds.[8] Presumably a luxury commodity,[9] the odorless oil was served as food, used for cooking, in medicine, and as an ideal base for perfumes and cosmetics.[10] In Egypt today, *M. peregrina* is known as an aromatic and medicinal desert plant. Bedouins collect the behen-nuts to gain fine oil for lubrication[11] and use seed powder for water purification.[12]

Moringa species grow fast and perform well on marginal lands in arid climates. The leaves of Moringa species are edible and very rich in vitamins, proteins and minerals reaching values many times higher than other food items,[13] a superfood for humans and animals.[14] Various active compounds[15] positively affect the skin, the immune system, the blood sugar and cholesterol and are beneficial in treating diseases.[16] *M. peregrina* came into focus as an alternative source for biodiesel because in contrast to other toxic biodiesel plants[17] it is also good animal fodder. Showing similar characteristics to olive oil, ben oil is promising for cosmetics, lubricants and domestic consumption. Being a coagulant to purify water, a soil stabilizer and a suitable tree for agroforestry, moringa is a cornerstone for livelihoods, environmental services and economic development. Moringa can be grown either as trees organized in rows, as clusters or orchards or as commercial shrubby field crop with spacings of 10 – 15 cm[18] which can be harvested more frequently.

M. oleifera has broadly been screened by researchers of various disciplines, while *M. peregrina* started to receive more attention only recently. A broader use of all plant parts, commercial cultivation and industrial processing of *M. peregrina* were not yet established. Given its many benefits and significance as cultural heritage and an ornamental tree, *M. peregrina* holds great potential. As a fast-growing pioneer with impressive pink blooms and an airy form, it can serve as a single specimen tree in private gardens, for example in the New Urban Communities. A light crown throwing permeable shadow allows for plants to grow beneath it, marking it suitable for permaculture. As a versatile and beautiful tree, it is a perfect species for edible landscapes in arid urban and rural contexts – both locally on a small scale, and commercially.

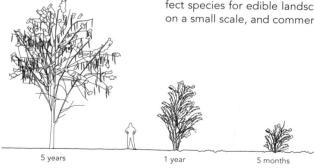

5 years   1 year   5 months

Cyperus papyrus, Orman Gardens, Cairo
Photo: Monique Jüttner

water requirement	sun requirement	drought resistance	wind resistance	salinity tolerance	growth rate	shade
very high	high	moderate	moderate	low	very fast	very light

Width 0.6 – 1.2 m **Height** 1.2 – 1.5 m

Habitat Egypt to tropical Africa

Soil nutrient-rich, peaty and wet soils, submerged in 15 – 30 cm deep water

Form a perennial, clump forming aquatic plant with ornamental value, a macrophyte capable to improve water quality by removing fecal pathogens in wastewater

Foliage tall, 3 angled leafless stem, globe-like compound umbels of 100 – 200 thread-like rays 12 – 30 cm long

Flowers small brown flowers, all year round with the peak of flowering during spring and summer[2], become pendent with age

Bloom June – August

Fruits seeds

Trunk leafy, thin, green stems

Roots fibrous roots, 30 – 50 cm deep rhizomatous or tuberous underground stems

Aroma -

Propagation seeds and division in spring

Maintenance low, year-round growth with rapid accumulation of biomass requires management[3]

Ecosystem Services

Provisioning – Economic rapid biomass production[4] (fuel), basketry, fiber, paper, fodder

Regulating - Environmental water purification, good habitat for animals, water, climate and air regulation

Cultural - Social a local cultural heritage, an iconic and inspirational plant, an illustrative and educational natural system

Aesthetic - Spatial an ornamental feature to frame or create private niches or public larger spaces, provides light permeable shade

Papyrus
البردية

com. name   Egyptian Paper Rush
gen. sp.   *Cyperus papyrus*[1]
arab. name   Papyrus -Albardi

a rhizome with roots and emerging culms / b young umbel / c flowering umbel / d stands of *Papyrus alternifolius*

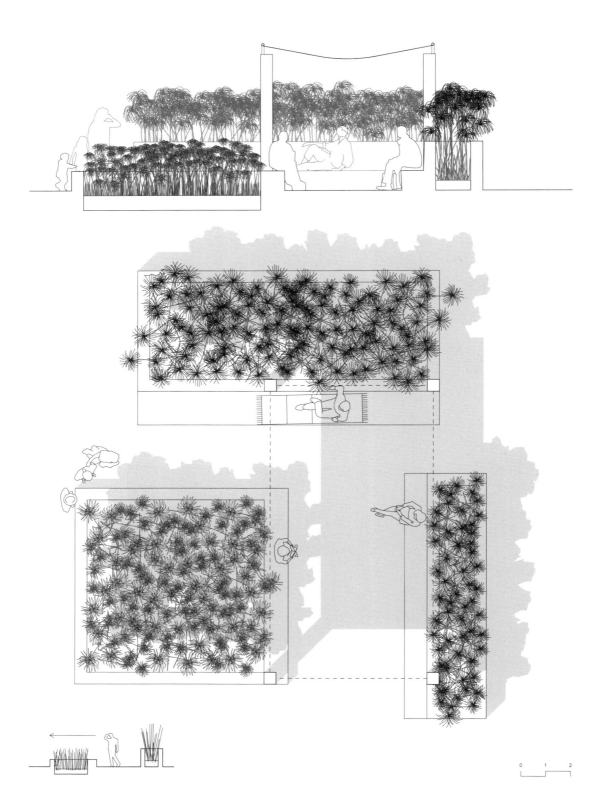

Papyrus
البردية

Papyrus alternifolius,
Orman Gardens, Cairo
Photo: Monique Jüttner

The papyrus is an aquatic plant that grows into large wetlands floating as clumps or rooted in shallow water. Ancient depictions and hieroglyph writings reflect the wide distribution and intensive use of this sedge-type plant in ancient Egypt. *C. papyrus* was of the highest cultural and economic significance as the raw material for paper production,[5] for everyday items,[6] for fodder as well as for food. The construction of dams[7] regulating the annual Nile floods in 19th century Egypt very likely challenged the papyrus' natural habitat, causing near extinction.[8] Today, papyrus rarely occurs in natural stands, but is still a popular ornamental grass whose values other than its beauty are broadly forgotten.

Through the excretion of antimicrobial substances and the metabolism of micro-organisms[9] active in the root zone, the plant acts as a natural filter to improve water quality. Constructed wetlands[10] (CWs) planted with papyrus or other water cleansing plants[11] use this natural effect to remove pollutants like pathogens, nutrients and organic and inorganic contaminants[12] from wastewater. In the context of water scarcity, this can be a valuable source for irrigation water. Where households[13] are not connected to central water treatment plants and domestic wastewater is discharged untreated contaminating soil and groundwater, CWs can be a considerable improvement for public health and the environment (see Chapter 03 Learning from – Constructed Wetlands). Papyrus grows fast and is thus rapidly accumulating biomass that can be harvested, dried and processed into compressed or carbonized briquettes, being a good biofuel for cooking and heating. Already small papyrus stands can significantly purify water, contribute to an aggregable microclimate and act as a vital biotope to insects, fish and birds. They can provide fodder or fuel and can be a valuable carbon store.

Cyperus alternifolius, a popular sedge used to buffer water bodies or to give fine texture to the landscape, shows similar water cleansing characteristics to *C. papyrus*, but grows smaller. Integrated into appealing garden objects forming entrances, framing spaces or fencing properties, both sedges are beautiful and at the same time economically beneficial[14] and environmentally active. Capable of tackling some of the major challenges of urbanization today, the ancient cultural heritage plant *C. papyrus* may regain attention and importance.

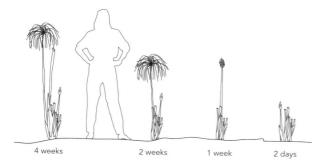

4 weeks   2 weeks   1 week   2 days

Bamboo stands, Orman Gardens, Cairo
Photo: Monique Jüttner

water requirement	sun requirement	drought resistance	wind resistance	salinity tolerance	growth rate	shade
moderate	high	no tol. low	high	moderate	fast	good

Width various **Height** up to 15 – 20 m

Habitat Asia, subtropical Africa, not native to Egypt

Soil humus rich, fertile, well drained

Form an impressive clump-forming, evergreen grass with slender hollow culms, producing slender branches at each node

Foliage linear lance-shaped leaves (20 cm long) growing on branches arising from midculm nodes

Flowers rarely seen, once the bamboo flowers, it dies

Bloom August - September

Fruits rarely seen

Trunk glossy light-dark green, hollow trunk (diameter 5 – 15 cm) with nodes, rich in fiber

Roots rhizome root system, 70 – 90 cm deep

Aroma -

Propagation sections, cuttings and division in spring

Maintenance moderate, invasive growth management, rapid biomass accumulation 6.5 – 167 t/ha[1]

Ecosystem Services

Provisioning – Economic young shoots as nutritious vegetable, animal fodder, furniture, building construction (scaffolding, fences, roofs, shelter), engineered bamboo, flooring, panels, pulp, paper, cloth, medicine, skin care cosmetics, charcoal[2], biofuel, a source of livelihood

Regulating - Environmental carbon sink (sequestration of 17 t/ha/y carbon[3]), wind break, erosion control, restores degraded lands, prevents desertification

Cultural - Social recreational and inspirational plant

Aesthetic - Spatial urban refuge and green lung, an ornamental feature, a framing or barrier applicable in public and private spaces, providing light, permeable or dense shade dependant on plant size

Bamboo
البامبو

com. name Bamboo
gen. sp. *Bambusa vulgaris*
arab. name Bamboo

a midculm nodes / b midculm node with young shoot

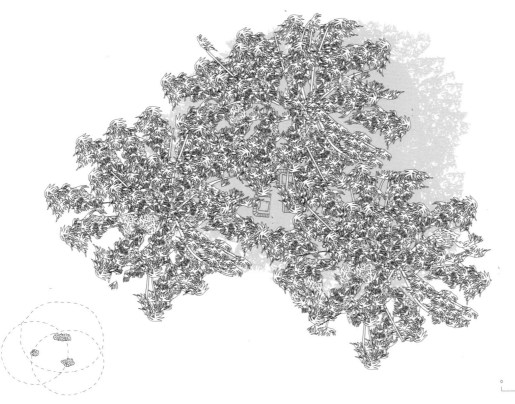

Bamboo
البامبو

Bamboo is a woody grass spread across all regions of the world.[4] In the regions of its origin, bamboo is strongly intertwined with local tradition: all parts of the plant are used, for construction work, furniture, food, fodder, fuel, charcoal or medicine.[5] In Egypt, bamboo grows along water bodies and is cultivated for basketry and furniture. Bamboo has drawn global attention for its exceptionally fast growth[6] and undemanding[7] cultivation, successively substituting wood.[8] Intense technical and material research has led to the development of innovative high-value products, establishing bamboo as a low-cost, lightweight material with high tensile strength, and elasticity[9] in design and architecture.[10]

Suitable for mixed farming systems with other woody plants, intercrops or animal husbandry, it is a low-end livelihood opportunity for rural communities as well as a high-end commercial industry providing jobs. The leaves of some species are a source of flavonoids, antioxidants[11] and other active compounds triggering the attention of medicine and cosmetic industries.

The plants' dense root networks stabilize slopes, watersheds or degraded landscapes, reduce erosion and act as a windbreak. Binding larger amounts of CO_2 than other plants, bamboo forests are a large-scale carbon sink, considerably purifying the air. With a high nutritional value[12] and a very fast reproduction rate bamboo is a highly renewable source of biofuel, animal fodder and soil nutrients.[13] Recent studies have identified the potential of bamboo stands to treat greywater (see Chapter 03 Learning from – Constructed Wetlands) from food industries[14] and for the phytoremediation of Chromium contaminated soils from tanneries.[15]

A dense canopy provides cooling shade, but also competes with neighboring plants for resources. With pruning, spacing and trenching, its invasive growth can be managed.[16]

Bamboo is a rare, appreciated landscape element because of its finely structured canopy and arching clustered stems. Primarily known as a luxury plant, its environmental and economic potentials to sustain rural livelihoods or to cater to new markets have not yet materialized in Egypt. Offering solutions to pressing questions such as environmental degradation, desertification, climate change and rural development, it absolutely deserves to be explored further within the Egyptian context.

6 years   3 years   1 year

Phragmites australis stands, Nile banks, Aswan
Photo: Monique Jüttner

water requirement	sun requirement	drought resistance	wind resistance	salinity tolerance	growth rate	shade
high	flexible	moderate	high	moderate	very fast	light

Width diameter of stems reaching from 1 – 4 cm

Height 3 m up to 8 m

Habitat Mediterranean region, Coastal N. and E. Africa, in Egypt in the Nile Delta and Valley

Soil prefers slightly alkaline, heavy, moist soils, can also grow on sandy soil when ground water is close to the surface

Form a submerged evergreen perennial, a wetland grass of tall habit

Foliage alternating green elongated leaves with a 5 – 8 cm wide base, growing from the stem

Flowers small flowers in a 70 cm long, feathered pinnacle at the end of the stem

Bloom July - December

Fruits -

Trunk hollow stem

Roots thick network of extensive roots and rhizomes, reaching up to 1 m into the ground

Aroma -

Propagation easy propagation by dividing rhizomes, tubers or stem cuttings

Maintenance low, a rapid biomass accumulation[2] may require a management of invasiveness

Ecosystem Services

Provisioning – Economic building and roofing material, basketry, fiber, paper pulp, musical instruments, fences, fodder, bioenergy[3]

Regulating – Environmental erosion control, river bank stabilization, phytoremediation (soils, water), tolerance of environmental and pollution stresses, carbon sink, animal habitat, air purification

Cultural – Social a plant with educational and recreational potential

Aesthetic – Spatial an ornamental feature of small private and large public open spaces, good to create a softly shaded urban micro refuge (no shade roof), spatial and visual barriers

Reed
الغاب

com. name   Giant Reed, Persian Reed
gen. sp.   *Arundo donax L.*[1]
arab. name   ghaab baladi, ghaab rhumi

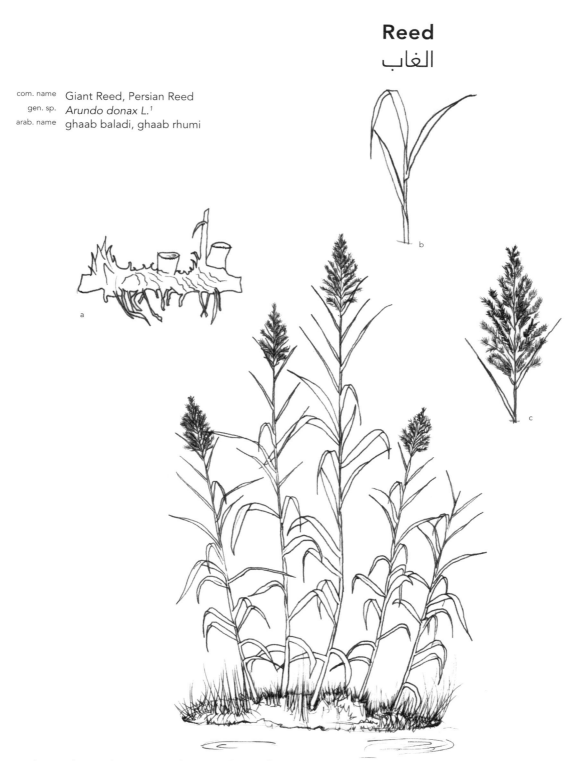

a rhizome with roots and emerging stems / b vegetative shoot / c inflorescence

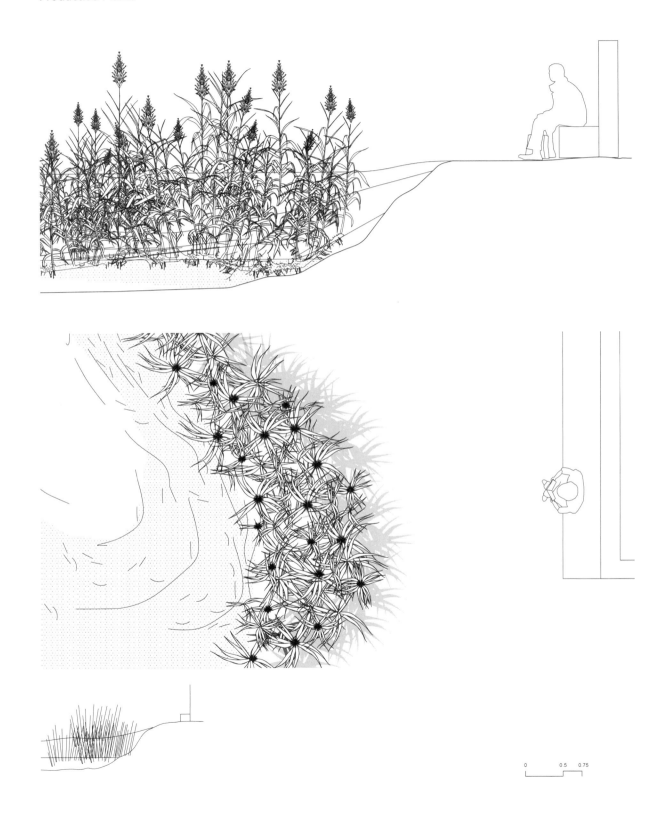

Reed
الغاب

Phragmites australis stands, Siwa Oasis
Photo: Monique Jüttner

Reeds are fast-growing wetland grasses widespread throughout the world. In Egypt, reeds can be found on the coast, in the oases, in some watersheds in Sinai, along the Nile, irrigation canals, or water bodies as well as in dryer and less fertile soils such as roadsides or wastelands. *Arundo donax* and *Phragmites australis* are common reeds in Egypt with similar characteristics and properties.[4] We describe *A. donax* in more in detail, as it has a long history of cultivation in Egypt since its introduction in prehistoric and ancient times.[5] Remains were found in pharaonic tombs, early primitive pipes were manufactured from the culms and Ancient Greeks used the reed for pens and arrows. As a very fast-growing[6] grass it has been cultivated for construction,[7] fibre and musical instruments and has many uses today as a fence and windbreak on agricultural fields or as an ornamental grass.

Growing in a wide range of habitats and tolerating stresses such as polluted water and soils, salinity and drought,[8] it is a robust and versatile plant that is also invasive[9] and water-intensive.[10] A dense and deep rhizome root system stabilizes soils and protects the plant from strong winds. Rapid biomass accumulation renders *A. donax* a valuable biomass crop and a source of bioenergy.[11] Good growth even on marginal or saline lands qualifies it as suitable for land reclamation, simultaneously reducing soil erosion. The significant accumulation of trace metals in the plant[12] earmark it as a good phytoremediator on polluted lands. As a plant filter[13] in constructed wetland (CW)[14] systems, *A. donax* removes pathogens, nutrients and pollutants from effluents. Depending on the achieved quality, the treated water can be reused as irrigation water for gardens and agriculture or in households, or discharged without environmental damage. (see Chapter 03 Learning from – Constructed Wetlands)

As a beautiful feature in gardens, framing water bodies, enclosing spaces or marking borders, it also requires management regarding its invasiveness. Integrating it as green infrastructure to purify water in small private courtyards or gardens as well as in public open spaces on a larger scale would be a ground-breaking approach to the aggravating water shortage and insufficient water treatment in off-grid areas. Water-deficient new urban and rural areas of Egypt would benefit long-term from CWs as a particularly efficient, small-scale and low-cost technology.

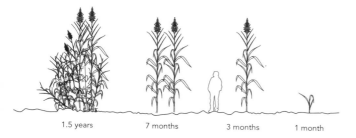

1.5 years   7 months   3 months   1 month

Tamarix aphylla as specimen tree, Fayoum
Photo: Monique Jüttner

water requirement	sun requirement	drought resistance	wind resistance	salinity tolerance	growth rate	shade
low	high	moderate	high	very high	fast-moderate	good

Width 2 – 4 m up to 10 m **Height** 10 – 15 m

Habitat widespread in the Middle East, North, East and Central Africa; Egypt: throughout the Nile Valley and Delta, the Oases, Mediterranean and Red Sea Coast

Soil heavy and light soil, sandy as well as saline is possible, well-drained, grows in riverine, desert, and seashore habitats, can withstand long inundation periods

Form an evergreen tree or shrub

Foliage attractive feathery foliage of green-whitish colour with very small leaves to minimize water losses, slender branches

Flowers small off-white flowers in the shape of bottle brushes

Bloom July-August

Fruits bell-shaped with a hairy tuft, cylindrical seeds

Trunk grey bark, old stems can reach 1 m in diameter

Roots horizontally wide spreading fibrous root system and deep tap root (15 – 20 m) to absorb underground water

Aroma -

Propagation from seeds and wood cuttings

Maintenance low, pruning necessary for hedges

Ecosystem Services

Provisioning – Economic construction timber, medicine, fuel, shade, forestry, dye, agro-forestry

Regulating – Environmental tolerance of heat, drought, soil salinity; erosion control, windbreak, shade, fire barrier, air improvement

Cultural – Social a tree of local identity

Aesthetic – Spatial a suitable tree for public and private spaces of small or large scale, as alley or hedge, a specimen and shade tree because of its attractive feathery foliage

Tamarisk
الطرفاء

com. name   Tamarisk
gen. sp.   *Tamarix aphylla*[1]
arab. name Altorfah, Athel

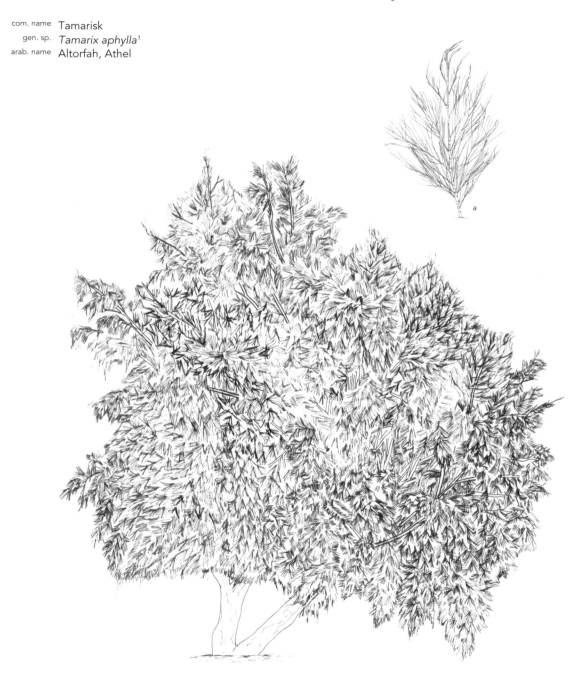

a branch

Tamarisk
الطرفاء

Tamarix nilotica as spatial enclosure,
Oases, Western Desert
Photo: Monique Jüttner

Tamarisk species are halophytes and xerophytes[2] native to the Middle East. They can be found throughout Egypt, naturally growing or cultivated, either as a shrub (*T. nilotica*) or as a tall tree *(T. aphylla)*. Preferred habitats are sand dunes, the desert, riparian areas, wadi beds, salt marshes and coastal plains.

Associated with religious beliefs and medicinal uses, the tamarisk was known and cultivated since ancient times in Egypt for shade, as a windbreaker and for its valuable timber.[3] *T. nilotica* is known for its diaphoretic and diuretic effect; it is used to cure wounds, skin diseases and liver disorders.[4] *T. aphylla* shows anti-fungal, anti-inflammatory, antibacterial and anti-tumor activities.[5] The bark and leaves of *T. aphylla* are used for tanning and dyeing, while its dense wood is good fuel and valuable timber for construction or furniture, rendering the tree interesting for agro-forestry.

Tamarisk species are particularly tolerant towards high concentrations of salt. They secrete excess salt through salt glands that deposit whitish salt droplets on the branchlets, resulting in a greyish-green leaf colour and a high salinity in branches and leaves. The nutritive values of *T. aphylla* and *T. nilotica* were found to be low.[6] As saline leaves are unpalatable to most livestock and increase the need for livestock watering, tamarisk is rather unsuitable as animal fodder. Leaf litter consequently raises soil salinity under the tree inhibiting the growth of non-salt-tolerant plants under its canopy. It is an effective fire barrier as high salt content in the leaves prevent the tree from rapid burning.

Extreme tolerance of environmental stresses, like salinity, heat, drought or inundation make tamarisk a perfect plant for marginal land, capable of stabilizing soils and sand dunes, preventing desertification and protecting from wind or dust. As a versatile tree it serves the ecosystem on a large scale as part of a forestation belt around urban areas or as windbreak or shelter from the sun. It is a tall tree with an impressive feathery foliage, forming sweeping crowns and reaching trunk diameters of 1 – 3 m. The tamarisk is a sublime as well as ecologically valuable plant that can be an imposing specimen tree in private gardens, while an avenue of trees creates a grand prelude of the type typical of ancient temples or tombs.[7]

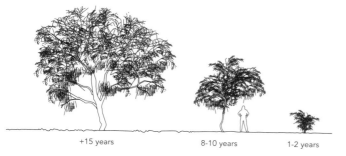

+15 years   8-10 years   1-2 years

Natural stands of Argoun Palm, Dungul Oases
Photo: Hala Barakat

water requirement	sun requirement	drought resistance	wind resistance	salinity tolerance	growth rate	shade
very low	high	very high	no data	no data	very slow	good-medium

Width 3 – 5 m   **Height** 5 – 10.5 m

Habitat Northern part of Sudan, Desert oases, Egypt: Upper Egypt, in Dungul and Nakhla Oasis (Western Desert) in very small populations

Soil sandy soil

Form a rare evergreen fan palm with a large, spherical crown of very stiff and strong leaves, well adapted to aridity

Foliage leaflets are leathery and large, sword shaped, dissected, young green leaves on the top point straight upward, old dry leaves drop from trunk

Flowers dioecious (male and female flowers on separate trees), small flowers in a large inflorescence

Bloom May

Fruits shiny brown-purplish fruits (ellipsoid 2 – 5 cm long), with dry, yellow flesh, bitter, but with a sweet taste if buried in the sand for some time

Trunk single stem

Roots deep main root (to tap ground water) and many side roots

Aroma -

Propagation from seeds

Maintenance low-moderate, propagation very difficult

Ecosystem Services

Provisioning – Economic edible fruits, fuel, leaves for mats and ropes

Regulating – Environmental shade, a habitat in the harshest environment, adaptation to hyper-aridity

Cultural – Social nature and cultural heritage, spiritual, educational

Aesthetic – Spatial specimen tree, small scale (due to propagation difficulties), public and private spaces

Argoun Palm
نخيل العرجون

com. name	Argoun Palm, Nubian Desert Palm
gen. sp.	*Medemia argun (Mart.) Württemb. Ex H. Wendl*[1]
arab. name	Argoun Palm

a cross-section of a fruit / b cluster of fruits / c leaf

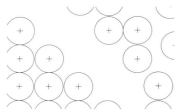

0   1   3

Argoun Palm
نخيل العرجون

The argoun palm is an indigenous and extremely rare evergreen fan palm persisting in the harshest desert environments of Egypt. Its appearance resembles the doum palm except that the trunk does not fork until it reaches 10 m above the ground. *M. argun* was considered extinct in Egypt, as the only evidence of the palm were fruits found in tombs of the 5th Dynasty (2500 BC) up until Roman Times (6 – 7th century AD).[2] Small populations of living plants were discovered in the 1950s[3] in remote desert sites of Nakhla and Dungul Oasis.

The presence of *Medemia* fruits as tomb offerings and depictions in wall drawings or hieroglyph writings indicate that it was cultivated in Ancient Egyptian gardens[4] either for its valuable edible fruits or for its cultural significance. While the taste of the fruits is rather bitter and becomes sweet only after burying them in the sand, the leaves are strong and soft. For desert dwellers, they offer an ideal material for mat or rope making and a source of fuel.

In harsh desert conditions where few species survive, *Medemia* contributes to biodiversity and is a habitat for animals, offering shade and food in extreme desert environments. Overexploitation and climate change led to its near extinction, rendering it a threatened plant and part of Egypt's biodiversity heritage.

While contributing to nature conservation, this desert plant can be an element of hyper-arid landscape design appropriate for New Urban Communities as well as historic sites. Planted as a line or arranged as a group, the palm can offer good shade and an agreeable microclimate. Little is known about its germination and cultivation due to its rareness, and its slow and wild growth. *Medemia* is not available in plant nurseries, as propagation proved to be difficult. Therefore, the plant is not yet ready to be applied in landscape design. Further research could foster the introduction of this specimen plant to gardens and landscape design and could save an almost lost species while re-establishing an ancient heritage of cultivation.

30 years   20 years   12 years   7 years

Weeping fig as street tree cut into geometric shapes, New Cairo
Photo: Peter Blodau

water requirement	sun requirement	drought resistance	wind resistance	salinity tolerance	growth rate	shade
moderate	flexible	moderate	high	moderate	fast	very good

Width up to 15 m   **Height** 6 – 30 m

Habitat South- and Southwest Asia, North Australia

Soil humus-rich and sandy soils, moist to well-drained

Form an evergreen tree or large shrub with slender, arching stems, can be trained as hedge or climber against walls

Foliage ovate-elliptic, leathery glossy leaves, 5 – 13 cm long, causes significant litter

Flowers petal-less flowers borne in the leaf axis, enlarges to form fig fruit

Bloom July – August

Fruits spherical to oblong figs (1.5 cm long), mature from green to pink or orange to black, can be found on the tree throughout the year

Trunk single or multi stemmed, can be trained

Roots extensive surface roots (can lift sidewalks) and deep roots (1 – 1.2 m deep)

Aroma -

Propagation semi-ripe or leaf-bud cuttings and seeds

Maintenance moderate, temporary pruning, fertilizer needed

Ecosystem Services

Provisioning – Economic animal fodder (leaves, fruits), medicine, wood

Regulating – Environmental air purification, cooling, erosion control, tolerance to environmental stresses

Cultural – Social recreation

Aesthetic – Spatial the tree provides an iconic habit and large shade when not cut, a spatially versatile plant for multiple scales in the public and private realm

Weeping Fig
الفيكس بنجامينا

com. name   Weeping Fig
gen. sp.   *Ficus benjamina*[1]
arab. name   Ficus Benjamina

a fruits / b twig with fruits

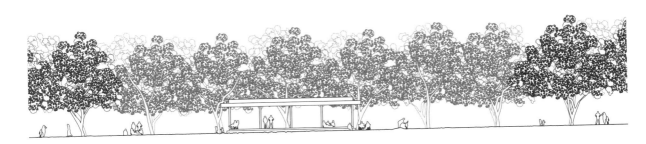

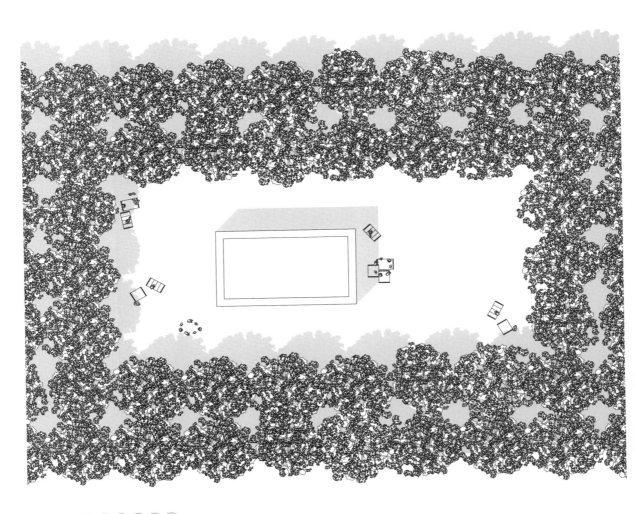

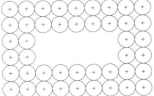

0   6   9

Weeping Fig
الفيكس بنجامينا

above: weeping fig as specimen tree, Elephantine Island, Awan; below: as green belt forest, New Cairo
Photos: Monique Jüttner

F. benjamina is one of the most useful and ornamental figs out of a genus of 800 species in the Moraceae family. Originating from tropic to subtropic regions of Asia, Malaysia and Australia, *F. benjamina* has been introduced to large parts of the world. As a relatively unpretentious plant, it became a popular indoor plant and designated street tree, as well as a frequent ornamental specimen in landscape design. In the areas of its origin, *F. benjamina* has a long tradition as a medicinal plant.[2] For Hindus and Buddhists in Nepal,[3] it is a sacred tree. Twigs are used as insect repellent; its sap is poisonous, and in many areas the leaves are a source of fodder for small ruminants.

Tolerant to dust and stress caused by inappropriate pruning or injuries, *F. benjamina* is a popular street tree. Cities worldwide benefit from its particular adaptability to urban environments and its high CO_2 fixation potential (air purification). In Egypt, *F. benjamina* and *F. Nitida Thunb*[4] from the Moraceae family belong to the basic repertoire of landscape design as a shading street tree, windbreak, protection belt or ornamental specimen tree.

Growing large with an impressive habit, it can dominate the scene, also displacing plants beneath it. Trained as a hedge, it is a good visual shield and ornamental feature of a garden. A spacing of 50 – 75 cm is advisable for hedges, while larger spacing applies for rows, alleys or single specimen trees (distances more than 15m). Fruits can be found on the tree throughout the year, providing a source of nutrition for birds and thus a good habitat.

Branches spread extensively and roots can go very deep. Exerting strangling power, they can cause damage to buildings, foundations, streets or subterranean infrastructure. Subsequent maintenance and repair costs can be a considerable burden, rendering the selection of appropriate plantation sites, design context and plant spacing an imperative. As key element of public open space in the new cities and older urban areas alike, *F. benjamina* is considerably shaping urban environments all over Egypt. If not trimmed to geometrical shapes, the tree unfolds its large and dense canopy that throws a deep shadow, locally lowering temperatures by 10° C.[5] This is an essential quality for open spaces, especially in hot climates.

+50 years   25 years   15 years   2-3 years

Acacia ehrenbergiana, Sahara, New Valley Aswan
Photo: Harald Kehl

water requirement	sun requirement	drought resistance	wind resistance	salinity tolerance	growth rate	shade
moderate	high	moderate	high	moderate	fast	medium

Width 5 – 7 cm **Height** 4 – 6 m

Habitat common in the driest parts of Egypt: the Southeastern Desert, oases of the Western Desert; widespread in the Western and Central Sahara, extending to Arabia

Soil sandy soil, rocky grounds, desert plains

Form a spiny, evergreen tall shrub, rarely a small tree with an irregular crown, twigs pointing straight up

Foliage bipinnate leaves, feather-like compound leaves divided into 8 – 10 leaflets per pinna, twigs are spinescent with thorns of up to 6 cm length, being longer than the leaves

Flowers inflorescences in light-yellow globular heads of about 1.5 cm in diameter

Bloom March – April

Fruits long brownish pods (up to 8 cm) containing 5 – 7 seeds

Trunk multi-stemmed, dark brown trunk, sharp long spines; peeling bark, strong wood

Roots very deep tap roots and widely spread shallow roots

Aroma sweet flowers

Propagation from seeds, long dormant periods, germination can be enhanced by soaking them in hot water[2]

Maintenance -

Ecosystem Services

Provisioning – Economic slowly burning fuel, nutritious livestock fodder, wood

Regulating – Environmental microhabitat, soil improvement, dune and soil fixation, halts gully erosion and desertification

Cultural – Social a symbol of the desert with recreational value

Aesthetic – Spatial a shrubby tree to enclose or define spaces, depending on size it provides soft shade

Acacia ehrenbergiana
السلام

com. name   no recorded name
gen. sp.   *Acacia ehrenbergiana Hayne*[1]
arab. name   Alsalam, Alselem

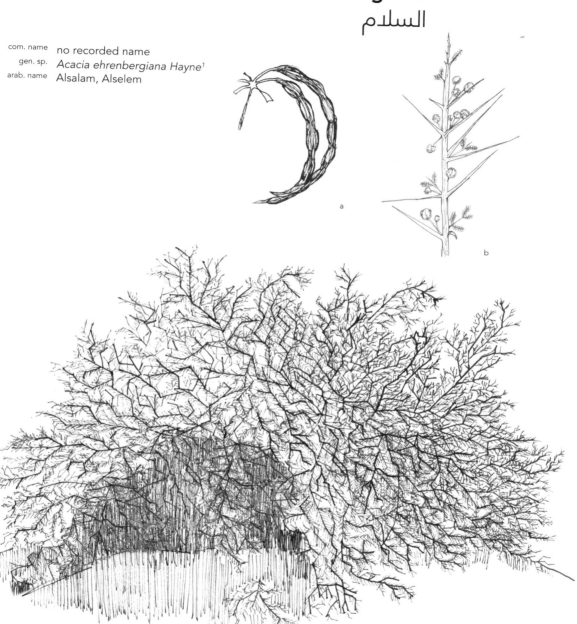

a pods / b twig with spines, leaves and flower heads

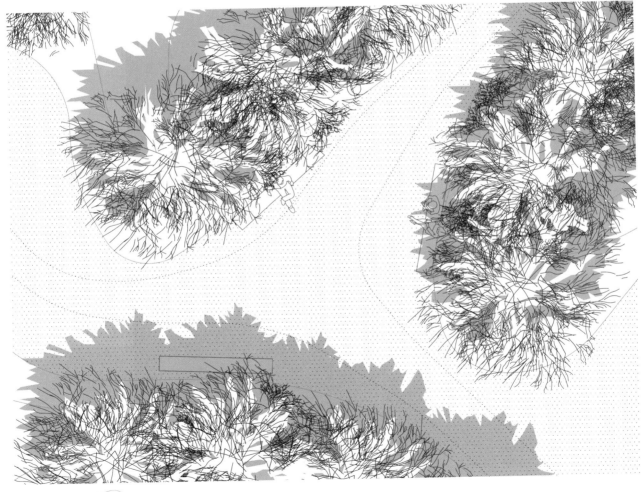

0   1   1.5

Acacia ehrenbergiana
السلام

Amongst 1,200 acacia species that are widespread in many regions of the world, ten are indigenous to Egypt. As ancient tomb paintings frequently depict the acacia tree with birds[3] on its branches it seems to have been a keystone species of ancient Egyptian landscapes. Acacia wood was used in boat, furniture and coffin building, while its peculiar yellow flowers were associated with the sun and woven into garlands.[4]

A. ehrenbergiana prefers habitats with water availability. Amongst desert acacias, it is, however, the most well-adapted species to extreme heat, salinity and drought[5] allowing its cultivation in different parts of Egypt, especially on degraded land and in harshest environments.

In the desert, it rarely grows as a tree, but predominantly as a shrub.[6] By inducing sand accumulation, shrubs form small and large hillocks and stabilize dunes or slopes of watersheds. The plant's ability to form a symbiosis with nitrogen-fixing bacteria in the root zone allows it to fertilize poor desert soils, encouraging further plant growth and offering microhabitats. *A. ehrenbergiana* not only supports the desert ecosystem but also nomadic Bedouin livelihoods based on pastoralism that heavily rely on this plant for palatable livestock fodder for camels and goats, but also as fuel or as a source of hard wood. Stress resulting from salinity[7] limits propagation success on a large scale, demanding pre-germination treatment.

The potential of *A. ehrenbergiana* for landscape design has not yet been fully explored as the plant is primarily known in the context of silviculture and ecosystem services to prevent desertification and erosion, to rehabilitate degraded lands, for afforestation of reclaimed lands as well as to support rural livelihoods. The yellow flowers alone are an ornamental highlight, but additionally the habit of the shrub can be modelled as a topographic feature offering a wide scope of design possibilities for landscape design, such as flat planes structured with hillocks to form intimate spaces. Planted as a fence-like boundary its thorny branches can act as a barrier. As a fully grown tree it can be the focus of a walled garden. *A. ehrenbergiana* may become a keystone species for desert landscape design through synergizing its ecosystemic capacity with its landscaping features.

+30 years   15 years   5 years   2-3 years

Nile acacia on the Nile banks, Aswan
Photo: Monique Jüttner

water requirement	sun requirement	drought resistance	wind resistance	salinity tolerance	growth rate	shade
low-moderate	high	moderate	high	moderate	moderate	good

Width 5 – 10 m **Height** 7 – 15 m

Habitat widespread in North Africa, extending to Asia (India, Pakistan), in Egypt it grows along the Nile Valley and the oases of the Western Desert, along irrigation canals and moist places beside water bodies in the oases or along the Nile banks

Soil moderately fertile, moist, well-drained soils, can withstand long inundation periods and short drought periods

Form an evergreen spiny tree, forming a compact round crown with horizontally spread twigs

Foliage bipinnate leaves, paired white spines at each base of the leaf

Flowers round flowering heads, bright yellow, sweet-scented

Bloom May – June

Fruits long green/brown pods with constriction between seeds, remaining on the tree for almost a year after breaking up

Trunk single stem, rough, dark green or black bark, deeply fissured, gum dark reddish

Roots deep tap roots 5 – 6m deep, intensive lateral roots

Aroma flower

Propagation from seeds with pre-treatment or semi-ripe cuttings

Maintenance low, with good irrigation it can grow fast

Ecosystem Services

Provisioning – Economic leaves and pods as nutritious fodder for livestock, firewood, charcoal, timber for carving and fencing, bark for tanning, medicine, Arabic gum, pulp for paper

Regulating – Environmental stabilizes soil, nitrogen fixing, habitat for animals, wind break, air purification

Cultural – Social a local cultural and natural heritage, a tree closely linked to traditional knowledge

Aesthetic – Spatial grouped trees form a dense canopy defining space and providing good shade; as a hedge, boundaries can be marked and spaces enclosed

Acacia nilotica
السنط

com. name Nile Acacia, Egyptian Thorn, Gum Arabic
gen. sp. *Acacia nilotica (L.) Delile*[1]
arab. name Alsant, Alsont

a spiney twig with leaves, pods and flower heads

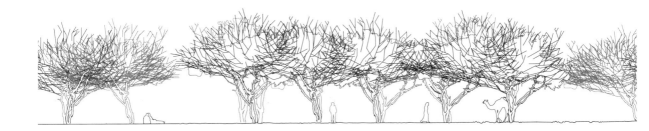

Acacia nilotica
السنط

In contrast to desert acacias, the Nile acacia prefers moist soils along irrigation canals, pools or wells. Indigenous to Egypt, its preferred habitats are the Nile Valley, the Delta and the oases.

In pharaonic times the Nile acacia was important as a source both of timber for boat construction[2] and a dye for leather or cotton[3] due to the high concentration of tannins in its pods, bark and leaves. All parts of the plant were processed for medicinal uses, while the bark was a source of gum to produce inks, paints, confectionary and soft drinks.[4] Flowers were used as ornaments in garlands. To this day, Egyptian thorn is widespread in North and East Africa, where it is a source of timber, fuel, gum and highly nutritious livestock fodder and an important medicinal plant with anti-inflammatory, antidiabetic, and antihypertensive properties. All parts of the plant (pods, bark, leaves, gum, root and flower) are used for various treatments.[5] Being a part of the traditional knowledge and cultural heritage of many tribal communities in Egypt and other countries in East and South Africa, the plant is still medicinally and economically relevant.[6] Like other acacia species, A. nilotica is characterized by its soil-improving (nitrogen fixation) and soil-binding capacities. If watered well, it grows fast and can be invasive even on marginal soils.

In India, in response to a growing population with a growing demand for timber, fuelwood and livestock fodder, A. nilotica has been successfully implemented on a larger scale to establish social forestry programs[7] and to reclaim degraded lands for agroforestry.[8] If planted for economic purposes, a spacing of 4 x 4 m[9] is recommended; to serve as a windbreak it should be planted as a strip. On a household level, it provides shade. It can be planted as a thorny hedge to keep animals out and prevent trespass. Not only is it an ideal plant for forestation to halt desertification, to reclaim desert land and to support local livelihoods, it is also an appealing ornamental tree with an impressive blossom and leaf structure. Urban planners and landscape designers should therefore give this plant and its multiple valuable aspects more attention.

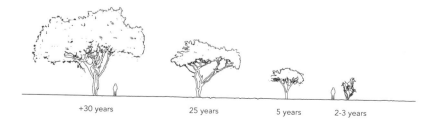

+30 years   25 years   5 years   2-3 years

Acacia tortilis subsp. raddiana in Wadi Hammamat
Photo: Monique Jüttner

water requirement	sun requirement	drought resistance	wind resistance	salinity tolerance	growth rate	shade
low	moderate	moderate	high	moderate	slow	good

Width up to 15 m **Height** 7 – 10 m

Habitat Northern Sahara, spreading to Palestine and Arab Peninsula, in the Egyptian deserts mostly in watersheds, the oases and Sinai

Soil different soil types, poor to moderately fertile, well drained, prefers non saline soils but tolerates salinity

Form an evergreen, thorny tree with broad, rounded, umbrella-shaped crown when mature

Foliage bipinnate leaves, with short, hooked or long, straight spines at each base of the leaf, leaves can drop during dry periods

Flowers spherical, white-yellowish flowers

Bloom May – June, possible twice a year depending on rain

Fruits curved or spirally twisted pods, hairless when mature, contains 8 – 12 seeds

Trunk dark grey bark, a distinctive trunk, that can reach considerable diameters in old trees

Roots tap roots penetrate deep into the soil, surface roots develop later after rain

Aroma flowers

Propagation from seeds

Maintenance low

Ecosystem Services

Provisioning – Economic livestock fodder, hard wood, construction and furniture wood, fuel and charcoal, traditional medicine (gum, pods, bark, bronchitis)

Regulating – Environmental fixing sand dunes, afforestation, nitrogen fixing, habitat for animals, water regulation, air purification

Cultural – Social a symbol of desert culture, combining knowledge of nomadic life and inspiration

Aesthetic – Spatial a large arching canopy provides good shade, a specimen with impressive habitus

Acacia tortilis subsp. raddiana
السنط الملتوي

com. name   Acacia
gen. sp.   *Acacia tortilis subsp. raddiana (Savi) Brenan*[1]
arab. name   Alsayaal

a spiny twig with leaves and flower heads / b pods

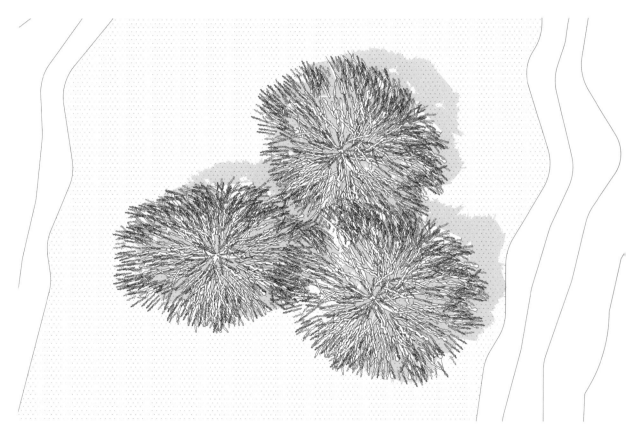

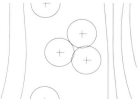

0   1   2

Acacia tortilis subsp. raddiana
السنط الملتوي

Acacia tortilis subsp. raddiana
in Wadi Durunkat, Egypt
Photo: Gidske L Andersens

As one of ten indigenous acacia species in Egypt, *A. tortilis subsp. raddiana* typically grows along watersheds in the desert, in depressions, in the oases as well as in higher altitude in Sinai.

The plant's habitat in Egypt corresponds to the traditional nomadic pastoral life of Bedouins. The leaves and pods are valuable fodder for livestock, the hard wood of this acacia is the source of timber, fuel or charcoal for the area, and parts of the plant are used for medicinal purposes. Through living in unity with a landscape of scarcity for centuries, a special ecological knowledge emerged. A study on traditional knowledge of plant species amongst local communities in Wadi Allaqi[2] found that acacia species are still widely associated with medicinal, grazing, fuel and charcoal use today. As cultural heritage[3] acacias mutually shape the appearance of the landscape and the people living in it.

In desert environments that are subjected to land degradation resulting from floods, wind or climate change, *A. tortilis subsp. raddiana* provides valuable ecosystem services. Like other acacia species, it considerably improves the soil quality through its nitrogen-fixing ability (see *A. ehrenbergiana* and *A. nilotica*). The wide crown provides shade, whilst deep tap roots and surface roots stabilize the ground and increase the water storage of the soil. People, animals and other plants directly benefit from this essential plant that is often the only species persisting in harsh desert areas.[4]

With its emblematic form, the *A. tortilis subsp. raddiana* is an impressive shadow tree, accentuating a distant view on a plane. As a mature tree in a courtyard it can be the center of a home while also supplying livestock with fodder and offering traditional medicine. As an intercrop for other plants or in agroforestry, it can improve plant growth and harvests. As a symbol of local heritage, performing extraordinarily well in arid environments and being full of character, acacias can become distinguished "keystone species"[5] of garden design in arid landscapes.

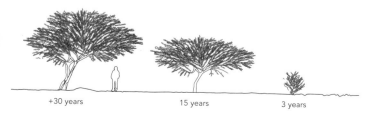

+30 years   15 years   3 years

A aesthetic landscape مساحة خضراء جمالية
misahat khadarra' jamalia
the scenic quality of landscape formed by color, form, texture and lines, the role of focal points, scale, layering, etc.

afforestation عمليات تشجير/ غرس الغابات
eamaliat tashjir / ghars alghabat
the process of planting trees, or sowing seeds, in a barren land devoid of any trees to create a forest.

anthropocene عصر الأنثروبوسين
easr al'antharubusin
relating to or denoting the current geological age, viewed as the period during which human activity has been the dominant influence on climate and the environment

aquaponics زراعة سمكية نباتية
ziraea samakia nabatia
the combination of aquaculture (raising fish) and hydroponics (the soil-less growing of plants) that grows fish and plants together in a closed cycle as one integrated system

aquifer المياه الجوفية
almiah aljawfia
an underground layer of rock that holds groundwater

arid environment البيئة القاحلة
albiya alqahila
can be defined as one in which the amount of precipitation an area receives, divided by the amount which is lost to evapotranspiration, yields a fraction which is less than 0.50

awareness توعية
taweia
knowledge or perception of a situation or fact

B barrage وابل
wabil
artificial barrier across a river to prevent flooding, aid irrigation or navigation, or to generate electricity

basin irrigation حوض الري
hawd alriy
irrigation of land by surrounding it with embankments to form a basin and flooding it with water

biodiversity التنوع البيولوجي
altnw'e albiology
the variety of living species on Earth, including plants, animals, bacteria, and fungi

biodigester هاضم حيوي
hadim hayawi
a device or structure in which the digestion of organic waste matter by bacteria takes place with the production of a burnable biogas and a nutrient-rich slurry

biological control التحكم البيولوجي
altahakum albiology
an environmentally sound and effective means of reducing or mitigating pests and pest effects through the use of natural enemies

black water مياه سوداء
miah sawda'
the mixture of urine, feces and flushwater along with anal cleansing water (if water is used for cleansing) and/or dry cleansing materials

botany علم النبات
eulim alnabat
science of plants

C canopy ظلة
zullah
the aboveground portion of a plant community or crop, formed by the collection of individual plant crowns

chaddar تشادار
tashadar
a textured stone chute often with a zigzag pattern creating bounces or ripples in the waterfall that enhance the sound of water movement

chahar bagh شهار باغ
Islamic quadrilateral garden layout based on the four gardens of Paradise mentioned in the Qur'an divided by walkways or flowing water into four smaller parts
a textured stone chute often with a zigzag pattern creating bounces or ripples in the waterfall that enhance the sound of the water movement

cistern صهريج
sahrij
sub-surface water reservoirs or storage tanks built to catch and store (rain) water

climate change تغير المناخ
taghayar almunakh
the shift of climate conditions increasingly as a result of human behaviour globally creating complex urgencies such as global warmig, flooding and aridity

climate regulation (micro+macro) تنظيم المناخ
tanzim almunakh
ecosystem service regulating processes related to atmospheric chemical compositions, the greenhouse effect, the ozone layer, precipitation, air quality, and moderation of temerpature and weather patterns (including cloud formation) at both global and local scales (Constanza et al, 1997)

CO_2 sequestration عزل ثاني أكسيد الكربون
eazl thani 'uksid alkarbun
describes long-term storage of carbon dioxide or other forms of carbon to either mitigate or defer global warming and avoid dangerous climate change; proposed as a way to slow the atmospheric and marine accumulation of greenhouse gases released by burning fossil fuels.

commodification سلعة
silea
transformation of resources, services, goods, or people into objects of trade within a capitalist economic system; in the context of a general commodification of the real estate market globally and in specific in Egypt, landscapes became a prominent factor in the marketability of middle and upper income housing

constructed wetlands معالجة الأراضي الرطبة
muealajat al'aradi alrutba
water treatment systems that use natural processes involving wetland vegetation, soils, and their associated microbial assemblages to improve water quality

corridor الرواق
alrowaq
a belt of land linking two other areas or following a road or river

corvée السخرة
alsakhra
a day's unpaid labour owed by a vassal to his feudal lord

cultivar صنف
sinf
a plant variety that has been produced in cultivation by selective breeding

cultural landscape ثقافية
thaqafiah
cultural properties that represent the combined works of nature and of man

D desertification تصحر
tasahur
process by which fertile land becomes desert, typically as a result of drought, deforestation, inappropriate agriculture and urbanization

drainage تصريف المياه
tasrif almiah
removal of excess water from soil surface and below to permit optimum growth for plants and to avert damage to adjoining buildings

drinking water مياه شرب
miah shurb
aka potable water, is water that is safe to drink or to use for food preparation

drip irrigation ري بالتنقيط
raiy biltanqit
a micro-irrigation system to save water and nutrients by slowly dripping water to the roots of plants above or below the soil surface to bring water directly to the root zone and minimize evaporation

drought-resistant plants نباتات مقاومة للجفاف
nabatat muqawamah liljafaf
plants able to maintain their biomass production during arid or drought conditions

E ecosystemic services خدمات النظام البيئي
khadamat alnizam albi'iy
benefits to humans by the natural environment from healthy ecosystems grouped into four broad categories: provisioning, such as the production of food and water; regulating, such as the control of climate and disease; supporting, such as nutrient cycles and oxygen production; and cultural, such as spiritual and recreational benefits

environment البيئة
albi'a
surroundings or conditions in which a person, animal, or plant lives or operates

environmental adaptability القدرة على التكيف البيئي
alqudrat ealaa altakayuf albi'iy
ability to cope with unexpected disturbances in the environment

environmental damage الأضرار البيئية
al'adrar albi'iya
deterioration of the environment through depletion of resources such as air, water and soil; the destruction of ecosystems and the extinction of wildlife

erosion التعرية
altaeria
surface processes (wind and water) that remove soil, rock, or dissolved material and redeposit them in other places

erosion control   مكافحة تآكل التربة
mukafahat takul altorbah
practice of preventing or controlling wind or water erosion in agriculture, land development, coastal areas, river banks and construction

evaporation   تبخر
tabakhor
loss of water from a surface as it changes into a gas phase leading to water loss, but potentially improving micro-climate

F fauna   الحيوانات
alhayawanat
animals of a particular region, habitat, or geological period

feddan   فدّان
faddān
unit of area equal to 4,200 sqm used in Egypt, Sudan, Syria and the Sultanate of Oman; in Classical Arabic, the word means 'a yoke of oxen': implying the area of ground that could be tilled by them in a certain time

flora   النباتية
alnabatia
plants of a particular region, habitat, or geological period

fodder   علف
ealf
food, especially dried hay or straw, for cattle and other livestock

food heritage   التراث الغذائي
alturath alghidha'iy
knowledge and practices related to the production, transformation, distribution and consumption of food, across generations within a region or community

food security   أمن غذائي
aman ghidha'iy
availability of adequate, nourishing, diverse, balanced and affordable food supplies of basic food stocks at all times

food sovereignty   السيادة الغذائية
alsiyadah alghidha'iya
ability of people who produce, distribute and consume food to also control the mechanisms and policies of food production and distribution instead of being reliant on global corporations and markets

G grafting   تطعيم النبات
tateim alnabat
horticultural technique whereby tissues of plants are joined so as to continue their growth together and to optimize properties

grain size   حجم الحبوب
hajm alhubub
the diameter of individual grains of sediment, or the lithified particles in clastic rocks or other granular materials, ranging from very small colloidal particles, through clay, silt, sand, and gravel, to boulders

green lung   الرئة الخضراء
alri'a alkhadra
An area of natural parkland within an urban region to replenish the air with oxygen

green roof   السطح الأخضر
alsath al'akhdar
a roof that is covered in plants, which may retain water to reduce stormwater runoff and lower cooling costs through insulation as well as contribute to urban food production

greenhouse gases   غازات الاحتباس الحراري
ghazat alihtibas alharariy
primary gases (H_2O, CO_2, CH_4, N_2O, O_3) in the earth atmosphere causing the greenhouse effect which causes global warming

greywater   مياه رمادية
miah ramadeyah
Water coming from domestic equipment other than toilets (e.g., bathtubs, showers, sinks, washing machines)

groundwater   مياه الجوفية
miah aljawfeya
water found underground in the cracks and spaces in soil, sand and rock stored and moving slowly through aquifers

H habitat   موطن
mawtin
natural home or environment of an animal, plant, or other organism; those places where it can find food, shelter, protection and mates for reproduction

halophyte   الملحية
almalahiya
a plant that is salt-tolerant through different adaptation strategies

heritage   التراث
alturath
tangible and intangible features belonging to a specific culture (e.g. language, buildings, traditions, food, etc.) that were created in the past and are still relevant today

heritage conservation   حفظ التراث
hifz alturath
actions or processes that are aimed at safeguarding the character-defining elements of a cultural resource

horticulture   بستنة
bastana
the agriculture of plants, mainly for food, materials, comfort and beauty for decoration excluding classical field farming

hortus conclusus   حديقة مغلقة
hadiqah mughlaqa
enclosed garden

hydroponics   الزراعة المائية
alziraeah alma'iya
a multiscalar method of growing plants in a water-based, nutrient-rich solution without the use of soil, using around 80% less water

hydrozone   هيدروزون
a portion of landscape area where plants with similar water needs are grouped in an effort to use less water

I infrastructure   بنية تحتية
binyah tahtiah
basic structure of an organization or system which is necessary for its operation, esp. public water, energy, and systems for communication and transport

intercrop   زراعة بينية
ziraeat bayneya
to grow one crop between the rows of another, as in an orchard or field contributing to biodiversity and biological control

interdisciplinarity
combining more than one academic disciplines into one activity

inundation pool   بركة
birka
temporary man-made lake filled during Nile floods

K kirat   قيراط
qirāt
One kirat equals 175 sqm; 24 kirat make up one feddan

L land reclamation   استصلاح الأراضي
estislah al'aradi
to allocate desert land for other purposes, mainly agriculture and urbanization

landscape as infrastructure   المناظر الطبيعية كبنية التحتية
almanazir altabiya kabniah althahtiah
alignment of the disciplines of landscape architecture, civil engineering, and urban planning

landscape ecology   بيئة المناظر الطبيعية
bayyat almanazir altabiya
the study of interactions between the temporal and spatial aspects of a landscape and the organisms within it

landscape element   عنصر المناظر الطبيعية
unsur almanazir altabiya
geophysically defined landforms such as mountains or hills, water bodies such as rivers, lakes, living elements of land cover including indigenous vegetation, human elements including different forms of land use, buildings, and structures, and transitory elements such as lighting and weather conditions

large-scale   نطاق واسع
nitaq wasea
involving many people or things, or happening over a large area

lawn   العشب
aleaushb
open, close-cut grasslands, especially near to a house or in a park, originating in the moist, mild, climate of Europe

M macro-catchment water harvesting   مستجمعات المياه الكبيرة
mustajmaeat almiah alkabira
an area for rainwater harvesting consisting of four components: the catchment area, the runoff conveyance system, the storage system and the application area where the ratio of the catchment to the application area (usually cultivated) varies between 10:1 and 100:1

macrophyte   الضامة
aldama
aquatic plant growing in or near water (emergent, submergent, or floating)

maintenance   صيانة
siana
the work needed to keep a road, building, machine, etc. in good condition

matrix   قالب
qalib
the cultural, social, or political environment in which something develops

micro-catchment water harvesting   مستجمعات المياه الكبيرة
(MicroWH)
mustajmaeat almiah alsaghirah
designed to trap and collect runoff from a relatively small catchment area, usually
(10 – 500 m2) where the ratio between the catchment (collection) area to the cultivated (application) area can vary between 2:1 and 10:1

micro-gardening   زراعة ميكروسكوبية
ziraeat mikroskobeya
the practice of intensively food 'farming' in containers and well-designed, small
urban spaces designed to be highly productive; energy and space efficient; sustainable; affordable; and grown in healthy living soil

multi-scalar   متعدد المقاييس
mutaeadid almaqayis
relating to multiple scales

N natural heritage   التراث الطبيعي
alturath altabieaiy
Natural features consisting of physical and biological formations or groups of such
formations, which are of outstanding universal value from the aesthetic or scientific
point of view; geological and physiographical formations and precisely delineated
areas which constitute the habitat of threatened species of animals and plants of outstanding universal value from the point of view of science or conservation; natural sites
or precisely delineated natural areas of outstanding universal value from the point
of view of science, conservation or natural beauty. World Heritage Convention 1972

network   شبكة
shabakah
a large system consisting of many similar parts that are connected together to
allow movement or communication between or along the parts, or between the
parts and a control centre

nitrogen-fixing plants   محطات تثبيت النيتروجين
mahattat tathbit alnitrujin
plants growing in symbiosis with bacteria in the root zone producing nitrogen, a
major nutrient for all plants

not suitable for human use   غير صالحة للاستخدام الآدمي
ghayr saliha lilaistikhdam ladamiy

nutrient-film technique   تقنية فيلم المغذيات
taqneyet film almughdhiat
an approach where roots are suspended in a trough through which a thin layer of
nutrient solution is continually recirculated

O oasis   واحة
wahah
an ecosystem providing habitat for flora and fauna based on the presence of water,
in arid or semi-arid environments that permit human settlement and cultivation
provided that the technical and social know-how is available

orchard   بستان
bustan
intentional planting of trees or shrubs that is maintained for food production

ornamental plants   نباتات الزينة
nabatat alziyna
plants that are grown for decorative purposes in gardens and landscape design
projects, as houseplants, cut flowers and specimen display

P patch   رقعة
ruqea
a small area that is different in some way from the area that surrounds it

perennial agriculture   الزراعة المعمرة
alziraeat almueamara
the cultivation of crop species that live longer than two years without the need for
replanting each year

permaculture
an innovative framework of closed-loop systems creating sustainable ways of
living by imitating resilient features of natural ecosystems that can be used by
anyone, anywhere

phytoremediation   علاج النبات
eilaj alnabat
the use of plants to remove, contain, or degrade environmental contaminants in
water, soil or air

plant nursery   مَشتَل
mashtal
a place where plants are grown to a desired age, specializing in propagation,
growing out, or retail sale and conditioning for replanting

polished treated waste water   مياه الصرف الصحى المعالج
miah el sarf el sehhy el moalaj
primarily treated waste water polished in constructed wetland or treatment reservoir

pollination   التلقيح
altalqih
the transfer of pollen grains from the anther, which is the male part of the flower,
to the stigma, which is on the female part

potting soil system   نظام تربة وعائي
nizam turbat weaiy
a medium in which you can grow vegetables, plants, and herbs in a pot or a container

private space   مساحة خاصة
misahat khassah
a location in which a person has a reasonable expectation of privacy

productive landscape   مساحة خضراء منتجة
misahat khadara' muntijah
an emerging strategy integrating productivity in cities via landscape and planning tools

protectorate   محمية
mahmeyah
Law 102, issued in 1983 empowered the prime minister to protect certain areas in
order to set basic principles for the management and protection of their resources;
today, there are 30 protectorates in Egypt making up 15% of the country's total
area

pruning   تقليم
taqlim
cutting away dead or overgrown branches or stems, especially to encourage growth

public space   مساحة عامة
misahat eamah
a place that is generally open and accessible to people such as streets (including
the pavement), public squares, parks and beaches

Q quanat   كانات
kanat
ancient water infrastructure in arid and semi-arid climates transporting water for
irrigation and drinking from an aquifer or wellthrough a gently sloping underground channel

R rainwater   مياه الأمطار
miah al'amtar
water fallen as rain that has not collected soluble matter from soil and is therefore soft

rainwater harvesting   حصاد مياه الأمطار
hisad miah al'amtar
technology that collects and stores rainwater for human use

recreational landscape   مساحة خضراء ترفيهية
misahat khadirra' tarfihia
a rich natural or man-made potential for active recreational and tourism development given availability of resources and infrastructure provision

recreational park   حديقة ترفيهية
hadiqah tarfiheyah
a plot of land used for formal and informal recreational activities

recycled water   المياه المعاد تدويرها
almiah almoaead tadwiruha
the process of converting wastewater into water that can be reused for other
purposes such as irrigating gardens and agricultural fields or replenishing surface
water and groundwater bodies, fulfilling certain residential needs (e.g. toilet flushing), businesses, and industry; can even be treated to reach drinking water standards

reservoirs   خزانات
khazzanat
a natural or artificial lake for storing and supplying water for an area created using
a dam or lock

resilience   المرونة
almuruna
the ability of systems to absorb changes and still persist

S sabil kuttab   سبيل وكتاب
sabil wakuttab
drinking water fountain with school on upper level

saquia   ساقية
saquia
a water wheel/water-lifting device using animals still in use in some parts of Egypt

schaduf   شادوف
schaduf
hand-operated device for lifting water to irrigate land, typically consisting of a
long, tapering nearly-horizontal pole mounted like a seesaw

sedimentation
tathaful ; trasub ; rusub
تَثَفُّل ؛ تَرَسُّب ؛ رُسْوب
when water has little or no movement, suspended solids sink to the bottom under the force of gravity and form a sediment

septic tank
bayarat / khazzan lilsarf alsihiy
بيارة / خزان للصرف الصحي
an underground tank to collect sewage for decomposition through bacterial activity before draining by means of a soakaway

sericulture
iintaj alharir min dud alqazz
إنتاج الحرير من دود القز
silk farming; the cultivation of silkworms to produce silk

sewage water
miah majari
مياه مجاري
wastewater from people living in a community consisting of grey and black water

sha'
sha'
garden as well as lake and pond in ancient Egypt

shade
zil
ظل
darkness and coolness caused by shelter from direct sunlight

sickle
manjil
منجل
a single-handed agricultural tool designed with variously curved blades and typically used for harvesting, or reaping, grain crops or cutting succulent forage chiefly for feeding livestock, either freshly cut or dried as hay

sludge
hama'a
حمأة
a semi-solid slurry that can be produced from a range of industrial processes, from water- and wastewater treatment or on-site sanitation systems' of limited size or extent

small-scale
nitaq saghir
نطاق صغير
opening, feeding, adding organic matter, mulching and deeply watering the soil are some ways to increase the quality of soil

soil improvement
tahsin altorba
تحسين التربة

storm protection
himayatan min aleawasif
حماية من العواصف
Coral reefs, mangrove forests, dunes, and wetlands are all examples of natural barriers that protect the hinterland from rising sea levels and storm surges

stubble burning
harq alqash
حرق القش
intentionally setting fire to straw stubble that remains after harvesting, thus turning plant remains into ash as a natural fertilizer; burning rice straw in Egypt is considered the main cause of what is known as "the black cloud," a thick layer of smog from burning rice straw that spreads across Cairo for an extended period of time

succulents
aleasara
العصارة
plants that develop special features such as thick, fleshy parts to retain water in arid conditions

sustainability
alaistidama
الاستدامة
to meet the needs of the present without compromising the ability of future generations to meet their own needs; originating in forestry in the 17th century, the definition of sustainable development was extended by the Brundtland Commission in 1987 to include three pillars: the economic, the environmental, and the social

sustainable park
hadiqah mustadama
حديقة مستدامة
a park made to preserve natural resources and promote quality of life for the people using native plants and geographic features to be more efficient

swale
sawal
سوال
a natural or man-made trench to redirect water to where it can be released safely

symbiotic cycle
dawrat nafea mutabadil
دورة نفع متبادل
any type of closed and long-term biological interaction between different biological organisms, be it mutualistic, commensalistic, or parasitic

T transdisciplinarity
eabr altakhasusat
عبر التخصصات
the crossing of many disciplinary boundaries to create a holistic approach

treated waste water
miah alsirf alsihiy almuealaja
مياه الصرف الصحي المعالجة
treated wastewater can be used directly as a source for agriculture or used indirectly

U urban agriculture
alziraeat alhadaria
الزراعة الحضرية
provides fresh food, generates employment, recycles urban wastes, creates greenbelts, and strengthens cities' resilience to climate change (FAO)

urban connectivity
alaitisa alhadariu
الاتصال الحضري
to facilitate neighborhood connections through pedestrian mobillity via the street network, paths, etc.; it also refers to socio-economic connectivity: accessibility of urban system services (transportation, sanitation, water, etc.) across different socio-economic groups providing equality and ecological connectivity: access to natural and semi-natural habitats in cities (green parks, urban forests, domestic gardens. etc.) providing city dwellers with ecosystem services

urban heat island effect
uzur hirariat hadaria
جزر حرارية حضرية
a phenomenon of higher temperatures in cities mainly due to impermeable surfaces and the accumulated use of concrete asphalt and stone, as well as increased anthropogenic heat production

urban park
hadiqatan eumrania
حديقة عمرانية
communal green spaces in the city that serve multiple, evolving functions

urban refuge
malja hadriun
ملجأ حضري
a place to escape from the hustle and bustle of the city like a pocket park or a community garden

V vacant land
ard fada'
ارض فضاء
land that has no buildings on it and is not being used

W wadi
wādē dry riverbed
وادي

waste collection points
niqat tajmae alqamama
نقاط تجميع القمامة
the point of disposal of waste for transporation, the point of a treatment, recycling plant or landfill

waste water
miah alsarf
مياه الصرف
used water from any combination of domestic, industrial, commercial or agricultural activities, surface runoff or stormwater, and any sewer inflow or sewer infiltration

waste water treatment plant (WWTP)
mahatat muealajat miah alsir alsihiyi
محطة معالجة مياه الصرف الصحي
a plant to clean sewage and water by removing solids and pollutants, break down organic matter and restore the oxygen content of treated water so that they can be returned to the environment and reused again

water diversion
tawjih almiah
توجيه المياه
dams are installed to raise the water level of a body of water to allow the water to be redirected and used to supply irrigation systems, reservoirs, or hydroelectric power generation facilities

water regulation
tanzim almiah
تنظيم المياه
policy to ensure the safety of drinking-water to protect public health and to ensure limited use through taxation

water runnels
gadwal almiah
جدول المياه
a small stream in a stone bed featured in Islamic gardens that aligns a path and provides the sound of water

water-sensitive urban design (WSUD)
altasmim alhadariu alhassas tijah almiah
التصميم الحضاري الحساس تجاه المياه
a land planning and engineering design approach which integrates the urban water cycle, including stormwater, groundwater and wastewater management and water supply, into urban design to minimise environmental degradation and improve aesthetic and recreational appeal

watershed
hawd asarf
حوض الصرف
an area of land that drains all the streams and rainfall to a common outlet such as the outflow of a reservoir, mouth of a bay, or any point along a stream channel

windbreak
masadat riah
مصدات رياح
a planting usually made up of one or more rows of trees or shrubs planted in such a manner as to provide shelter from the wind and to protect soil from erosion

X xerophyte
nabat sahrawi
نبات صحراوي
plants that are morphologically adapted to extreme arid conditions

INTRODUCING THE NARRATIVE
1   see Hill, J. (2010). Hapi. Available at: https://ancientegyptonline.co.uk/hapi/ [accessed 22 July. 2019]
2   see https://www.theguardian.com/world/2015/aug/04/egypt-water-crisis-intensifies-scarcity [accessed 18 August, 2017]
3   Arab Republic of Egypt Ministry of Environment (2016). EGYPTIAN BIODIVERSITY STRATEGY AND ACTION PLAN (2015 – 2030).
4   See Atta-Allah Kafafy, Nezar, 2010. The dynamics of urban green space in an arid city; the case of Cairo-Egypt, Cardiff University
5   Egypt Independent (12 Feb, 2013). Preserving one of Egypt's most efficient ecosystems. Egypt Independent [online]. Available at: https://egyptindependent.com/preserving-one-egypt-s-most-efficient-ecosystems-mangrove/ [accessed 22 July. 2019]
6   see Isaksson, C. (2019). Impact of Urbanization on Birds In: Bird Species – How They Arise, Modify and Vanish pp 235 – 257. Available at: https://link.springer.com/chapter/10.1007/978-3-319-91689-7_13 [accessed 30 July. 2019]

01 LANDSCAPE CONDITIONS
Evolving Landscapes
1   Arab Republic of Egypt Ministry of Environment, 2016
2   ibid
3   Luck and Smallbone 2010; Aronson et al. 2014 cited by Isaksson, 2018 https://link.springer.com/chapter/10.1007/978-3-319-91689-7_13
4   (https://www.adaptation-undp.org/explore/northern-africa/egypt)
5   Agrawala et al., 2004
6   GOPP and UNDP, 2009
7   A study for Wadi Bili west of El Gouna concluded that during heavy rainfalls in March 2014 large parts of the roughly 35 million cubic meters of rainwater infiltrated into the aquifer. However, one million cubic meters passed through the Bili canyon to be lost to the salty waters of the Red Sea, enought to provide the city of El Gouna with drinking water for a year (see Hadidi, 2016).
8   see http://www.eeaa.gov.eg/en-us/topics/nature/afforestation/greenbelts.aspx
9   Oswald, 2015
10 Dabaieh, 2015
11 Fathy, 1986
12 see Whittaker-Wood, 2018

Landscaping Practices - From Symbiosis to Commodification
1   Bowman, 1996 p. 19
2   see Sampsell, 2014
3   ibid
4   see Loeben, 2016
5   Daines, 2008
6   Wilkinson, 1994
7   ElMasry, 2015
8   Daines, 2008
9   Bowman and Rogan, 1999 p. 3
10 see Frantz-Murphy, 1999
11 see Cuno, 1980 p. 246
12 Ruggles, 2008 p. xi, 41
13 Petruccioli, 1998 p. 357
14 Piri Reis (1465/70 – 1533) was an Ottoman cartographer who is mostly known for his maps published between 1513 and 1524 in his book of navigation.
15 Ratte, 2015 p. 56 – 79
16 Khasraw, N. 1046 – 1052. Safarnamah. Translated by Yahia Al-Khashab. p. 116 – 117
17 Ruggles, 2008 p. 170
18 Dobrowolska, Fahmy, 2004
19 Al Maqrizi (1364 – 1442) was an Egyptian historian and writer whose writings describe Egypt and the Arab world during the 14th and 15th Centuries as well as a certain focus on the Fatimid rule.
20 Echols, Nassar, 2007
21 Waqf is a land or property endowed to Muslim charitable to religious purposes and benefits. Large parts of waqf land were ahli or family waqfs benefitting from tax exemptions and with revenues only being designated to charitable work once the family line became extinct (see Cuno, 1980).
22 Ruggles, 2008 p.169; El Masry, 2015 p. 59
23 For the evolving role of water and leisure in the city of Cairo see Sadik, H. (2019)
24 Sims, 2018 p. 33
25 Hamdy et al, 2007
26 Sims, 2018 p. 33
27 From 1882 – 1914, Egypt was a veiled protectorate of Britain: the British controlled most of Egypt without any real legal authority.From 1914 – 1922, it was a formal protectorate, until Britain

declared the nation to be independent. Still, the British maintained a strong presence until the 1956 Suez Crisis.
28 see Cuno, 1980
29 Rabbat, 2018. Egypt went bankrupt after Khedive Isma'il borrowed heavily during the construction of downtown Cairo and the Suez Canal in his attempts to modernize Egypt. As a result, the British occupied Egypt in 1879.
30 ETH Basel, 2009
31 In Egypt, waqfs represented a significant part of the economy. In 1942, endowed land property made up 11.5 % of all private agricultural land in the country (Baer, 1969, 80).
32 Abooelroos et al, 2017. BCM = Billion Cubic Meters
33 Sims, 2012
34 Sims, 2018 p. 190
35 Sims, 2018
36 Denis, 2018
37 Diester, 2013 p. 9
38 Sims, 2012 p. 3; Denis, 2017 p. 44
39 Denis, 2017 p. 36, see in comparison LSE study: peak population in administrative area 153,606 residents / sq.km

Timeline
1   Lutz, Trotha, and Museum Rietberg, 2016 p. 42)
2   Sampsell, 2003
3   Sampsell, 2003 p. 39
4   Wuttmann, Gonon, and Thiers, 2000
5   Sims, 2014
6   Barakat, 2017
7   Ruggles 2008, p. 40
8   Khusraw, 1993
9   Ruggles 2008, p. 34, Rabbat, 2004
10 Rabbat 2004, p. 45
11 Ruggles, 2008, Rabbat, 2004
12 Rabbat 2004, p. 45
13 Ruggles 2008, p. 169, Volait 2005, p. 113
14 Abdel-Rahma,n 2016
15 Sampsell 2003, p. 33
16 New York Times, 1864
17 Volait 2005, p. 113, Ruggles 2008, p. 170
18 Rabbat, 2004
19 El Quosy and Khalifa 2017, p. 34
20 Dobrowolska and Dobrowolski, 2006
21 Kafafy 2010, p. 153
22 El Quosy and Khalifa, 2017)
23 Sims, 2010
24 Herzog et al, 2010
25 Deng, 2007; Sims 2014
26 Abdel-Kader and Ettouney, 2009
27 Sims 2014, p. 100
28 Abdel-Kader and Ettouney, 2009
29 Denis, 2006
30 Sims 2014, p. 194
31 Sims 2014, p. 81
32 Sims 2018, p. 51
33 New Urban Communities Authority, 2019
34 Denis, 2006
35 El Kateb et al, 2015
36 ElMasry, 2014
37 Responsible and Inclusive Business Hub MENA Egypt, 2015
38 Mohamed, 2018
39 Sims 2018, p. xxxvii
40 Stanley and Clemente, 2017
41 Graphic Agricultural Land Egypt in km2: Pre Ptolemaic: up to 8000 Km2 (Noaman and El Quosy, 2017 p. 18); Ptolemaic – Roman Egypt: 10 000 Km2 (Sampsell, 2003); Islamic Period 645: 6000 km2; 1517: 12 000 km2 (2.8 Million Feddan) (Noaman and El Quosy 2017:16); Ottoman period: 8 400 km2 (2 million Feddan) (Noaman and El Quosy, 2017 p. 17); 1805: 8 400 km2 (2 million feddan) (Sims 2014); 1952: 25 200 km2 (6 million Feddan) (Sims 2014); 1960-2016: (1961: 25 680 km2; 1964: 25 060 km2; 1966: 27 800 km2; 1970: 28 430 km2; 1974: 28 430 km2; 1978: 25 400 km2; 1982: 24 452 km2; 1986: 25 670 km2; 1990: 26 480 km2; 1994: 32 460 km2; 1998: 32 596 km2; 1999: 34 830 km2; 2000: 32 910 km2; 2004: 34 780; 2008: 35 420; 2009: 36 890, 2011: 36 200; 2013: 37 309; 2014: 37 151; 2015: 37 898; 2016: 37 337) (The World Bank Group and FAO, 2019)
42 Graphic Population Egypt: 3000 BC: 1-1.5 million; late Dynastic period:3-4 mil., early Roman period: 6-8 mil. (F. Dorman et al, 2019); early 15th Century: 3mil (Berkey in: Petry, 1998:380); 1798:3mil.; 1947:19mil.; 1960: 26mil.; 1976: 36.6mil.; 1986: 47.7mil.; 1996: 58.8mil.; 2013: 85mil.; 2020: 100mil. (Noaman, 2017)

43 definition of water stress levels by UN (United Nations 2018); Graphic available renewable water resources per capita/year in Egypt: 1949: 2526 m3 (20 mil. Inh.) (Amer et al, 2018) 1962: 2041 m3 (Wahba, Scott, and Steinberger, 2018) (1960: 26.6 mil. inh.); 1970: 1972 m3 (CAPMAS, 2014); 2014: 663 m3 (Samir) (90 mil. Inh.); 2018: 570 m3 (Samir, 2018) (98 mil. inh.); 2030: expected to drop below 500 m3 (Wahba, Scott, and Steinberger, 2018)
44 with a 2 % increase per year, a population growth of 60 million is expected for the next 30 years (Maged, 2019)
45 Agricultural Land Loss: 619,177 feddan between 1993 and 2015 (Radwan et al, 2019)
46 Anglo-Egyptian Treaty (1929) Egypt receives 48 billion m³ / year; update of Anglo-Egyptian Treaty (1959) Egypt receives 55 billion m3 / year (S. Kimenyi and Mukum Mbaku, 2015)
47 Lewis, 2019

02 LEARNING FROM
Al Azhar Park
1 see Ibrahim
2 ibid
3 Otte, 2005
4 Musgrave
5 El Masry, 2017
6 Musgrave, see also El Masry 2014 a+b
7 Ibrahim
8 Otte, 2005

Geziret El Dahab
1 Sleem, Hassan, 2010
2 Fawzi, Abdelmaksoud., Azer, 2010
3 See Barthel 2009, ETH Studio Basel 2010, Redeker, Nazer, 2016
4 Cairo's green area/inhabitant ratio estimated at only 1.5 sqm (global average 10 – 18 sqm) see El-Zafarany
5 CAPMAS 2017 census
6 ibid
7 References for Ecovillage Park calculations: BiogasWorld, 2016, Cia.gov., 2016, Irena.org., 2016, Vymazal, J., 2007, Frearson, A., 2016

Desert Afforestation
1 FAO, 2005
2 Goldmann, 2001
3 see El Kateb et al, 2015
4 see El Tawil, 2018
5 El Kateb and Mosandl, 2012
6 El Kateb et al, 2013
7 see MEDENEC, 2012
8 see El Kateb et al, 2015
9 El Kateb and Mosandl, 2012
10 Becker et al, 2013
11 El Tawil, 2018

Wadi Agriculture
1 see Plan Bleu UNEP Map Regional Activty Center Sustainability Profile Mediterranean Destinations, 2011
2 Akhtar et al, 2009
3 Mekdaschi, Studer, Liniger, 2013
4 see Hadidi, 2016
5 see Jones et al, 2019
6 Prinz, 1996; Prinz, 2002

Water-Sensitive Open Space Design
1 see Sims, 2015
2 (according to agricultural groups A, B or C defined in the Egyptian code for the use of treated wastewater in agriculture (Abu Zeid et al, 2014, p. 30)
3 for a detailed analysis see 2030 Strategic vision for treated wastewater reuse in Egypt

Urban Microfarms
1 see Khasraw, N. 1046 – 1052. Safarnamah. Translated by Yahia Al-Khashab p.116 – 117
2 see "Cairo to Begin Planting Gardens on Rooftops"
3 see El Kateb and Mosandl, 2012

Constructed Wetlands
1 see Egyptian Law for Reuse of Treated Waste Water 2016
2 see Eid, 2014
3 see Masi et al, 2010
4 Hoffmann et al, 2011
5 Eid, 2014

Aquaponic Farming
1 Mollison, 1992
2 Pearson et al, 2010
3 www.bustanaquaponics.com

Essays URBANIZATION
The Larger Scale – Urbanization, Agriculture, Land Reclamation
1 Egyptian unit of area equivalent to 1.038 acres (0.42 ha). The measure of land is the feddan, equal to 1.03 acres, subdivided into 24 kirats.
2 Radwan, Blackburn, Whayatt, & Atkinson, 2019
3 Brand, 2017
4 Sims, 2012
5 Askoura, 2005
6 ibid
7 Salem, 2016
8 Noeman, 2000; cited by Warner, 2013
9 Warner, 2013
10 Fecteau, 2012
11 ibid
12 Egypt Today Staff, 2019
13 Shawkat and Hendawy, 2012
14 Tadamun, 2015
15 Sims, 2012
16 ibid
17 Shawkat and Khalil, 2016

03 REVISITED AND PROJECTED
Ancient Gardens
1 see Loeben, C.E. (2016)
2 see ibid

Islamic Gardens
1 Jodidio, P. (ed.) (2018). Agha Khan Garden. Aga Khan Trust for Culture, Geneva, Switzerland

Desert Gardens
1 see Gerot, 2016 also for the elaboration on terrain vague which we may anticipate as a future design condition when we take the vast realm of desert development into account
2 Most prominently by the botanist Irina Sprenguel elaborates desert gardening based on her research of desert plants specifically in the Egyptian context, as well as the creation of an educational desert garden in Aswan documented in her book The Desert Garden – A Practical Guide.

Essays FOOD
Planning for Egypt's Food System and Heritage
1 this paragraph is a shortened version of a text published by Hala N. Barakat in 2017 (Barakat, 2017)
2 such as Panicum and Cenchrus that were ground into flour and couscous
3 (Wasylikowa and Dahlberg, 1999 p. 29, Barakat and Fahmy, 1999 p. 40)
4 5300 BC – 3000 BC
5 (Vartavan and Asensi Amoros, 1997)
6 Melon, fig, sycomore fig, grape, christ thorn
7 3200 BC – 332 BC
8 lettuce, green onions, cucumber, celery, purslane, coriander, cichorium, fenugreek leaves, green broad beans
9 cowpea, purslane, carthamus, vetch, cichorium, spinach, mallow and jews mallow
10 (Barakat, 2017)
11 desheish (similar to bulgur), freek (green roasted crushed wheat), keshk (dry crushed wheat with sour milk balls)
12 332 BC – 30 BC Ptolemaic Period; 30 BC – 395 AD Roman Period; Byzantian rule 395 AD – 641 AD
13 Arab Conquest 641 AD and Arab Empire in the Mediterranean till 15th century
14 1st wave: tomato, chili pepper, pumpkin, zucchini, sunflower, sweet potato, maize, peanut, potato, guava, prickly pear; 2nd wave: cocoa, papaya, avocado, passion fruit, pecan, oregano, strawberry hybrid, quinoa, cashew, pineapple, vanilla, jojoba
15 such as cinnamon, cloves, cardamom, nutmeg, balanos and peppercorns which became a major expensive commodity as chili pepper did not exist in the old world yet.
16 originally from New Guinea, sugar cane was introduced to China and India, then brought to Persia where medieval Arabs spread the knowledge of cultivation and processing to wherever they went.
17 Nazeera and Baheya, 1942
18 Noaman and El Quosy, 2017
19 El Quosy and Khalifa, 2017 p. 34
20 El Quosy and Khalifa, 2017 p. 44

Endnotes

21 The reform overturned a feudal social system in which large land owners held the majority of all agricultural lands, renting small pieces to farmer families. Previously, large land estates were redistributed into small farms, guaranteeing permanent tenure to renters while requiring cooperative membership. (Hopkins et al., 1995)

22 to a considerable share of 12.3 % of the national expenditures in 1980 - compared to 0.2 % ten years earlier (Tschirgi, 1995 p. 33)

23 A food policy permitting lower wages and leaving dispensable income for the consumption of domestically produced goods through food subsidies proved to be supportive for industrialization efforts.

24 (Tschirgi, 1995 p. 33)

25 The global food crisis occurring from crop shortfalls of export countries in 2007 is implicated as a trigger for price hikes and subsequent protests in Egypt. (Hopkins et al., 1995)

26 across all income levels: obesity for children under five: 20.5 percent in 2006-2012; adult obesity: 46.3 % of women and 22.5 % for men in 2008; world median: 6.2 %; world average 23.4 % (FAO, 2015, p. 31)

27 Cereals dominate human diets in Egypt accounting for 62.3 % (including a share of 33 % for wheat) of daily calorie intake per capita, followed by sugar, milk, maize, soybean oil and olive oil while meat consumption with 3 % is very low compared to the world average of 8 %(FAO, 2015, p. 29f).

28 only 17 % of subsidies reached the poorest quintile of population while 24 % went to the richest quintile (Lorenzon, 2016 p. 123)

29 de Koning, 2006 p. 232

30 FAO, 2015 p. 30

31 Since seed breeder associations in the 1960s had called for the protection of their interests, PVP (plant varieties protection) laws – a form of intellectual property (IP) protection similar to patent rights (UPOV laws) were adopted in most industrialized countries (Braunschweig et al., 2014 p. 11). To benefit from international trade also less developed or developing countries adopted UPOV based laws either forced by bilateral trade agreements such as TRIPS (Agreement on Trade-Related Aspects of Intellectual Property Rights within the framework of the World Trade Organization, enforced in 1995) requiring UPOV based laws or because of unawareness towards the impacts of the laws. These countries traditionally are organized around smallholders, which can be negatively impacted by the laws. Smallholder farming builds on traditional knowledge and prospers through informal breeding, exchanging, saving or trading seeds amongst farmers, which UPOV laws prohibit. Farmers' livelihoods may be at stake in favour of a sectoral positive impact, hampering the right to food (Braunschweig et al., 2014 p. 6). Agricultural production being highly dependent on a limited set of improved varieties that are tied to tailor-made fertilizer regimes that must be purchased from monopolized global markets are major downsides of formal seed markets.

32 Near East and North Africa (NENA) including Algeria, Bahrain, Egypt, Iran, Iraq, Jordan, Kuwait, Lebanon, Libya, Morocco, Oman, Qatar, Saudi Arabia, Sudan, Syria, Tunisia, United Arab Emirates, Yemen, and Palestine

33 Hadjichristodoulou, 2000

34 Article 189, 192, 193, 194 of law 82 Pertaining to the Protection of Intellectual Property Rights

35 such as the TRIPS and other European-Egyptian partnerships

36 Pothukuchi, K., and J. Kaufman,1999; Morton 2009

37 http://www.milanurbanfoodpolicypact.org/

38 Friis, 2018

39 Rapid Planning Consortium, 2015, p.6

04 PRODUCTIVE PLANTS

1 Täckholm and Drar, 1956; Hadidi and Boulos, 1988; Springuel, 2006; ElMasry, 2014

2 such as nature sciences, medicine as well as agricultural sciences, arts and engineering

3 de Groot, Wilson, and Boumans 2002

4 de Groot, Wilson, and Boumans 2002; Alcamo, Bennett, and Millennium Ecosystem Assessment (Program) 2003

Doum Palm

1 ElMasry, 2014 p. 39
2 Aboshora et al, 2014 p. 180 – 181
3 Stauffer et al., 2014 p. 336
4 Seleem, 2015
5 Aamer, 2016
6 Springuel, 2006 p. 26

Date Palm

1 ElMasry, 2014 p. 46
2 average yield in Egypt 75 up to 90 – 102 kg/palm/year while the world average is about 50 kg/palm/year (FAO/RNE, 2008, p. 26)
3 Irrigation amounts vary depending on palm type, soil type, availability

of ground water and plant maturity. Annual gross water use in Egypt: 86 – 124 cubic meters/palm; 10,280 – 14,880 (cubic meters/ha)(FAO/RNE, 2008 p. 5) Optimal fruit production of a mature palm in Aswan could be achieved with irrigation 12 times per year; average annual water use for date cultivation in different regions (cubic meters/fed): Lower Egypt: 4,547; Middle Egypt 5,391; Upper Egypt: 6,253 (FAO/RNE, 2008 p. 27)

4 artificial pollination was introduced from Mesopotamia during the 18th century BC and established as agricultural practice from the New Kingdom onwards (Hadidi and Boulos, 1988 p. 84)

5 Dates have antibacterial, anti-inflammatory and antioxidant activity and antifungal properties.

6 fresh dates: 213 kcal/100 g; carbohydrates: 32.99-38.20 %; fats: 0.14 g/100 g, proteins: 1.50 g/100 g; dried dates: 314 kcal/100 g, carbohydrates: 77.97- 79.39 %; fats: 0.38 g/100 g, proteins: 2.14 g/100 g (Al-Orf et al., 2012:100-101)

7 Egypt 2016: cultivation of 11.5 million palm trees, annual production of 1.16 million tonnes dates (faostat, 2018)

8 date ripening stages: Kimri=immature green, Khalal: mature full coloured, Rutab/Tamr: soft brown, raisin like

9 dry date cultivars commonly grown in the hottest regions of Aswan and Quena Govenorates: El-Barakawi, El-Abrimi, El-Sakouti (Riad, 1993 p. 49)

10 half-dry date cultivars commonly grown in the New Valley: Sewi/Saidi, Amri, El-Aglani (Riad, 1993 p. 49)

11 high-moisture date cultivars commonly grown on the Mediterranean and in the delta: Zagloul, Samani, Hayani (Riad, 1993 p. 49)

12 Ripe-dry dates attain maximum sugar contents through extreme heat and few water during ripening.

13 95 % of ownerships are of less than 5 feddan (Riad, 1993, p. 51)

14 date palms support 1million families in Egypt by generating additional income (FAO/RNE, 2008 p. 27)

15 mono-cultures use a regular grid of 8/10 – 10m distances, plant densities range from 100 to 200 plants/ha, the average is 120 plants/ha (FAO/RNE, 2008 p. 6)

16 approx. 6 million date palms are not planted in groves but cultivated along with other crops on the farms (FAO/RNE, 2008:26)

17 about 90 % in Egypt are irrigated with surface methods, modern irrigation systems with less water loss are not widely used for date palm cultivation as farmers fear drawbacks on their long-term crop if switching the irrigation techniques. (FAO/RNE, 2008 p. 11).

Egyptian Sycamore

1 ElMasry, 2014 p. 125
2 Galil and Eisikowitch, 1968 p. 745
3 In the excavated tomb of Ineni, an official in the reign of Thutmose I (1504 – 1442), depictions of his garden included a list of species grown: 73 sycomores, 31 persea, 170 date palm, 120 doum palm, 5fig, 2 moringa, 5 pomegranate, 16 carob, 5 garland thorn, 1 argoun palm, 8 willow, 10 tamarisk, 2 myrtle, 5 acacia, 12 vines and further 5 unidentified species. (Bigelow, 2000)
4 Lutz et al., 2016 p. 47
5 Springuel, 2006 p. 34
6 Abd-el-hak et al., 2016 p. 647
7 against ringworm (bark and sap), scorpion or snake bites (sap), cough, chest diseases or dysenteries (bark), inflammations and tuberculosis (Abd-el-Hak et al., 2016 p. 647)
8 Galil, 1967 p. 188

Pomegranate

1 ElMasry, 2014 p. 264
2 Holland et al, 2009 p. 153
3 harvest depends on cultivar (Holland et al, 2009 p. 155), e. g. cultivar Wonderful with up to 30t/ha (Melgarejo and Valero These, 2012 p. 12)
4 harvest per mature tree if well-kept ("Pomegranate Growing," 2018)
5 around 1500 BC (Diab, 2018)
6 as depictions and offerings in ancient tombs and writings state (Diab, 2018 p. 83)
7 in 2011 Egypt produced around 6500 tons of fruit (Ismail et al., 2014 p. 227)
8 as recycled water is very often slightly saline (Holland et al., 2009 p. 152)
9 average nutritional value 83 Kcal/100g
10 grains in tubs, dehydrated seeds, jams, jellies, liquors and other drinks, pomegranate extracts for cosmetics, food supplements (Melgarejo and Valero These, 2012 p. 24)
11 to treat high blood pressure, cholesterol, oxidative stress, hyperglycemia, and inflammatory activities (Zarfeshany et al, 2014)

Olive

1 (ElMasry, 2014, p. 149)
2 Fruit yields vary from 2 – 20t/ha/y. Average yields of 9 – 10 t/ha/y are common for conventional production (MedAgri, 2018a); and 7.38 kg/ha/y

for organic orchards (International Olive Council, 2012). Olive oil yields range from 10 – 55 gallons (=37.8 – 207.9 liter) from 1 t of olives.
3 Springuel, 2006 p. 98f
4 Gilbert and Zalat, 2016
5 such as controlling blood cholesterol level, reducing cardiovascular diseases and cancers
6 Market Research Future MRFR, 2017
7 Sixteen-fold increase of annual olive production in the past 25 years in Egypt: 1990: 41,962 t; 2000: 281,745 t; 2010: 390,932 t; 2016: 694,309 t (faostat, 2018)
8 Important local varieties are: Aggezi Shami (table olive well adapted to environment, 20 % of olive area); Hamed and Toffahi (green pickling, large fruit, low oil content, 6 % of olive area); Wateken (high fruit weight, mainly used for oil production, 5 % of olive area); Maraki (heavy fruit, oil production, 2 % of olive area), Aggizi Akse (very heavy fruit for green pickling) (International Olive Council, 2012 p. 6)
9 olive production 2013 on new land: 487,053 t compared to 76,017 t on old land (Hussein Mohamed, 2017 p. 4)
10 Egypt 2012/13 produced 300 000 t table olives of which 80,000 t were exported. The olive oil production 2012/13 amounted to 6,500 t, which is still marginal compared to 220,000 t of olive oil produced, for example, in Tunisia 2012/13. (MedAgri, 2018b)
11 Plants in rain-fed orchards compete for water catchment area and thus require low planting densities of 70-100 trees/ha while irrigated orchards allow 333 – 400 trees/ha or even 800 trees/ha entailing small tree sizes. Spacing of 8.5 m x 8.5 m (138 trees/ha) or 5m x 8 m (250 trees/ha) allow mechanical harvesting and pruning while row distances below 6 m restrain mechanical methods. (Emam et al., 2016)
12 MARSADEV Matrouh Rural Sustainable Development Project, implemented by CIHEAM Bari, Ministry of Agriculture, Desert Research Center (DRC) of Marsa Matrouh, Egypt, Feb. 2014 – Feb. 2017

Banana
1 Australian Government, 2016
2 Productivity depends on environmental conditions, variety and production type, average yields: commercial industries approx. 60 t/ha, small producers approx. 30 t/ha (FAO, 2018)
3 between the 5th and 11th century AD (Barakat, 2017)
4 Egypt was the 16th largest producer of bananas worldwide with 1.341.478 t (=48.5 t/ha/y) in 2016. (1st: India with 29,124,000 t in 2016). Area and production increased manifold from 1991 (14.147 ha / 392.887 t) to 2016 (27.632 ha / 1.341.478 t) (FAO, Faostat Crops Egypt, Banana, http://www.fao.org/faostat/en/#data/QC, [accessed 09.27.2018])
5 Dwarf Cavendish Hindi, Mohammed Ali, Baradika, Sindh, Williams and Grandnain(e) are most frequent cultivars in Egypt (De Langhe, 2002).
6 of approx. 80 kcal per 100 g as they are rich in carbohydrates and natural sugar
7 Australian Government, 2016
8 De Langhe, 2002
9 ibid
10 single row system: suckers within the row are narrow, while the space between the rows is wide to allow aeration; paired row patterns: spacing of 0.90-1.20 m, distances between pair of rows is 1.2-2.0 m allowing good management and decreasing costs for drip irrigation; square systems: plants in equal distances of 1.8 m spacing, allow short lived intercrop; triangular systems: like square systems but one row shifted halfway.

Sweet Orange
1 ElMasry, 2014, p. 99
2 average fruit yield in Egypt 24.31 t/ha/y (Abobatta, 2018a)
3 Citrus medica arrived first via Persia and Mesopotamia and was presumably cultivated since the Second and Third Century AD while further citrus species (lime, lemon, sour and sweet orange) arrived later in the 11th century AD (Bouchaud et al., 2017 p. 44)
4 (faostat, 2018) world orange production in 2016: Brazil 17,251,291 t (1st); China 8,550,865 t (2nd); Egypt 3,438,030 t (7th)
5 Orange production in Egypt: 46 % consumed fresh, 3 % processed; 51 % exported to Russia, Saudi Arabia, Netherlands, China (Abobatta, 2018 p. 9); varieties for local fresh consumption: Sweet Orange Sukkari or local juice production: Baladi Orange, Blood orange, Khalily orange (Hamza and Tate, 2017)
6 Abobatta, 2018a
7 F Ahmed, 2012
8 Oranges account for 30 % of total Egyptian fruit production and 65 % of citrus production. (W. Abobatta, 2018 p. 8)
9 (W. Abobatta, 2018 p. 40) Many orchards consist of old trees reaching up to 50 years while productivity is best at the age of 4-15 years.
10 Flood irrigation prevails in the delta fostering weed and not allowing a fine-tuned water and nutrition regime. Old land suffers from deficient

management and harvesting techniques while newly reclaimed land suffers from increased salinity. (Abobatta, 2018b)
11 Sims, 2014
12 Ssebunya and Kilcher, 2011
13 Planting patterns of monoculture orchards vary from 4 m x 6 m (ca. 400 trees/ha) or 3 x 5 – 6 m to very dense plantings of 2 m x 3 m (1,650 trees/ha). Spacing relates to harvesting and irrigation methods, pruning frequency and productivity of an orchard. (United Nations Conference on Trade & Development, 2003)
14 Intercropping positively effects the ecosystem (see: permaculture) and requires a wider spacing of 7.5 m – 8 m x 7.5 m – 8 m.

Grape
1 Gilbert and Zalat, 2016 p. 75
2 walls, scaffolding, cordon or wire, trellis, gazebos
3 light green in spring and summer; yellow, red, green, orange or bronze in fall
4 In Egypt 170,000 feddan were cultivated with vines in 2007 with an average yield of 9.9 t/feddan which equals 23.6t/ha (Ministry of Agriculture and Land Reclamation, 2009 p. 80, 142). Yields vary from 3 – 20 kg/plant depending on cultivar, yard density and local conditions. For example, in France table grape yields range between 6 – 12 t/ha and wine grape yields range between 5 – 15 t/ha (FAO-OIV, 2016 p. 27).
5 probably between the 7 – 4th century BC (Terral et al, 2010 p. 444)
6 around 2700BC (E. McGovern, 1997 p. 5)
7 to treat skin diseases and diarrhoea
8 which were found to have cardio- and neuroprotective, antimicrobial and antiaging properties (FAO-OIV, 2016 p. 20)
9 65 kcal/100 g (Ibid)
10 (FAO-OIV, 2016 p. 34) Global table grape production and consumption almost doubled since 2000 (FAO-OIV, 2016 p. 32)
11 (Tellioglu and Konandreas, 2017 p. 29)
12 Common table grape varieties in Egypt are: white seedless: Early Superior, Thompson; Rish Baba white seeded: Muscat of Alexandria; coloured seedless: Flame, Beauty, Ruby; Monukka; coloured seeded: Red Globe, Cardinal, Emperor, Ribier (FAO-OIV, 2016), Shafik D. et al., 2016)
13 Common wine making varieties in Egypt are: French Colombard, Muscat Blanc, Cabernet Sauvignon, Palomino, Ruby Cabernet. Older vineyards are planted mainly with the local varieties Red Roomy and Thompson Seedless (Mohamed and El-Sese, 2009 p. 194).
14 such as arbours or wire trellis (T-shaped, y-shaped or overhead arbour) or trained as bush (FAO-OIV, 2016 p. 26)
15 varying from approx. 1100 – 1900 up to 3000 plants per hectare (high density cultivation) (Kok, 2014 p. 1239)
16 Commercial vineyards mostly are laid out in rows of 3m-4m spacing and plants are placed in 1,5m-3m distances allowing farm vehicles and farmers to pass for pruning (mechanical or manual), harvesting and management. (Kok, 2014 p. 1239)
17 reaching ages of 50 or even 100 years

Prickly Pear
1 ElMasry, 2014 p. 378
2 fruit yields vary from 1-5 t to 15-20 t/ha/yield, yields with traditional orchard planting methods:1-5 tons/ha; intensive orchard practices:15 – 30 tons/ha (FAO and ICARDIA, 2017 p. 63).
3 3.44 g/sqm/day CO_2 uptake under optimal conditions (Ibid p. 33).
4 by the Spanish conquistadors 1552, discovery of the "indies"
5 anti-inflammatory, antiviral, anticancer, anti ulcerogenic and cholesterol reducing (Ibid p. 155), high antioxidant activities help to prevent cancer, diabetes, hyperglycemia, arteriosclerosis and gastric diseases (M. Abou Elella, 2014)
6 A health promoting food in Mexico where also the leaves are a typical vegetable (nopalito) in the human diet.
7 fruits contain 85 % water, cladodes 91% (FAO, ICARDIA, 2017 p. 152)
8 WUE (Water Use Efficiency) describes the ratio of water processed by the plant to water lost by transpiration.
9 Precipitations of 400-600 mm per year are required for cactus pear production, thus rainfall below 300mm/y requires irrigation for fruit production. (Ibid p. 60)
10 Other countries like Mexico, Italy, Chile, South Africa, Argentina and Israel cultivate cactus fruits commercially on a large scale but produce only small amounts for export markets (Ibid p. 197).
11 (Yousry, 2013)
12 like plants medicinal and cosmetic properties
13 (FAO, 2013)
14 (Ibid p. 56) The layout is determined by farm size and system, cultivar, harvesting method, management, soil and climate, irrigation as well as training systems. Trees in rows need distances of 4-6 m (for farm machinery to pass); planted densely as hedges, distances range from 1.5-2 m or even 4 m.

Moringa
1   (ElMasry, 2014 p. 145)
2   plants that morphological are adapted to extreme arid conditions
3   composed of 59 % kernel and 41 % husk (Salaheldeen et al, 2014 p. 49)
4   high yields of leaves, e.g. on a plantation in Nicaragua without irrigation and fertilizer green matter harvested every 75 days: 100 t/ha (1st year); 57 t/ha (2nd year); with irrigation and fertilizer harvested every 35days: 650 – 700t/ha (Trees For Life International, 2005a p. 32)
5   up to 1000 pods per tree/year yielded, containing each 8 – 15 seeds with kernel containing 38 % oil (Senthilkumar et al., 2018 p. 2)
6   Moringaceae family includes 13 species
7   during the new kingdom (Springuel, 2006 p. 96)
8   since the middle kingdom (Kondo, 1991 p. 45)
9   (Kondo, 1991 p. 46)
10 (Lucas and Harris, 2012 p. 331)
11 (Zahran and Willis, 1992 p. 173)
12 (Ezzo et al, 2017)
13 7 times the vitamin C of oranges, 4 times the calcium of milk, 3 times the potassium of bananas, 2 times the protein of yogurt (Trees For Life International, 2005b)
14 In sub-Saharan Africa and Asia Moringa balances diets and fights malnutrition (ibid).
15 including anti-inflammatory, antimicrobial (Senthilkumar et al., 2018 p. 8), anticancer, antioxidant, antibacterial, compounds and antiproliferation activities (Abd El Baky and El-Baroty, 2013 p. 98)
16 inflammation, cardiovascular, liver and memory diseases
17 Jatropa curcas is a conventional plant for biodiesel production but not simultaneously a livestock fodder (Salaheldeen et al., 2014 p. 50)
18 10 – 15 cm spacings were experimented with at research plantations in Nicaragua (Trees For Life International, 2005b p. 31)

Papyrus
1   ElMasry, 2014 p. 410
2   Serag, 2003 p. 19
3   Papyrus is considered as invasive in habitats outside its native range.
4   fresh biomass production above ground in managed and natural stands equals max. 30 kg/sqm in June – 10.1 kg/sqm in January; dry mass above-ground in the Nile in natural stands: 5 – 8 kg DM/sqm, managed stands: 2.8 – 4.4 kg DM/sqm (Serag, 2003 p. 20-22)
5   since 3000 BC (Pacini et al., 2018 p. 143)
6   basketry, sandals, ropes, blankets, tables, chairs, mattresses, medicine, perfume, food, and clothes, cartonnage e. g. mummy masks
7   Aswan Low Dam (1903) and Aswan High Dam (1970)
8   (Serag, 2000 p. 195)
9   bacteria and viruses active when exposed to oxygen (Kipasika et al., 2016 p. 654)
10 as horizontal or vertical flow systems, (see Chapter 03 Learning from – Constructed Wetlands)
11 for example Arundo donax, Bambusa vulgaris (see Chapter 04 – Productive plants), Cyperus alternifolius, Phragmites australis, Typha latifolia, Canna
12 (Abou-Elela and S. Hellal, 2012 p. 209)
13 as it often is the case in informal or rural areas of Egypt
14 source of raw material, fuel and fodder provisioning the family or the community

Bamboo
1   "The average bamboo biomass ranges from 6.5 tons per hectare in Pakistan to 167 tonnes per hectare in China." (Lobovikov et al., 2007 p. 26)
2   Bamboo charcoal has the calorific value of half that of oil of the same weight (Lobovikov et al., 2007 p. 31).
3   value calculated for plantations in Costa Rica (Janssen, 2000 p. 38)
4   in tropical, subtropical and mild temperate zones (Lobovikov et al., 2007)
5   to treat cough or colds
6   bamboo can be harvested after 3 – 5 years while woody trees (depending on species) need 20 – 60 years till they can be harvested
7   "bamboo thrives on poor soils, requires little or no inputs and is prone to few diseases." (International Network for Bamboo and Rattan (INBAR), 2015)
8   Janssen, 2000
9   similar to steel (Janssen, 2000)
10 as columns, beams or bamboo composites like laminated lumber, ply bamboo, bamboo MDF (Coen, 2015)
11 reducing inflammation, promoting circulation, and inhibiting allergic reactions (Shukla et al., 2012 p. 10)
12 similar to alfalfa (Tewari et al., 2015 p. 268)
13 when decomposing (Tewari et al., 2015 p. 278)
14 EU Cordis, 2013

15 Were et al., 2017
16 recommended spacing in agroforestry: 9 m x 9 m for large sized species or 4 m x 4 m for small sized species (Tewari et al., 2015 p. 266); trenches with barriers hindering underground root spreading: 30 – 40 cm width and 50 – 60 cm depth

Reed
1   Springuel, 2006 p. 135
2   A total above-ground biomass of 2.2 – 13.7 kg DM/sqm/y of A. donax populations were measured in the Nile Delta in Egypt (Eid et al., 2016 p. 6). Biomass values vary greatly from 15 t – 30 t – 40t DM/ha/y depending on growth conditions such as e.g. climate and soils (Nsanganwimana et al., 2014 p. 25).
3   Heating value of A. donax in constructed wetlands: 19.6 MJ/kg; 496 – 637 GJ/ha (Nsanganwimana et al., 2014 p. 67,72)
4   Often confused at a first glance, both reeds are easily distinguished by their height. P. australis reaches up to 3 m and is more widely spread in Egypt while A.donax reaches up to 8 - 9 m and has a longer tradition of cultivation.
5   (Springuel, 2006) From the Mediterranean region it spread in Asia, North Africa, southern Europe, the Middle East and elsewhere.
6   A. donax is one of the fastest growing plants worldwide with a rapid growth rate of up to 10 cm per day. (Eid et al., 2016)
7   smoking pipes, fishing rods, baskets and mats
8   A. donax tolerates rainfall ranging from 300 mm – 4000 mm per year. (Nsanganwimana et al., 2014 p. 8)
9   Eid et al., 2016 p. 7
10 Stands of A. donax can consume up to 2000 liters of water/sqm of plants (Csurhes, 2016 p. 12).
11 Biofuel, bioethanol are valuable alternatives to fossil fuels (Palmer et al., 2014), while products such as timber, biochemicals and animal fodder (the palatability of A. donax is limited to some animals only) serve local processing industries and livelihoods. (Nsanganwimana et al., 2014 p. 5)
12 (Galal and Shehata, 2016)
13 Various water cleansing plants (e. g. papyrus, reeds, bamboo – amongst others) are applicable.
14 Water, media, microbes and vegetation are the main components in CW systems directly affecting the results of the treatment process.

Tamarisk
1   ElMasry, 2014 p. 176
2   Mekki and El-Meleigy, 2012
3   Springuel, 2006 p. 104f
4   Ama Abdelgawad, 2017
5   Soliman Yu and Ibrahin Al, 2011
6   El-Beheiry and El-Kady, 1998
7   Bigelow, 2000

Argoun Palm
1   Springuel, 2006 p. 113
2   Ibrahim and Baker, 2009 p. 10
3   Springuel, 2006 p. 113
4   Springuel, 2006 p. 32

Weeping Fig
1   ElMasry, 2014 p. 117
2   for treating influenza, dysentery, malaria and respiratory diseases, leave extracts, sap, bark and roots are known for antitumor, antibacterial, antiviral and analgesic activities (Abdelkader and Aldughaish, 2016 p.63)
3   Kunwar and Bussmann, 2006
4   Hadidi and Boulos, 1988 p. 68
5   Vargas-Garzón and Molina-Prieto, 2012

Acacia ehrenbergiana
1   Springuel, 2006, p. 69
2   Acacia seeds are impermeable to water which delays germination (physical dormancy) (Ben Zetta, 2017 p. 356)
3   David, 2014 p. 247
4   Lucas and Harris, 2012 p. 335
5   Ben Zetta, 2017 p. 356
6   Springuel, 2006 p. 3
7   Khalil et al., 2016 p. 68

Acacia nilotica
1   Springuel, 2006 p. 75
2   ibid
3   Orwa et al., 2009 p. 3
4   Orwa et al., 2009 p. 3
5   against for example hemorrhages, cold, tuberculosis and leprosy (Malviya et al, 2011 p. 833)

6 Bargali and Bargali, 2009
7 Kumar, 2015
8 Bargali and Bargali, 2009 p. 12
9 Indian Council of Forestry Research and Education, Dehradun. Forest Research Institute, n.d.

Acacia tortilis subsp. raddiana
1 Springuel, 2006, p. 81
2 Kandal et al, 2016 p. 498-500
3 Hobbs et al, 2014
4 Abdallah et al, 2008
5 Springuel, 2006 p. 64

INTRODUCING THE NARRATIVE

Quotes below images

Ahmed, O. A. (2020). Guiding Egypt Hiking Community through Siwa House. 2 January

Arab Republic of Egypt Ministry of Environment (2016). Egyptian Biodiversity Strategy and Action Plan (2015 – 2030)

Kafafy, N.A. (2010). The dynamics of urban green space in an arid city; the case of Cairo- Egypt, Cardiff University

Egypt Independent (12 Feb, 2013). Preserving one of Egypt's most efficient ecosystems. Egypt Independent [online]. Available at: https://egyptinde-pendent.com/preserving-one-egypt-s-most-efficient-ecosystems-mangrove/ [accessed 22 July, 2019]

Van Eyck, J. (2017). The Insatiable Human Desire to Imagine, Explore, and Create. extract of abstract Landscaping Egypt – From the Aesthetic to the Productive, int. conference May 5-6, 2017

Ezz, M. Arafat, N. (2015). Guardian Africa network Egypt 'We woke up in a desert' – the water crisis taking hold across Egypt. Available at: www.theguard-ian.com/world/2015/aug/04/egypt-water-crisis-intensifies-scarcity [accessed 18 August, 2017]

Hill, J. (2010). Hapi. Available at: https://ancientegyptonline.co.uk/hapi/ [accessed 22 July, 2019]

Isaksson, C. (2019). Impact of Urbanization on Birds In: Bird Species – How They Arise, Modify and Vanish pp 235-257. Available at: https://link.springer.com/chapter/10.1007/978-3-319-91689-7_13 [accessed 30 July, 2019]

Rashed, A. (2017). Innovative Approach and Technology in the Lake Manzala Engineered Wetlands Project (A Success Story). abstract Landscaping Egypt – From the Aesthetic to the Productive, May 5-6, 2017

Shakir. Qur'an 9.72. Quranic Arabic Corpus. Available at: http://corpus.quran.com/translation.jsp?chapter=9&verse=72 [accessed 30 July, 2019]

Editorial

Hadidi, N., Boulos, L. Makar, S. Gohary, M. (1968). Street Trees of Egypt. Cairo University Herbarium

Sprenguel, I. (2004). Desert Garden – A Practical Guide. The American University in Cairo Press

El Masry, L. (2014). A Plant Guidebook for Al Azhar Park and The City Of Cairo. El-Shorouk International Bookshop, Cairo

El Masry, L. (2014). Landscape Architecture and the Planting Design of Al Azhar Park. El-Shorouk International Bookshop, Cairo

01 LANDSCAPE CONDITIONS

Evolving Landscapes

Advisory and Technical Advisory Council in the Interest of Urban Planning (1971). The Desert House. Arab Urban Architecture in the Middle East, Beirut Arab University

Arab Republic of Egypt Ministry of Environment (2016). Egyptian Biodiversity Strategy and Action Plan (2015 – 2030).

UNDP Climate Change Adaptation (n.d.) Egypt, <https://www.adaptation-un-dp.org/explore/northern-africa/egypt> [accessed 22 July, 2019]

Dabaieh, Marwa (2015). More than Vernacular: vernacular architecture be-tween past tradition and future vision. 1 ed. Lund: Media-Tryck

Fathy, Hassan (1986). Natural Energy and Vernacular Architecture: Principles and Examples. University of Chicago Press (The Arab Foundation for Studies and Publishing, 1st ed. 1988)

GOPP and UNDP (General Organization for Physical Planning, Ministry of Housing and Urban Development and United Nations Development Pro-gramme) (2009). Participatory Urban Planning for Alexandria City till 2032.

Hadidi. A (2016). Wadi Bili Catchment in the Eastern Desert -Flash Floods, Geological Model and Hydrogeology. TU Berlin

Isaksson, Caroline (2018). Impact of Urbanization on Birds, in: Bird Spe-cies. Springer, pp 235-257. Available at: https://link.springer.com/chap-ter/10.1007/978-3-319-91689-7_13 [accessed 22 July, 2019]

Oswald, Ferdinand (2015). Reduce A/C: Reducing the Utilisation of Air Con-ditioning in High-Rise Buildings in Subtropical and Tropical Climate Regions, Institute of Architec-ture Technology, Technical University Graz

Whittaker-Wood, Fran (2018). The Most Polluted Cities in the World. Avail-able at: https://blog.theecoexperts.co.uk/most-polluted-cities 25July 2018 [Accessed 22 July, 2019]

Landscaping Practices – From Symbiosis to Commodification

Aboulroos, S., Satoh, M. (2017). Irrigated Agriculture in Egypt: Past, Present and Future. Springer Nature, Cham, Switzerland

Ahmed, T. (2014). New spatial cultures: a landscape story from Egypt, in: Roe, M. Taylor, K. (eds.). New Cultural Landscape. Taylor and Francis Group

Angélil, M., Maltesse-Barthes, C. (eds.) (2018). Cairo Desert Cities. Ruby Press, Berlin

Baer G. (1969). Waqf Reform. In: Studies in the Social History of Modern Egypt. Chicago: University of Chicago Press

Behrens Abou-Seif, D. (1985). Azbakiyya and its Environs from Azbak to Ismail 1476 – 1879. Institute Francaise d' Archeologie Orientale

Bowman, A.K. (1996). Egypt after the Pharaohs, 332 BC-AD 642: From Alexan-der to the Arab Conquest, Revised edition, 2nd ed. University of California Press

Bowman, A.K. Rogan, E. (1999). Agriculture in Egypt from Pharaonic to Mod-ern Times, Proceedings of the British Academy. British Academy

Cuno, C. M. (1980). The Origins of Private Ownership of Land in Egypt: A Reappraisal. Int. J. Middle East Studies 12 (1980) pp. 245 – 275. Cambridge University Press

Daines, A. (2008). Egyptian Gardens. Studia Antiqua 6 no.1, pp. 15–25

Deister, L. (2013). Designing Landscape as Infrastructure Water Sensitive Open Space Design in Cairo. Ain Shams University, Stuttgart University, Cairo, Stuttgart

Denis, E. (2018). Cairo's New Towns: From One Revolution to Another, in: Cairo Desert Cities. Ruby Press, Berlin

Echols, S. Nassar, H. (2007). Canals and Lakes of Cairo: Influence of Traditional Water Systems on the Development of Urban Form. Retrieved from Urban Design International

Fahmy, K. Dobrowolska, A. (2004). Muhammad 'Ali Pasha and His Sabil. Amer-ican University in Cairo Press

Fairchild Ruggles, D. (2008). Islamic Gardens and Landscapes. University of Pennsylvania Press, Philadelphia, Pennsylvania

Frantz-Murphy, G. (1999). Land Tenure in Egypt in the First Five Centuries of Islamic Rule (Seventh – Twelfth Centuries AD). Proceedings of the British Academy, 96, 237 – 266 Available at: https://www.thebritishacademy.ac.uk/sites/default/files/96p237.pdf [accessed 07 Jan 2020]

Hamdy, R., Abd El-Ghani, M., Youssef, T., El-Sayed, M. (2007). The Floristic Composition of Some Historical Botanical Gardens in the Metropolitan of Cairo, Egypt. AJAR 2. pp. 610 – 648

Loeben, C.E. Die Ältesten Gärten der Welt. In: Lutz, A., von Trotha, H. (eds.) (2016). Gärten der Welt. Wienand Verlag, Köln

Makhzoumi, J. (2018). Borrowed or Rooted? The Discourse of 'Landscape' in the Arab Middle East, in: Landscape Culture – Culturing Landscapes: The Differentiated Construction of Landscapes. Springer SV, pp. 111–126

Makhzoumi, J., Moosavi, S., Grose, M. (2015). Landscape Practice in the Mid-dle East between Local and Global Aspirations. Landscape Research: 41, 16. https://doi.org/10.1080/01426397.2015.1078888

Petruccioli, A. (1998). Rethinking the Islamic Garden, in: Transformation of Middle Eastern Natural Environments: Legacies and Lessons, Bulletin Series 103, 349–365. Yale University Press, New Haven

Rabbat, N. (2018). A Brief History of Green Spaces in Cairo. In: Jodidio, P. (ed.). Cairo: Renewing the Historic City, The Aga Khan Historic Cities Programme Prestel, Munich pp. 77 – 89

Ratte, F. (2015). Understanding the City through Travellers' Tales: Cairo as seen and experienced by two Fourteenth Century Italians, in: The City in the Muslim World: Depictions by Western Travel Writers, Culture and Civilization in the Middle East. Routledge, New York, pp. 56 – 79

Sadik, H. (2019). From Bath to A Pool – A Research of Bathing Cultures up until the Contemporary Trend of Natural Swimming Pools. Master thesis GUC Architecture and Urban Design Program

Sampsell, Bonnie M. (2014). The Geology of Egypt. 2nd ed. American University in Cairo Press, Cairo

Sims, D. (2018). Egypt's Desert Dreams: Development or Disaster? 2nd ed. American University in Cairo Press, Cairo

Thackston, W M ed. (1986). Naser-e Khosraw's book of travels = (Safarnama). Bibliotheca Persica, Albany, N.Y.

Wilkinson, A. (1994). Symbolism and Design in Ancient Egyptian Gardens. Garden History 22, pp. 1–17. Available at: https://doi.org/10.2307/1586999

https://urbanage.lsecities.net/data/residential-density-cairo data published December 2018 [accessed 19 December, 2019]

Timeline

Abdel-Kader, Nasamat, and Sayed Ettouney. 2009. "The Egyptian New Communities, Between Objectives and Realization – A Critical Discourse, Three Decades Later." ARCHCAIRO 2009 5th International Conference.

Abdel-Rahman, Nourhan H. 2016. "Egyptian Historical Parks, Authenticity vs. Change in Cairo's Cultural Landscapes." Procedia - Social and Behavioral Sciences 225 (July): 391–409. https://doi.org/10.1016/j.sbspro.2016.06.086.

Amer, Abd El Hafez, Abd El Ghany (eds.) (2017). Water Saving In Irrigated Agriculture in Egypt, LAP Lampert Academic Publishing

Barakat, Hala N. 2017. "We Are What We Eat, We Were What We Ate." In The Food Question in the Middle East. Vol. 34. CAIRO PAPERS IN SOCIAL SCIENCE 4. Cairo: American University in Cairo Press.

CAPMAS (2014). Water Resources and Means to Rationalise their Use, report

Denis, Eric. 2006. "Cairo as Neoliberal Capital?" In Diane Singerman and Paul Amar. Cairo Cosmopolitan, 47–71. American University in Cairo Press.

Dobrowolska, Agnieszka, and Jarosław Dobrowolski. 2006. Heliopolis: Rebirth of the City of the Sun. Cairo: American Univ. in Cairo Press.

El Kateb, Hany, A El-Gindy, Bernd Stimm, and Manfred Mosandl. 2015. "German-Egyptian Collaboration to Afforestation in Desert Lands of Egypt: Information Summary and Description of the Field Experiments." SILVICULTURAL EXPERIMENTS 4.

El Quosy, D., and H. E. H. Khalifa. 2017. "Control of the Nile's Flow: The Introduction of Perennial Irrigation for Modern Agriculture." In Irrigated Agriculture in Egypt, edited by Masayoshi Satoh and Samir Aboulroos, 29–45. Cham: Springer International Publishing. https://doi.org/10.1007/978-3-319-30216-4_3.

ElMasry, Laila. 2014. Landscape Architecture and the Planning Design of Al-Azhar Park. Vol. Volume I. Cairo: Shorouk Intl. Bookshop.

F. Dorman, Peter, Alan Edouard, Samuel John R. Baines, Alan K. Bowman, and Edward F. Wente. 2019. "Ancient Egypt." In Encyclopædia Britannica. Encyclopædia Britannica, Inc. https://www.britannica.com/place/ancient-Egypt/Macedonian-and-Ptolemaic-Egypt-332-30-bce.

Herzog, Jaques, Pierre de Meuron, Manuel Herz, Shadi Rahbaran, and Ying Zhou. 2010. Nasr City. Zurich: ETH Studio Basel.

Kafafy, Nezar. 2010. The Dynamics of Urban Green Spaces in an Arid City: The Case of Cairo-Egypt. Cardiff: Cardiff University.

Khusraw, Nasir. 1993. "Safarnāmāh" رضان رسخ .ورسخ رفسن نامز .ةمجرت ةمصخ يدحي الخشاب، (الهنة المصرية الكتاب.) Translated by Yayá al-Khashshāb. 2nd Edition. Cairo: al-Hay'ah al-Mirīyah al-'Ama lil-Kitāb.

Lewis, Aidan. 2019. "Factbox: Key Facts about Ethiopia's Giant Nile Dam." Thomson Reuters, November. https://www.reuters.com/article/us-ethiopia-dam-factbox/factbox-key-facts-about-ethiopias-giant-nile-dam-idUSKBN1XG21L.

Lutz, Albert, Hans von Trotha, and Museum Rietberg, eds. 2016. Gärten Der Welt: Orte Der Sehnsucht Und Inspiration. Zürich : Köln: Museum Rietberg Zürich ; Wienand.

Maged, Mira. 2019. "UN Recent Report: Egypt's Population to Increase 60 Million by 2050." Egypt Independent, July 5, 2019. https://egyptindependent.com/un-recent-report-egypts-population-to-increase-60-million-by-2050/.

Mohamed, Hanan. 2018. "Egypt to Establish 15 New 4th Generation Cities: PM." Egypttoday, March 1, 2018. https://www.egypttoday.com/Article/3/44156/Egypt-to-establish-15-new-4th-generation-cities-PM.

New Urban Communities Authority. 2019. "New Urban Communities Authority." Www.Newcities.Gov.Eg. 2019. http://www.newcities.gov.eg.

New York Times. 1864. "Egyptian Cotton: Its Modern Origin and the Importance of the Supply." New York Times, June, 5.

Noaman, M. N., and D. El Quosy. 2017. "Hydrology of the Nile and Ancient Agriculture." In Irrigated Agriculture in Egypt, edited by Masayoshi Satoh and Samir Aboulroos, 9–28. Cham: Springer International Publishing. https://doi.org/10.1007/978-3-319-30216-4_2.

Noaman, M.N. 2017. "Chapter 1 Country Profile." In Irrigated Agriculture in Egypt Past, Present and Future Masayoshi Satoh, Samir Aboulroos (Eds.). Cham: Springer International Publishing.

Petry, Carl F., ed. 1998. Islamic Egypt 640-1517. 1st ed. Cambridge University Press. https://doi.org/10.1017/CHOL9780521471374.

Rabbat, N. 2004. "A Brief History of Green Spaces in Cairo, Cairo: Renewing the Historic City." In Revitalising a Historic Metropolis. (Stefano Bianca and Philip Jodidio, Eds.). Turin: Umberto Allemandi & C. for Aga Khan Trust for Culture.

Radwan, Taher, George Alan Blackburn, James Duncan Whyatt, and Peter Atkinson. 2019. "Dramatic Loss of Agricultural Land Due to Urban Expansion Threatens Food Security in the Nile Delta, Egypt." Remote Sensing 11 (3): 332. https://doi.org/10.3390/rs11030332.

Responsible and Inclusive Business Hub MENA Egypt. 2015. "Sustainable Startup Handbook Egypt En." https://issuu.com/ribhmena/docs/sustainable_startup_handbook_egypt_.

Ruggles, D. Fairchild. 2008. Islamic Gardens and Landscapes. Penn Studies in Landscape Architecture. Philadelphia: University of Pennsylvania Press.

S. Kimenyi, Mwangi, and John Mukum Mbaku. 2015. "The Limits of the New 'Nile Agreement.'" https://www.brookings.edu/blog/africa-in-focus/2015/04/28/the-limits-of-the-new-nile-agreement/.

Samir, Samar. 2018. "Egypt Holds on to Water Rights amid 'Critical Situation,'" June. https://www.egypttoday.com/Article/2/52549/Egypt-holds-on-to-water-rights-amid-%E2%80%98critical-situation%E2%80%99.

Sampsell, Bonnie M. 2003. A Traveler's Guide to the Geology of Egypt. Cairo, Egypt ; New York: American University in Cairo Press.

Sims, David. 2010. Understanding Cairo: The Logic of a City out of Control. 1st paperback ed. Cairo ; New York: The American University in Cairo Press.

Sims, David E. 2014. Egypt's Desert Dreams: Development or Disaster? Cairo: The American University in Cairo Press.

Sims, David E. 2018. Egypt's Desert Dreams: Development or Disaster? Cairo New York: The American University in Cairo Press.

Stanley, Jean-Daniel, and Pablo L. Clemente. 2017. "Increased Land Subsidence and Sea-Level Rise Are Submerging Egypt's Nile Delta Coastal Margin." GSA Today, May, 4–11. https://doi.org/10.1130/GSATG312A.1.

The World Bank Group, and FAO. 2019. "Agricultural Land (Sq. Km) - Egypt, Arab Rep." 2019. https://data.worldbank.org/indicator/AG.LND.AGRI.K2?locations=EG.

United Nations. 2018. "Water Scarcity." https://www.unwater.org/water-facts/scarcity/.

Volait, Mercedes. 2005. Architectes et Architectures de l'Egypte Moderne (1830-1950): Genèse et Essor d'une Expertise Locale. Collection Architectures Modernes En Méditerranée. Paris, France: Maisonneuve et Larose.

Wahba, Shimaa M., Kate Scott, and Julia K. Steinberger. 2018. "Analyzing Egypt's Water Footprint Based on Trade Balance and Expenditure Inequality." Journal of Cleaner Production 198 (October): 1526–35. https://doi.org/10.1016/j.jclepro.2018.06.266.

Wuttmann, Michel, Thierry Gonon, and Christophe Thiers. 2000. "The Qanats of 'Ayn-Manâwîr (Kharga Oasis, Egypt)." Edited by Institut français d'archéologie orientale, Cairo. Journal of Achaemenid Studies and Researches.

Essays WATER

Water Conditions in Egypt

Abdel-Wahab, R., (2015): Wastewater Reuse In Egypt: Opportunities and Challenges. IFAT Entsorga 2012 Messe München Germany.

Ahmed, G. Yehia, Khaled, M. Fahmy, Mahmoud, A. S. Mehany, Gehad G. Mohamed (2017); "Impact of Extreme Climate Events on Water Supply Sustainability in Egypt: Case Studies in Alexandria region and Upper Egypt", Journal of Water and Climate Change (2017) 8 (3) pp. 484-494. https://doi.org/10.2166/wcc.2017.111.

Allam, M. N., & Allam, G. I. (2007). Water Resources in Egypt: Future Challenges and Opportunities. Water International, 32(2). pp. 205-218 http://dx.doi.org/10.1080/02508060708692201.

Elshamy, M, E, Wheater, H, S (2009): Performance assessment of a GCM land surface scheme using a fine-scale calibrated hydrological model: An evaluation of MOSES for the Nile Basin. Hydrol. Process, 23, pp. 1548-1564

Kotb, A (2015): Impacts of Climate Change on Nile Flood Predictions from Regional Climate Model. Master Thesis, the Institute of African Research and Studies, Cairo University.

Liersch, S., Koch, H., and Hattermann, F. F., (2017): Management Scenarios of the Grand Ethiopian Renaissance Dam and Their Impacts under Recent and Future Climates, Water, 9, 728, https://doi.org/10.3390/w9100728, 2017.

MWRI (2010). Draft Report on Strategy of Development and Management of Water Resources up to 2050.

Omar, M.E.M., and Moussa, A.. (2016): Water management in Egypt for facing the future challenges, Journal of Advanced Research (2016) 7, pp. 403 – 412

Shaalan, M., El-Mahdy, M., Salah, M., El-Matbouli, M., (2018): Aquaculture in Egypt: Insights on the Current Trends and Future Perspectives for Sustainable Development. Journal of Reviews in Fisheries Science and Aquaculture, Volume 26, 2018-Issue1.

Strzepek, K, McCluskey, A. (2007): The Impacts of Climate Change on Regional Water Resources and Agriculture in Africa. Policy Research Working Paper 4290.

Designing for Global Water Challenges: Appropriating nature-based Water Purification Systems as Part of the Urban Landscape

Ahern, J.: Green infrastructure for cities: The spatial dimension. In: Novotny, Vladimir; Brown, Paul (ed.): Cities of the Future: Towards Integrated Sustainable Water and Landscape Management. IWA Publishers, London 2007, p. 267-283

Bajc, K.; Stokman, A. (2018): Design for Resilience: Re-connecting communities and environments. In: La Frontiers, Issue No. 4/ 2018, S. 14-31

De Meulder, B.; Shannon, K. (2008): "Water and the City: the 'Great Stink' and Clean Urbanism". In: De Meulder, B.; Shannon, K. (Hg.): Water urbanisms. SUN Publishers, Amsterdam, p. 5 – 9

Chaouni, A.; Margolis, L. (2015): Out of Water: Designing Solutions for Arid Regions. Birkhäuser Publishers, Basel.

Hoyer, J.; Dickhaut, W.; Kronawitter, L.; Weber, B. (2011). Water sensitive urban design: Principles and inspiration for sustainable stormwater management in the city of the future. Berlin.

Lepik, A.; Giseke, U.; Keller, R.; Rekittke, J.; Stokman, A.; Werthmann, C. (Hrsg.) (2017): Out There. Landscape Architecture on Global Terrain. Hatje Cantz, München

McDowel, S.l (Hrsg.) 2015: Water Index - Design Strategies for Drought, Flooding and Contamination. Actar Publisher, Barcelona

Mossop, E. 2005: Affordable Landscapes. In: TOPOS Nr. 50, pp. 13 – 23

Mossop, Elisabeth: Landscapes of Infrastructure. In: Waldheim, Charles (Ed.): The Landscape Urbanism Reader. Princeton Architectural Press, New York, 2006, pp. 164 – 177

Nemcova, E.; Eisenberg, B., Poblet, R., Stokman, A. 2015: Water-Sensitive Design of Open Space Systems. Ecological Infrastructure Strategy for Metropolitan Lima. In: Czechowski/Hauck/Hausladen (Eds.): Revising Green Infrastructure: Concepts Between Nature and Design. CRC Press Taylor and Francis, London. pp. 357 – 387

Novotny, V.; Ahern, J.; Brown, P. (2010): Water centric sustainable communities: planning, retrofitting and building the next urban environment. John Wiley & Sons, New York.

Picon, A. 2005: Constructing Landscape by Engineering Water. In: Institute for Landscape Architecture, ETH Zurich (Hrsg.): Landscape Architecture in Mutation. Gta Verlag, Zurich, pp. 99 – 114

Shannon, K. (Ed.), Meulder, B., & Gosseye, J., & D'Auria, V. (2008): UFO1 Water Urbanisms. SUN Publishers, Amsterdam

Stokman, A. 2013: On Designing Infrastructure Systems as Landscape. In: ETH Zürich (Hrsg.): Topology. Landscript 3, Jovis Publishers, Berlin. pp. 285 – 311

Yu, K. (2006): Position Landscape Architecture. The Art of Survival. China Architecture and Building Press, Beijing.

02 LEARNING FROM

Groot, R. S. de, Wilson, M. A. Boumans, R.M.J. (2002). A Typology for the Classification, Description and Valuation of Ecosystem Functions, Goods and Services. Ecological Economics 41: 393–408.

Zakri, A.H. Watson, R. (2003).Ecosystems and Human Well-Beings. Millenium Assessment Reports. Island Press

Viljoen, A. M., Wiskerke, J. S. C. eds. (2012). Sustainable Food Planning: Evolving Theory and Practice. Wageningen: Wageningen Acad. Publ.

Al Azhar Park, Islamic Cairo, SITES International

El Masry, L., Al Azhar Park, Islamic Cairo, abstract Landscaping Egypt conference, GUC, May 5-6, 2017

El Masry , L. (2014a). Landscape Architecture and the Planting Design of Al Azhar Park. Shorouk International Bookshop, Cairo

El Masry , L. (2014b). A Plant Guidebook for Al Azhar Park and the City of Cairo. Shorouk International Bookshop, Cairo

Ibrahim, K. A "Green Lung" for Cairo: The Creation of the Al-Azhar Park https://www.akdn.org/project/green-lung-cairo [accessed July 10, 2019]

Musgrave, T. Al-Azhar Park. Available at https://www.gardenvisit.com/gardens/al-azhar_park [accessed August 11, 2019]

Otte, G. (2005). Al-Azhar Park, Cairo, Egypt. AKDN. Available at: from https://www.akdn.org/press-release/aga-khan-creates-new-30-hectare-park-historic-cairo-media-advisory [accessed July 10, 2019]

Khalifa Heritage and Environment Park, Cairo
Megawra - Built Environment Collective

Al Ibrashy, M. Khalifa Heritage And Environment Park: An Output Of The Athar Lina Ground Water Research Project, abstract Landscaping Egypt – From the Aesthetic to the Productive, int. conference, GUC, May 5-6, 2017

Khalifa Heritage & Environment Park Groundwater research project international school. documentation available at http://atharlina.com/wp-content/uploads/2017/01/Final-Booklet.pdf [accessed June 20, 2018]

Files for design update as adapted in deep section courtesy of Megawra - Built Environment Collective

Geziret El Dahab, Giza
Nil - Nile Islands Initiative

Barthel, P.-A. et al (2009) Dahab 2050. CEDEJ Cairo

BiogasWorld. (2016). Biogas Calculations -Biogas World. Available at: https://www.biogasworld.com/biogas-calculations/

CAPMAS – Central Agency for Public Mobilization and Statistics (2017)

CIA – Central Intelligence Agency (2016). Africa: Egypt — The World Factbook - Central Intelligence Agency. [online] Available at: https://www.cia.gov/library/publications/resources/the-world-factbook/geos/eg.html

El-Zafarany, A. M. Existing Green Areas in Cairo - Comparison with Planning Criteria and International Norms. Available at http://www.egyptarch.net/research/cairourbandesert.pdf [Accessed 2 Feb, 2018]

ETH Studio Basel The Middle East Studio (2010). Islands of the Nile

Fawzi, N. M., Abdelmaksoud, H. S., Azer, S. A. (2010). Floristic Composition of Dahab Island at Nile Region, Egypt; in: Current Science International Volume 06 Issue 04. Oct.- Dec. 2017 pp. 729 – 745

Frearson, A. (2016). EFFEKT designs villages that produce all food and energy. Available at: https://www.dezeen.com/2016/05/20/effekt-designs-regen-villages-produce-own-food-energy-danish-pavilion-venice-architecture-biennale-2016/ [accessed June 20, 2018]

Irena.org. (2020). [online] Available at: https://irena.org/-/media/Files/IRENA/Agency/Publication/2016/IRENA_Statistics_Measuring_smallscale_biogas_2016.pdf [accessed June 10, 2018]

IRENA (2016). Measuring small-scale biogas capacity and production. Abu Dhabi: International Renewable Energy Agency (IRENA).

Redeker, C. Nazer, H. (2016). Designing Cycles – Solid Waste Management Case Study Geziret El Dahab. SBE16 Cairo conference proceedings

Sleem, S. H. and Hassan, M. M. (2010). Impact of Pollution on Invertebrates Biodiversity in the River Nile Associated With Dahab and El-Warrak Islands, Egypt. International Journal of Environmental Science And Engineering (Ijese) Vol. 1: 15 – 25. Available at http://www.pvamu.edu/texged Prairie View A&M University, Texas, USA [accessed June 22, 2018]

Vymazal, J. (2007). Removal of nutrients in various types of constructed wetlands. Volume 380, Issues 1–3, 15 July 2007, pp. 48-65. Available at https://doi.org/10.1016/j.scitotenv.2006.09.014 [accessed June 22, 2018]

Desert Afforestation
National Program for Afforestation

El Kateb et al (2015). German Egyptian Research Collaboration to Afforestation in Desert Lands of Egypt: Information Summary and Description of the Field Experiments. Silvicultural Experiments 4

El Kateb H. & Mosandl R. (2012): Aufforstungen in ägyptischen Wüstengebieten. AFZ-Der Wald 67(19) pp. 36-39.

Becker K., Wulfmeyer V., Berger T., Gebel J. & Münch W. (2013): Carbon farming in hot, dry coastal areas: an option for climate change mitigation. Earth Syst. Dynam., 4, 237–251. Available at: http://www.earth-syst-dynam.net/4/237/2013/esd-4-237-2013.pdf. [accessed 14 August, 2018]

El Kateb H., Eger J. & Walterspacher D. (2013): Financial projections of large-scale afforestation in arid regions - An Example: Egypt. Munich & Bonn. Institute of Silviculture, Technische Universität München, & Forest-Finance Group, unpublished, 45 p.

El Tawil, N., First initial. (2018). Egypt Kuwait Holding cultivates forest for wood factory. Egypt Today Oct 31, 2018. Available at: https://www.egypttoday.com/Article/3/59754/Egypt-Kuwait-Holding-cultivates-forest-for-wood-factory [accessed 13.Dec. 2019]

Goldmann G. (2001): Wiege der Forstwirtschaft in Ägypten. Das Fatimiden-Kalifat. AFZ/Der Wald 56(2) pp. 74 – 75.

FAO - Food and Agriculture Organization of the United Nations (2005): State of the World's Forests 2005. Rome, FAO. Available at: ftp://ftp.fao.org/docrep/fao/007/y5574e/ y5574e00.pdf. [accessed 17 August, 2018]

FAO - Food and Agriculture Organization of the United Nations (2010): Global Forest Resources Assessment 2010 - Country Report: Egypt. Rome, FAO Forestry Department. Available at: http://www.fao.org/countryprofiles/index/en/?subj=5&iso3=EGY#sthash.xNZUTQeY.dpuf. [accessed 18 August, 2018]

MED-ENEC (2013). Energy Efficiency Urban Planning Guidelines for MENA region. Available at: http://www.cpas-egypt.com/pdf/MED-ENEC/Books/01Energy%20Efficiency%20Urban%20Planning%20Guidelines%20for%20MENA%20region-October%202013.pdf [accessed 13 Dec, 2018]

Wadi Agriculture
Marsadev Project, Wadi Kharouba, Marsa Matrouh
Desert Research Center Egypt, CIHEAM-Bari, Italy

Antipolis, S. (2011). PLAN BLEU. Sustainability Profile Mediterranean Destinations. UNEP/MAP Regional Activity Center

Ali A, Oweis T, Salkini AB and El-Naggar S. (2009). Rainwater cisterns: traditional technologies for dry areas. ICARDA, Aleppo, Syria. iv + 20 pp.

Hadidi. A (2016). Wadi Bili Catchment in the Eastern Desert – Flash Floods, Geological Model and Hydrogeology. TU Berlin

Jones, E. Qadira, M. van Vlietb, M.T.H., Smakhtina, V. Kangac, S. (2019). The State Of Desalination And Brine Production: A Global Outlook. In: Science of The Total Environment. Volume 657, 20 March 2019, pp. 1343-1356

Prinz, D. (1994) "Water Harvesting: Past and Future". In Sustainability of Irrigated Agriculture. Ed. by L. Pereira. 1994, pp. 135–144

Prinz, D. (2002). "The Role of Water Harvesting in Alleviating Water Scarcity in Arid Areas". In Keynote Lecture, Proceedings, International Conference on Water Resources Management in Arid Regions. 23 – 27 March, 2002. Vol. 3. Kuwait Institute for Scientific Research, 2002, pp. 107 – 112

Rima Mekdaschi, H. L. (2013). Water Harvesting: Guidelines to Good Practice. Centre for Development and Environment (CDE) and Institute of Geography, University of Bern; Rainwater Harvesting Implementation Network (RAIN), Amsterdam; MetaMeta, Wageningen; The International Fund for Agricultural Development (IFAD), Rome

Theib Y. Oweis, D. P. (2012). Water Harvesting for Agriculture in the Dry Areas . Leiden, Netherlands: CRC Press/Balkema

Orchard Park Al Burouj, Eastern Greater Cairo
Bustan Aquaponics

www.bustanaquaponics.com

https://alburoujeg.com

Water Sensitive Open Space Design
Al Rehab, New Cairo, IUSD Ain Shams University

Deister, L. (2013). Designing Landscape as Infrastructure – Water Sensitive Open Space Design in Cairo. Master thesis IUSD Ain Shams University

Abdel Wahaat, R. & El-Din Omar, M. (2011) Wastewater Reuse in Egypt: Opportunities and Challenges. Available at: http://www.arabwatercouncil.org/administrator/Modules/CMS/Egypt-Country-Report.pdf. [accessed March 5, 2019]

Sims, D. (2014). Egypt's Desert Dreams: Development or Disaster? The AUC Press, Cairo

AbuZeid, K., Elrawady, M. (2014), "2030 Strategic Vision for Treated Wastewater Reuse in Egypt", Water Resources Management Program, CEDARE

Urban Microfarms, Cairo
Schaduf Sustainable Living Solutions

El Kateb H. & Mosandl R. (2012): Aufforstungen in ägyptischen Wüstengebieten. AFZ-Der Wald 67(19) pp. 365 39.

Thackston, W M ed. (1986). Naser-e Khosraw's book of travels = (Safarnama). Bibliotheca Persica, Albany, N.Y.

Werr, P. (2015). Rich pickings at Egypt's rooftop gardens available at https://www.thenational.ae/business/rich-pickings-at-egypt-s-rooftop-gardens-1.129020 [accessed Dec. 15, 2015]

Cairo to Begin Planting Gardens on Rooftops available at https://egyptianstreets.com/2019/07/15/cairo-to-begin-planting-gardens-on-rooftops/?fbclid=IwAR0dHKImspicq4JeWBI2F8YJ2R8uHhd3sgSNEcMdv2iOLsOWR-5W8z25M1b8

https://www.unccd.int/convention [accessed July 20, 2019]

www.schaduf.com

Constructed Wetlands, Samaha Village, Dakhleya Governorate
National Water Research Center Egypt

Eid, M. (2014). Hydraulic Study Of Drainage System Constructed Subsurface Wetlands. El-Mansoura University. Faculty Of Engineering - Irrigation And Hydraulics Dept.

Hoffmann, H. Platzer, C. Winker, M. von Muench, E. (2011) Technology review of constructed wetlands - Subsurface flow constructed wetlands for greywater and domestic wastewater treatment. GIZ

Masi, F., El Hamouri, B., Abdel Shafi, H., Baban, A., Ghrabi, A., Regelsberger, M., 2010. Segregated black/grey domestic wastewater treatment by Constructed Wetlands in the Mediterranean basin: the Zer0-m experience. Water Sci. Technol. 61 (1), 97e105. Available at: https://doi.org/10.2166/wst.2010.780. [accessed Dec. 13, 2019]

Aquaponic Farming, Giza
Bustan Aquaponics

Mollison, Bill C. Permaculture: A Designers' Manual. 2nd ed. Tyalgum, Australia: Tagari, 2004.

Pearson LJ, Pearson L, Pearson CJ (2010) Sustainable urban agriculture: stocktake and opportunities. Int J Agric Sustain 8 pp. 7-19. Available at: https://doi.org/10.3763/ijas.2009.0468 [accessed May 5, 2019]

Proksch G., Ianchenko A., Kotzen B. (2019) Aquaponics in the Built Environment. In: Goddek S., Joyce A., Kotzen B., Burnell G. (eds.) Aquaponics Food Production Systems. Springer International Publishing

www.bustanaquaponics.com

Ten Medjool Date Palms, Nuweiba, South Sinai
Sinai Date Palm Foundation, Habiba Organic Farms

Maged El Said, Crowd Funding Medjool Date Palms in Sinai, Habiba Organic Farm, Nuweiba. Abstract Landscaping Egypt – From the Aesthetic to the Productive, int. conference, GUC, May 5 – 6, 2017

Sekem (2016). Bread of the Desert: Dates from Egypt. 05.12.16. Available at https://www.sekem.com/en/bread-of-the-desert-dates-from-egypt/ [accessed: June 7, 2019]

www.habibacommunity.com

Essays URBANIZATION

The Larger Scale – Urbanization, Agriculture, Land Reclamation

Askoura, Ibrahim E. "التوسع الحضري وآكل الأراضي الزراعية: دراسة تطبيقية على التكتل الحضري للقرى" (Urban Expansion and Agricultural Land Erosion: An Applied Study on Urban Clusters in Zakazik). "Arab Regional Conference on Rural Urban Integration," 2005.

Dorman, W. J. (2013). Exclusion and Informality: The Praetorian Politics of Land Management in C airo, E gypt. International Journal of Urban and Regional Research, 37(5), 1584 – 1610.

Egypt Today Staff, (2019): President Sisi inspects development projects in Toshka. Egypt Today. Available at: https://www.egypttoday.com/Article/1/67079/President-Sisi-inspects-development-projects-in-Toshka. [accessed July 7, 2019]

Fecteau, A., (2012): On Toshka New Valley's mega-failure, Egypt Independent. Available at: https://ww.egyptindependent.com/toshka-new-valleys-mega-failure-slideshow/ [accessed July 7, 2019]

Laurie Brand "The Politics of National Narratives." CIRS Monthly Dialogue on "The Politics of National Narratives: The Evolution of 'Revolution' in Egypt."23 Mar. 2015. Center for International and Regional Studies. Web. 23 Mar. 2017

Noeman, R., (2000): Egypt pours money into desert reclamation. Reuters.

Radwan, T. M., Blackburn, G. A., Whyatt, J. D., & Atkinson, P. M. (2019). Dramatic Loss of Agricultural Land Due to Urban Expansion Threatens Food Security in the Nile Delta, Egypt. Remote Sensing, 11(3), 332.

Shawkat, Y., Hendawy, M. (2016): Myths and Facts of Urban Planning in Egypt, The Built Environment Observatory. Available at: http://marsadomran.info/en/policy_analysis/2016/11/501/#_edn3 [accessed on July 8, 2019]

Shawkat, Y., Khalil, A. (2016): The Built Environment Budget 2015/16, An Analysis of Spatial Justice in Egypt. Cairo: The Built Environment Observatory. Available at: http://marsadomran.info/en/policy_analysis/urban-en/2016/11/589/ [accessed July 8, 2019]

Sims, D. (2012). Understanding Cairo: The logic of a city out of control. Oxford University Press.

Sims, D., (2014): Egypt's Desert Dreams: Development or Disaster. Cairo and New York: The American University in Cairo Press. Tadamun, (2015): Egypt's New Cities: Neither Just nor Efficient, TADAMUN. The Cairo Urban Solidarity Initiative. Available at: http://www.tadamun.co/egypts-new-cities-neither-just-efficient/?lang=en#.XSM-cBpMzbq0. [accessed July 8, 2019]

Voll, S., (1980): Egyptian Land Reclamation since the Revolution, Middle East Journal Vol. 34:2, pp. 127 – 148.

Warner, J., (2013): The Toshka mirage in the Egyptian desert – River diversion as political diversion, Environmental Science & Policy Vol. 30, pp. 102 – 112.

03 REVISITED AND PROJECTED

Fairchild Ruggles, D. (2008). Islamic Gardens and Landscapes. University of Pennsylvania Press, Philadelphia, Pennsylvania Girot, C. (2016). The Course of Landscape Architecture. Thames and Hudson, London, N.Y.

Jodidio, P. (ed.) (2018). Agha Khan Garden. Aga Khan Trust for Culture, Geneva, Switzerland

Loeben, C.E. Die Ältesten Gärten der Welt. In: Lutz, A., von Trotha, H. (eds.) (2016). Gärten der Welt. Wienand Verlag, Köln

Sprenguel, I. (2006). The Desert Garden – A Practical Guide. AUC Press, Cairo

Essays FOOD

Planning for Egypt's Food System and Heritage

http://www.milanurbanfoodpolicypact.org/signatory-cities/ [accessed on Sep. 23 , 2019] http://www.milanurbanfoodpolicypact.org/ [accessed on Sep. 23 , 2019]

https://sustainability-governance.net/category/telecoupling/

Barakat, H.N., and G. el-Din Fahmy. 1999. "Wild Grasses as 'Neolithic' Food Resources in the Eastern Sahara." In: M. van der Veen, ed., The Exploitation of Plant Resources in Ancient Africa. pp. 33 – 46. New York: Kluwer Academic/Plenum Publishers.

Barakat, H.N., 2017. We Are What We Eat, We Were What We Ate, in: The Food Question in the Middle East, CAIRO PAPERS IN SOCIAL SCIENCE. American University in Cairo Press, Cairo.

Braunschweig, T., François Meienberg, Carine Pionetti, Sangeeta Shashikant, Caroline Dommen, 2014. Owning Seeds, Accessing Food – A Human Rights Impact Assessment of UPOV 1991 based on Case Studies in Kenya, Peru and the Philippines.

de Koning, A., 2006. Café Latte and Caesar Salad: Cosmopolitan Belonging in Cairo's Coffee Shops, in: Cairo Cosmopolitan: Politics, Culture, and Urban Space in the New Globalized Middle East. Cairo, pp. 221 – 234.

El Quosy, D., Khalifa, H.E.H., 2017. Control of the Nile's Flow: The Introduction of Perennial Irrigation for Modern Agriculture, in: Satoh, M., Aboulroos, S. (Eds.), Irrigated Agriculture in Egypt. Springer International Publishing, Cham, pp. 29–45. https://doi.org/10.1007/978-3-319-30216-FAO, 2015. Egypt Wheat sector review, Report 21.

Giseke, Undine / Gerster-Bentaya, Maria / Helten, Frank / Kraume, Matthias / Scherer, Dieter / Spars, Guido / Adidi, Abdelaziz / Amraoui, Fouad / Berdouz, Said / Chlaida, Mohamed / Mansour, Majid / Mdafai, Mohamed (Hgs.) (2015): Urban Agriculture for Growing City Regions. Connecting Urban-Rural Spheres in Casablanca, Oxon, Abingdon, New York: Routledge

Hadjichristodoulou, A., 2000. Seed Legislation and Regulatory Measures in the Near East, in: Food and Agriculture Organization of the United Nations (Ed.), Seed Policy and Programmes in the Near East and North Africa: Proceedings of the Regional Technical Meeting on Seed Policy and Programmes in the Near East and North Africa: Larnaca, Cyprus, 27 June-2 July 1999, FAO Plant Production and Protection Paper. Food and Agriculture Organization of the United Nations, Rome.

Hopkins, N.S., Sohair, M., Abdelmaksoud, B., 1995. Farmers, Merchants and primary agricultural marketing in Egypt, in: The Metropolitain Food System of Cairo. Saarbrücken, pp. 43–67.

Lorenzon, F., 2016. The political economy of food subsidies in Egypt. Reforms and strengthening of social protection. Public Sphere J. Ssue 2016, pp. 105 – 133.

Nazeera, N., Baheya, O., 1942. Osul al-tahi al-nazari wa-l-'amali (The Basics of Theoretical and Practical Cooking). Cairo: Maktabet al-Nahda al-Misriya.

Noaman, M.N., El Quosy, D., 2017. Hydrology of the Nile and Ancient Agriculture, in: Satoh, M., Aboulroos, S. (Eds.), Irrigated Agriculture in Egypt. Springer International Publishing, Cham, pp. 9–28. https://doi.org/10.1007/978-3-319-30216-4_2

Tschirgi, D., 1995. Cairos Municipal food policy: "As he gets more, he can buy more" -, in: The Metrolopitan Food System of Cairo. Saarbrücken, pp. 27–41.

Vartavan, C. de, and V. Asensi Amoros. 1997. Codex of Ancient Egyptian Plant Remains. London: Triade Exploration.

Wasylikowa,K., and J. Dahlberg.1999. Sorghum in the Economy my of the Early Neolithic Nomadic Tribes at Nabta Playa, Southern Egypt In: M. van der Veen, ed., The Exploitation of Plant Resources in Ancient Africa, pp. 11-31. London: Kluwer Academic/Plenum Publishers.

04 PRODUCTIVE PLANTS
Groot, R. S. de, Wilson, M. A. Boumans, R.M.J. (2002). A Typology for the Classification, Description and Valuation of Ecosystem Functions, Goods and Services. Ecological Economics 41: 393–408.

Zakri, A.H. Watson, R. (2003).Ecosystems and Human Well-Beings. Millenium Assessment Reports. Island Press

Viljoen, A. M., Wiskerke, J. S. C. eds. (2012). Sustainable Food Planning: Evolving Theory and Practice. Wageningen: Wageningen Acad. Publ.

Aamer, R.A., 2016. Characteristics of aqueous doum fruit extract and its utilization in some novel products. Ann. Agric. Sci. 61(1), pp. 25 – 33.

Abd El Baky, H.H., El-Baroty, G., 2013. Egyptian Moringa peregrine seed oil and its bioactivities. Int. J. Manag. Sci. Bus. Res. 2, 98.

Abdallah, F., Noumi, Z., Touzard, B., Belgacem, A.O., Neffati, M., Chaieb, M., 2008. The influence of Acacia tortilis (Forssk.) Subsp. raddiana (Savi) and livestock grazing on grass species composition, yield and soil nutrients in arid environments of South Tunisia. Flora - Morphol. Distrib. Funct. Ecol. Plants 203, 116–125. https://doi.org/10.1016/j.flora.2007.02.002

Abd-el-hak, Nasra, A., Hanaa, S.M., Abd El-Rahman, Ritzk, A.E., 2016. Production and Evaluation of Sycamore and Fig blends jam. Agric Res 94 (3).

Abdelkader, A.F.A., Aldughaish, A.M., 2016. Physiological and Chemical Characteristics of Age-Differed Ficus benjamina L. Trees Cultivated in El-ahassa, Saudi Arabia. J. Plant Sci. 4, pp. 63–67

Abobatta, W., 2018a. Challenges for Citrus Production in Egypt. Acta Sci. Agric. 2.

Abobatta, W. (Ed.), 2018b. Improving Navel orange (Citrus sinensis L) productivity in Delta Region, Egypt. Adv. Agric. Environ. Sci. Open Access AAEOA 1, 36–38. https://doi.org/10.30881/aaeoa.00006

Aboshora, W., Lianfu, Z., Dahir, M., Gasmalla, M.A.A., 2014. Physicochemical, Nutritional and Functional Properties of the Epicarp, Flesh and Pitted Sample of Doum Fruit (Hyphaene Thebaica). J. Food Nutr. Res. Vol. 2, pp. 180 – 186.

Abou-Elela, S.I., S. Hellal, M., 2012. Municipal wastewater treatment using vertical flow constructed wetlands planted with Canna, Phragmites and Cyprus. Ecol. Eng. 47, pp. 209 – 213.

Al-Orf, S.M., Ahmed, M.H.M., Al-Atwai, N., Al-Zaidi, H., Dehwah, A., 2012. Review: Nutritional Properties and Benefits of the Date Fruits (Phoenix dactylifera L.). Bull. Natl. Nutr. Inst. Arab Repub. Egypt 39.

Ama Abdelgawad, A., 2017. Tamarix nilotica (Ehrenb) Bunge: A Review of Phytochemistry and Pharmacology. J. Microb. Biochem. Technol. 09. https://doi.org/10.4172/1948-5948.1000340

Australian Government, O. of the G.T.R., 2016. The Biology of Musa L. (banana).

Barakat, H.N., 2017. We Are What We Eat, We Were What We Ate, in: The Food Question in the Middle East, CAIRO PAPERS IN SOCIAL SCIENCE. American University in Cairo Press, Cairo.

Bargali, K., Bargali, S.S., 2009. Acacia nilotica: a multipurpose leguminous plant. Nat. Sci. 7.

Ben Zetta, H., 2017. EFFECTS OF PRE-GERMINATION TREATMENTS, Salt And Water Stresses On Germination Of Acacia Ehrenbergiana Hayne And Acacia Seyal Del. (Mimosoideae): Two Algerian Native Species. Appl. Ecol. Environ. Res. 15, 355–368. https://doi.org/10.15666/aeer/1504_355368

Bigelow, J.M.H., 2000. Ancient Egyptian Gardens. Ostracon J. Egypt. Study Soc. volume 11-1, pp. 7 – 10

Bouchaud, C., Morales, J., Schram, V., van der Veen, M., 2017. The earliest evidence for citrus in Egypt, in: Zech-Matterne, V., Fiorentino, G. (Eds.), AGRUMED: Archaeology and History of Citrus Fruit in the Mediterranean. Publications du Centre Jean Bérard. https://doi.org/10.4000/books.pcjb.2179

Coen, K., 2015. Bamboo, the building material of the future! An experimental research on glueless lamination of bamboo., student work conducted at the studio Architectural Engineering, TU Delft. Architectural Engineering, TU Delft

Csurhes, S., 2016. Giant reed Arundo donax Invasive plant risk assessment.

David, A., 2014. Hoopoes and Acacias: Decoding an Ancient Egyptian Funerary Scene. J. East. Stud. 73, pp. 235 – 252. https://doi.org/10.1086/677251

de Groot, R.S., Wilson, M.A., Boumans, R.M.J., 2002. A typology for the classification, description and valuation of ecosystem functions, goods and services. Ecol. Econ. 41, pp. 393 – 408

De Langhe, E., 2002. Banana diversity in the Middle East (Jordan, Egypt, Oman). INIBAP Programme Int. Plant Genet. Resour. Inst. IPGRI.

Diab, A.M., 2018. Representations of Pomegranate in Ancient Egypt during the New Kingdom. Int. J. Herit. Tour. Hosp. 12.

E. McGovern, P., 1997. The Beginnings of Winemaking and Viniculture in the Ancient Near East and Egypt, Expedition Magazine. Penn Museum.

Eid, E.M., Youssef, M.S.G., Shaltout, K.H., 2016. Population characteristics of giant reed (Arundo donax L.) in cultivated and naturalized habitats. Aquat. Bot. 129, pp. 1 – 8. https://doi.org/10.1016/j.aquabot.2015.11.001

El-Beheiry, M.A.H., El-Kady, H.F., 1998. Nutritive value of twoTamarixspecies in Egypt. J. Arid Environ. 38, pp. 529 – 539. https://doi.org/10.1006/jare.1998.0341

ElMasry, L., 2014. A Plant Guidebook for Al-Azhar Park and the City of Cairo. Shorouk Intl. Bookshop, Cairo

Emam, H.E., Abd El-Moniem, E.A.A., Saleh, M.M.S., 2016. The suitable planting distance for Koroneiki and Chemlali olives under Al-Nubaria district conditions. International Journal of PharmTech Research Vol.9, pp. 145 – 152

EU Cordis, 2013. Innovative system uses bamboo to treat wastewater [WWW Document]. Eur. Com. CORDIS EU Res. Results. URL https://cordis.europa.eu/article/id/36167-innovative-system-uses-bamboo-to-treat-wastewater/en [accessed Aug. 11, 2019]

Ezzo, M.I., Saleh, S.A., Glala, A.A., Abdalla, A.M., Adam, S.M., 2017. Surveying and preserving Moringa peregrina germplasm in Egypt. Acta Hortic. 79–84. https://doi.org/10.17660/ActaHortic.2017.1158.10

F. Ahmed, H., 2012. Phytohormones content and random amplified polymorphic DNA (RAPD) marker assessment of some Egyptian citrus cultivars. Afr. J. Biotechnol. 11, pp. 15755 – 15762. https://doi.org/10.5897/AJB12.2259

FAO, 2018. Banana facts and figures [WWW Document]. FAO Food Agric. Organ. U. N. URL http://www.fao.org/economic/est/est-commodities/bananas/bananafacts/en [accessed Oct. 26, 2018]

FAO, 2013. Agro-industrial utilization of cactus pear. Rome.

FAO, ICARDIA, 2017. CROP ECOLOGY, CULTIVATION AND USES OF CACTUS PEAR (Advance draft prepared for the IX INTERNATIONAL CONGRESS ON CACTUS PEAR AND COCHINEAL CAM crops for a hotter and drier world Coquimbo, Chile, 26 – 30 March 2017). Rome.

FAO-OIV, 2016. TABLE AND DRIED GRAPES Non-alcoholic products of the vitivinicultural sector intended for human consumption, FAO-OIV FOCUS 2016. Food and Agriculture Organization of the United Nations and the International Organisation of Vine and Wine.

FAO/RNE, 2008. Proceedings on Workshop on "Irrigation of Date Palm and Associated Crops".

faostat, 2018. FAOstat Crops Data, Food and Agriculture Organization of the United Nations [WWW Document]. FAOSTAT. URL http://www.fao.org/faostat/en/#data/QC [accessed Aug 11, 2019]

Galal, T.M., Shehata, H.S., 2016. Growth and nutrients accumulation potentials of giant reed (Arundo donax L.) in different habitats in Egypt. Int. J. Phytoremediation 18, pp. 1221 – 1230. https://doi.org/10.1080/15226514.2016.1193470

Galil, J., 1967. An Ancient Technique for Ripening Sycomore Fruit in East Mediterranean Countries. Econ Bot 22, pp. 178 – 190.

Galil, J., Eisikowitch, D., 1968. Flowering Cycles and Fruit types of Ficus Sycomorus in Israel. New Phytol pp. 745 – 758

Gilbert, F., Zalat, S., 2016. Gardens of a sacred landscape: Bedouin heritage and natural history in the high mountains of Sinai. American University in Cairo Press, Cairo

Hadidi, M.N., Boulos, L., 1988. The Street Trees of Egypt, revised edition, American University in Cairo Press

Hamza, M., Tate, B., 2017. Egypt Citrus Annual. Egyptian Orange Exports Thrives Thanks to Currency Devaluation., GAIN Report

Hobbs, J.J., Krzywinski, K., Andersen, G.L., Talib, M., Pierce, R.H., Saadallah, A.E.M., 2014. Acacia trees on the cultural landscapes of the Red Sea Hills. Biodivers. Conserv. 23, pp. 2923–2943. https://doi.org/10.1007/s10531-014-0755-x

Holland, D., Hatib, K., Bar-Ya'akov, I., 2009. Pomegranate: Botany, Horticulture, Breeding. Hortic. Rev. 35

Hussein Mohamed, D.M., 2017. Effect of some Chemical Thinning Compounds on Fruit Quality of Table Olives,thesis, Agricultural Sciences (Pomology) Department of Pomology Faculty of Agriculture Cairo University. Cairo

Ibrahim, H., Baker, W.J., 2009. Medemia argun – Past, Present and Future. Palms, Palms Vol. 53(1)

Indian Council of Forestry Research and Education, Dehradun. Forest Research Institute, n.d. Babul (Acacia nilotica). Indian Council of Forestry Research and Education, Dehradun. Forest Research Institute, Dehradun

International Network for Bamboo and Rattan (INBAR), 2015. Bamboo for Africa: A strategic resource to drive the continent's Green Economy. International Network for Bamboo and Rattan

International Olive Council, 2012. General description of Olive Growing in Egypt

Ismail, O.M., Younis, R.A.A., Ibrahim, A.M., 2014. Morphological and molecular evaluation of some Egyptian pomegranate cultivars. Afr. J. Biotechnol. Vol. 13(2), pp. 226 – 237

Janssen, J.J.A., 2000. Designing and building with bamboo, INBAR technical report

Kandal, H.A., Yacoub, H.A., Gerkema, M.P., Swart, Jac.A.A., 2016. Vanishing Knowledge of Plant Species in the Wadi Allaqi Desert Area of Egypt. Hum. Ecol. 44, pp. 493–504. https://doi.org/10.1007/s10745-016-9826-9

Khalil, C., El Houssei, B., Hassan, B., Fouad, M., 2016. Comparative Salt Tolerance Study of Some Acacia Species at Seed Germination Stage. Asian J. Plant Sci. 15, pp. 66 – 74. https://doi.org/10.3923/ajps.2016.66.74

Kipasika, H.J., Buza, J., Smith, W.A., Njau, K.N., 2016. Removal capacity of faecal pathogens from wastewater by four wetland vegetation: Typha latifolia, Cyperus papyrus, Cyperus alternifolius and Phragmites australis. Afr. J. Microbiol. Res. Vol. 10(19), pp. 654 – 661

Kok, D., 2014. A Review on Grape Growing in Tropical Regions. Turk. J. Agric. Nat. Sci. Special Issue: 1

Kondo, J., 1991. BEN-OIL IN ANCIENT EGYPT. Orient 27, pp. 44–55. https://doi.org/10.5356/orient1960.27.44

Kumar, V., 2015. Social forestry in India: concept and schemes. https://doi.org/10.13140/RG.2.1.1652.4243

Kunwar, R.M., Bussmann, R.W., 2006. Ficus (Fig) species in Nepal: a review of diversity and indigenous uses. Lyonia J. Ecol. Appl. 11.

Lobovikov, M., Piazza, M., Ren, H., Wu, J., 2007. World bamboo resources. A thematic study prepared in the framework of the Global Forest Resources Assessment 2005. FAO (Food And Agriculture Organization Of The United Nations), Rome.

Lucas, A., Harris, J.R., 2012. Ancient Egyptian Materials and Industries. Dover Publications.

Lutz, A., Trotha, H. von, Museum Rietberg (Eds.), 2016. Gärten der Welt: Orte der Sehnsucht und Inspiration. Museum Rietberg Zürich ; Wienand, Zürich : Köln.

M. Abou Elella, F., 2014. Antioxidant and Anticancer Activities of Different Constituents Extracted from Egyptian Prickly Pear Cactus (Opuntia ficus-indica) Peel. Biochem. Anal. Biochem. 03. https://doi.org/10.4172/2161-1009.1000158

Malviya, S., Rawat, S., Kharia, A., Verma, M., 2011. Medicinal attributes of Acacia nilotica Linn. - A comprehensive review on ethnopharmacological claims. Int. J. Pharm. Life Sci. 2.

Market Research Future MRFR, 2017. Extra Virgin Olive Oil Market: Global Survey, Trends, Outlook, Overview and 2023 Forecast Extra Virgin Olive Oil Market, press release of a market report by MRFR [WWW Document]. SBWire Press Releases. URL http://www.sbwire.com/press-releases/extra-virgin-olive-oil-market-global-survey-trends-outlook-overview-and-2023-forecast-884310.htm [accessed on Aug. 11, 2018]

MedAgri, 2018a. Understanding Olive Oil yield (factors affecting crop and extraction) [WWW Document]. URL http://www.medagri.org/sector_detail.php?id=4 [accessed on Aug. 11, 2018]

MedAgri, 2018b. Olives and Olive Oil [WWW Document]. Olives Olive Oil. URL http://www.medagri.org/sector_detail.php?id=4 [accessed on Aug. 11, 2018]

Mekki, L.E., El-Meleigy, E.-S.A., 2012. Genetical and Physiological Variability between Tamarix Aphylla And Tamarix Nilotica Species Of Oyoun Mousa Region, Sinai, Egypt. Egypt. J. Desert Res. 62/63, pp. 55 – 70

Melgarejo, P., Valero These, D., 2012. International Symposium on the Pomegranate. OPTIONS Méditerranéennes Ser. Mediter. Semin. Number 103 II.

Ministry of Agriculture and Land Reclamation, 2009. Sustainable Agricultural Development Strategy towards 2030. Arab Republic of Egypt, Cairo

Mohamed, Aiman.K.A., El-Sese, A.M., 2009. Chilling and Heat Requirements of Some Grape Cultivars (Vitis vinifera L). Int. J. Appl. Agric. Res. 4, pp. 193 – 202

Nsanganwimana, F., Marchand, L., Douay, F., Mench, M., 2014. Arundo donax L., a Candidate for Phytomanaging Water and Soils Contaminated by Trace Elements and Producing Plant-Based Feedstock. A Review. Int. J. Phytoremediation 16, pp. 982–1017. https://doi.org/10.1080/15226514.2013.810580

Orwa, C., Mutua, A., Kindt, R., Jamnadass, R., Anthony, S., 2009. Agroforestree Database:a tree reference and selection guide version 4.0 (http://www.worldagroforestry.org/sites/treedbs/treedatabases.asp) [WWW Document]. Acacia Nilotica Subsp Nilotica. URL http://www.worldagroforestry.org/sites/treedbs/treedatabases.asp (accessed 11.16.18)

Pacini, N., Hesslerova, P., Pokorny, J., Mwinami, T., Morrison, E., 2018. Papyrus as an ecohydrological tool for restoring ecosystem services in Afrotropical wetlands. Ecohydrol. Hydrobiol. 18, pp.142–154

Palmer, I.E., Gehl, R.J., Ranney, T.G., Touchell, D., George, N., 2014. Biomass yield, nitrogen response, and nutrient uptake of perennial bioenergy grasses in North Carolina. Biomass Bioenergy 63, pp. 218–228. https://doi.org/10.1016/j.biombioe.2014.02.016

Pomegranate Growing [WWW Document], 2018. . INFOAGRO.COM/AGRICULTURE. URL http://agriculture.infoagro.com/crops/print.asp?iddoc=41&idcap=1 [accessed on Oct. 22, 2018]

Riad, M., 1993. The date palm sector in Egypt. Ferry M Ed Grein Er Ed Palmier Dattier Dans Agric. Oasis Pays Méditerranéens Zaragoza CIHEAM Options Méditerranéennes Sér. Sémin. Méditerranéen S no. 28, pp. 45–53

Salaheldeen, M., Aroua, M.K., Mariod, A.A., Cheng, S.F., Abdelrahman, M.A., 2014. An evaluation of Moringa peregrina seeds as a source for bio-fuel. Ind. Crops Prod. 61, pp. 49–61. https://doi.org/10.1016/j.indcrop.2014.06.027

Seleem, H.A., 2015. Effect of Blending Doum (Hyphaene thebaica) Powder with Wheat Flour on the Nutritional Value and Quality of Cake. Food Nutr. Sci. pp. 622–632

Senthilkumar, A., Karuvantevida, N., Rastrelli, L., Kurup, S.S., Cheruth, A.J., 2018. Traditional Uses, Pharmacological Efficacy, and Phytochemistry of Moringa peregrina (Forssk.) Fiori. —A Review. Front. Pharmacol. Volume 9, Article 465

Serag, M.S., 2003. Ecology and biomass production of Cyperus papyrus L. on the Nile bank at Damietta, Egypt. J. Mediterr. Ecol. Vol. 4, No 3-4, 15–24.

Serag, M.S., 2000. Botanical Note - The Rediscovery of Papyrus (Cyperus papyrus L.), on the bank of the Damietta branch of the Nile Delta, Egypt. Taeckholmia 20, pp. 195–198

Shafik D., I., Adawy, S.S., Atia, M.A.M., Alsamman, A.M., Mokhtar, M.M., 2016. Genetic diversity, variety identification and gene detection in some Egyptian grape varieties by SSR and SCoT markers. Plant Omics 9, 311–318. https://doi.org/10.21475/poj.09.05.16.pne125

Shukla, R., Sumit, Sajal, S., Dwivedi, P.K., Sumit, G., 2012. MEDICINAL IMPORTANCE OF BAMBOO. Int. J. Biopharm Phytochem. Res. Vol. 1(1), pp. 9–15

Sims, D.E., 2014. Egypt's desert dreams: development or disaster? The American University in Cairo Press, Cairo

Soliman Yu, H., Ibrahin Al, S., 2011. Anti-inflammatory and Wound Healing Activities of Herbal Gel Containing an Antioxidant Tamarix aphylla Leaf Extract. Int. J. Pharmacol. 7, pp. 829–835. https://doi.org/10.3923/ijp.2011.829.835

Springuel, I., 2006. The Desert Garden. American University in Cairo PressSsebunya, B., Kilcher, L., 2011. African Organic Agriculture Training Manual. A Resource Manual for Trainers pp. 9-21 CITRUS. Frick

Stauffer, F.W., Ouattara, D., Stork, A.L., 2014. PALMAE (ARECACEAE) / 15 g. / 63 spp. Trop. Afr. Flower. Plants Monocotyledons 2 8., pp. 326-354 in Lebrun

Täckholm, V., Drar, M., 1956. Students' Flora of Egypt, second edition. ed. Anglo-Egyptian Bookshop

Tellioglu, I., Konandreas, P., 2017. Agricultural Policies, Trade and Sustainable Development in Egypt Issue Paper. Geneva: International Centre for Trade and Sustainable Development (ICTSD) and Rome: United Nations Food and Agriculture Organization (FAO)

Terral, J.-F., Tabard, E., Bouby, L., Ivorra, S., Pastor, T., Figueiral, I., Picq, S., Chevance, J.-B., Jung, C., Fabre, L., Tardy, C., Compan, M., Bacilieri, R., Lacombe, T., This, P., 2010. Evolution and history of grapevine (Vitis vinifera) under domestication: new morphometric perspectives to understand seed domestication syndrome and reveal origins of ancient European cultivars. Ann. Bot. 105, pp. 443–455. https://doi.org/10.1093/aob/mcp298

Tewari, S., Banik, R.L., Kaushal, R., Bhardwaj, D.R., Chaturvedi, O.P., Gupta, A., 2015. Bamboo Based Agroforestry Systems. ENVIS Cent. For. Natl. For. Libr. Inf. Cent. For. Res. Inst. ICFRE Dehradun 2015

Trees For Life International, 2005a. Moringa Presentation. Trees For Life International, W. St.Louis, Wichita

Trees For Life International (Ed.), 2005b. moringa-book. Trees For Life International, W. St.Louis, Wichita

United Nations Conference on Trade & Development, 2003. Organic Fruit and Vegetables from the Tropics Market, Certification and Production Information for Producers and International Trading Companies.

Vargas-Garzón, B., Molina-Prieto, L.F., 2012. Ficus benjamina L. in the cities: high number of individuals, severe damages to infrastructure and expensive economic losses. Rev. Nodo 13, pp. 93–101

Were, F.H., Wafula, G.A., Wairungu, S., 2017. Phytoremediation Using Bamboo to Reduce the Risk of Chromium Exposure from a Contaminated Tannery Site in Kenya. J. Health Pollut. Vol. 7, pp. 12–25

Yousry, O., 2013. The fruit beneath the thorns. Al-Ahram Wkly

Zahran, M.A., Willis, A.J., 1992. The vegetation of Egypt, 1. ed. ed. Chapman & Hall, London.

Zarfeshany, A., Asgary, S., Javanmard, S.H., 2014. Potent health effects of pomegranate. Adv Biomed Res 2014; 3: 100. https://doi.org/10.4103/2277-9175.129371

Introducing the Narrative
Cornelia Redeker and Monique Jüttner, Peter Blodau

01 Landscape Conditions
Intro Cornelia Redeker and Monique Jüttner

Graphics:
Nile section: Eman Farouk
Various maps Egypt (geography, climate, protectorates, etc.): Eman Farouk, Mariam Fouda, Yasmin Gizawy
Map of the Egyptian Nile (including water infrastructure irrigation and drainage canals): Eman Farouk
Rising sea levels and land reclamation: Cornelia Redeker, Hassan El Ghayesh adapted by Eman Farouk
Timeline: Eman Farouk, Cornelia Redeker and Monique Jüttner

Essays WATER
Water conditions Egypt: data Mohie El-Din Omar, graphics Eman Farouk
Designing for Global Water Challenges: images and graphics Antje Stokman

02 Learning From
Cornelia Redeker, Monique Jüttner
Overview Cornelia Redeker, Monique Jüttner
Graphics team: Youssef Ayman, Shaza Elba, Nourhan Sherif
with Omar Osman, Alaa Mubarak (Wadis North Coast Egypt),
Eman Farouk (Map of Desert Forestation in Egypt)
Al Azhar Park - From Landfill to Urban Infrastructure and Civic Park: Sites International
Khalifa Heritage and Environment Park – Conservation through Irrigation: Megawra Built Environment Collective
graphics Megawra adapted by Youssef Ayman, Manar Karam, Shaza Elba
Geziret El Dahab: Nil - Nile Islands Initiative
Scenario A Green Lung For The Megapolis: Youssef Ayman (Vertical Vacancies) / Aya Yasser, Menna Shokheir, Menatalla Ragaey, Radwa El-Sheikh (Ecotransportation Cairo) / Ethar Amr, Yara Essam (Ecotransportation Giza) / Bassant Adel, Sara Abu Henedy, Hassan Hussin (Dahab Island as Ecovillage Park)
Desert Afforestation: Hany El Kateb, Presidential Advisory Council Egypt, Institute of Silviculture, TU Munich
Scenario New Urban Forest: Youssef Ayman, Shaza Elba, Nourhan Sherif
Wadi Agriculture: Ashraf ElSadek National Desert Research Center Egypt, Mario Michelini, CIHEAM Bari
Scenario Wadi Agriculture - Wadi Urbanism: Yosra Malek
Orchard Park – Parks as Food Orchards: concept Bustan Aquaponics, graphics Sites International
Water Sensitive Open Space Design – Diversifying Water Sources, Plants and Uses: Lisa Deister, graphics adapted by Nourhan Sherif
Schaduf Microfarms: Schaduf Sustainable Living Solutions
Scenario Rooftop Gardens and Green Walls: Youssef Ayman
Constructed Wetlands: Ahmed Rashed, Egyptian National Water Research Center, Ministry of Water Resources and Irrigation / Collage Alshama Alfarraj, Rana Gharib
Scenario Site-Independent and Decentralized Ecosanitation: Youssef Ayman and Shaza Elba
Aquaponic Farming: Bustan Aquaponics
Scenario Food Production in the City: Youssef Ayman
Ten Medjool Date Palms: Maged El Said, Habiba Organic Farm
Scenario Shade, Food and Livelihood: Manar Karam, Nada Mansour

03 Revisited and Projected
Cornelia Redeker and Monique Jüttner
Graphics: Nourhan Sherif and Mai El-Shenawy

04 Productive Plants
Monique Jüttner, Cornelia Redeker
Overview Productive Plants: Monique Jüttner and Cornelia Redeker
Doum Palm hand drawing: Maha Aziz; design and life cycle: Monique Jüttner, Rana Mohamed
Date Palm hand drawing: Mahmoud Ebraheem; design and life cycle: Monique Jüttner
Egyptian Sycamore hand drawing: Salma Hassan; design and life cycle: Monique Jüttner, Salma Hassan
Pomegranate hand drawing: Mahmoud Ebraheem; design and life cycle: Monique Jüttner, Yasmine Khouzam
Olive hand drawing: Mahmoud Ebraheem; design and life cycle: Monique Jüttner, Salma Hassan
Banana hand drawing: Maha Aziz; design and life cycle:: Monique Jüttner, Maha Aziz, Yasmine Khouzam
Sweet Orange hand drawing: Yara Galal, Mahmoud Ebraheem; design and life cycle: Monique Jüttner
Grape hand drawing: Mahmoud Ebraheem, design and life cycle: Monique Jüttner
Prickly Pear hand drawing: Maha Aziz, design and life cycle: Monique Jüttner, Rana Mohamed
Moringa hand drawing: Maha Aziz, design and life cycle: Monique Jüttner
Papyrus hand drawing: Maha Aziz, design and life cycle: Monique Jüttner, Yasmine Khouzam
Bamboo hand drawing: Mahmoud Ebraheem; design and life cycle: Monique Jüttner
Reed hand drawing: Maha Aziz, design and life cycle: Rana Mohamed, Eman Farouk, Monique Jüttner
Tamarisk hand drawing: Yara Galal, design and life cycle: Monique Jüttner
Argoun Palm hand drawing: Maha Aziz, design and life cycle: Salma Hassan, Monique Jüttner
Weeping Fig hand drawing: Mahmoud Ebraheem, design and life cycle: Monique Jüttner
A. ehrenbergiana hand drawing: Yara Galal, design and life cycle: Monique Jüttner
A. nilotica hand drawing: Maha Aziz, design and life cycle: Monique Jüttner, Rana Mohamed
A. tortilis subsp. raddiana hand drawing: Mahmoud Ebraheem, design and life cycle: Monique Jüttner

Dictionary
Cornelia Redeker and Monique Jüttner
translation: Rana ElRashidy

Many of the proposals and illustrations evolved from the DESIGNING CYCLES course series at the German University in Cairo Architecture and Urban Design Program: *Decentralized and Small-Scale* design studio 7th semester, winter 2016 / *Green (Belt) Luxor* design studio 10th semester, spring 2017 / *Metro Nile Junction* Bachelor, spring 2017 / *Dahab Island in Context* design studio 10th semester, winter 2018 / *Landscaping Egypt*, elective seminar, winter 2016 / *Imagining Matrouh* design studio 7th semester, winter 2016 / *Landscaping Egypt - Climate Resilience* elective seminar, winter 2017, as well as the summer internship at the GUC Architecture and Urban Design Program in 2018 and a number of master theses under the umbrella of Landscaping Egypt.

Youssef Ayman is an illustrator and 3D designer based in Cairo. He graduated from the GUC Architecture and Urban Design Program to then pursue an international career in visual arts creating editorial illustrations and 3D artwork.

Hala Barakat is an archeobotanist, environmentalist, food researcher, author and yoga teacher. Previously affiliated to the Bibliotheca Alexandrina, she was in charge of the programs for the documentation of Egypt's natural and intangible cultural heritage.

Peter Blodau is a German-Irish artist and photographer based in Cairo and Berlin, teaching at the GUC Faculty of Applied Arts. His work over the past years has focused on urban transformation processes in Cairo.

Lisa Deister is a landscape architect. She is the author of the study Water-Sensitive Open Space Design Al Rehab, which was her master-thesis at the Integrated Urbanism and Sustainable Design Program at Ain Shams University Cairo.

Jerry van Eyck is a Dutch landscape architect. He is the founder and principal of !melk landscape architecture & urban design. !melk is involved in the park design of the New Administrative Capital, Egypt.

Eman Farouk graduated from the GUC Architecture and Urban Design Program, where she is currently teaching and doing research on Egypt's cultural landscapes.

Faris Farrag is an economist and the founder and managing director of Bustan Aquaponics - the first commercial aquaponics farm in Egypt established in 2011. As of 2019 he is also the managing director at Sara's Organic Farm.

Undine Giseke is a landscape architect and researcher focusing on open space, urban (food) systems and transdisciplinary design. She holds the Chair of Landscape Architecture and Open Space Planning at TU Berlin and is professor at TU Berlin El Gouna.

Sherif Hosny is the CEO and co-founder of Schaduf Sustainable Living Solutions, the pioneering company in the Middle East for hydroponic rooftop farming and green walls in both informal and commercial contexts.

Kareem Ibrahim is an Egyptian architect, researcher and urban development consultant working with international organizations in program development and implementation. He is the co-founder and managing director of Takween Integrated Community Development, Cairo.

May al-Ibrashy is an architect, architecture historian and adjunct lecturer at the American University in Cairo. She is founder and chair of the Built Environment Collective and director of Megawra, its commercial arm. She is coordinator of Athar Lina, a participatory initiative integrating conservation and community development based in Historic Cairo.

Manar Karam graduated from the GUC Architecture and Urban Design Program, where she is currently teaching and doing research on Nile waterfronts.

Hany El Kateb is a Member of the Egyptian Presidential Advisory Council of Scientists and Experts, a senior scientist at the Institute of Silviculture at TU Munich and an international senior consultant.

Deena Khalil, is an economist and a researcher at Takween Integrated Community Development

Yosra Malek graduated from the GUC Architecture and Urban Design Program where she is currently teaching and doing research on wadi urbanism.

Mario Michelini studied geography, international cooperation and project design. As international coordinator at CIHEAM Bari he managed the NEMO project and the rural coastal community development project in Marsa Matrouh, Egypt.

Hanaa Nazer is an Egyptian geographer, researcher and professor and head of the geography department at the Faculty of Arts at Fayoum University. Her research involves studies to resettle Nubian communities near Lake Nasser as well as various cartography projects in the Middle East such as the mapping of natural protectorates for the national Egyptian Atlas.

Mohie El-Din Omar is a civil engineer, specialized in water. After receiving his Phd from TU Berlin, he has worked as a consultant for various national and international organizations in the field of water resources management. He is currently working at the Egyptian National Water Research Center, Ministry of Water Resources and Irrigation.

Ahmed Rashed is a civil engineer, researcher and consultant in the field of water/wastewater treatment and environmental studies with a focus on natural/constructed wetlands as water treatment systems. Currently he is professor and head of department for Drainage Technologies at the Drainage Research Institute, National Water Research Center, Cairo.

Rana ElRashidy graduated from the GUC Architecture and Urban Design Program, where she is currently teaching and doing research on Egyptian urban policies.

Mohammed Refaat is an Egyptian landscape architect, founder of the landscape architecture and planning firm NATURE and professor for landscape architecture at the Faculty of Urban and Regional Planning, Cairo University.

Ashraf ElSadek is an Egyptian agronomist and director of Applied Research at the Sustainable Development Center of Matrouh Resources at the National Desert Research Center, Egypt. As national coordinator he managed the NEMO project and the Rural Coastal Community Development in Marsa Matrouh, Egypt.

Maged el Said is the founder and director of the Habiba Beach Lodge, Organic farm and Learning center. With the Sinai Date Palm Foundation, Habiba is seeking to expand the local production of palm date trees.

Mohamed Salheen is an Egyptian architect and urban planner. He is professor and director of the Integrated Urbanism and Sustainable Development Program at Ain Shams University, Cairo and a consultant to numerous national and international organizations in the fields of strategic, environmental and integrated planning and design. He holds a PhD from Edingburgh College of Art in Urban Design.

Salwa Salman is an urban sociologist and researcher at Takween Integrated Community Development, Cairo

Laila ElMasry Stino is co-founder and principal of Sites International Cairo, a multi-disciplinary consultancy firm specializing in designing integrated environments. She is Professor of Urban Design at the Faculty of Urban and Regional Planning at Cairo University and has taught at the University of Michigan, Ann Arbor, where she also obtained her PhD.

Antje Stokman is a landscape architect and professor for architecture and landscape at HafenCity University Hamburg. She co-founded the IUSD Program at Ain Shams University in cooperation with Stuttgart University. Her work focusses on strategies to develop infrastructural and ecological systems as a basis for sustainable urban form and design of urban landscapes.

Aurelia Weintz is a permaculture expert, trainer and co-founder of Nawaya, and co-founder of Slow Food Egypt. She is currently working on preserving Bedouin orchards in Sinai.

Editors Cornelia Redeker and Monique Jüttner

Project Team Eman Farouk, Manar Karam, Yosra Malek, Shaza Elba, Rana ElRashidy, Nourhan Sherif, Youssef Ayman, Menna Tawfik, Ibrahim Samy, Noha Salama

Cover Philipp Paulsen

Design and setting Cynthia-ël Hasbani, Raghda Moataz Zayed, Philipp Paulsen

Lithography Ramy Radwan

Printed in the European Union

Thank you to our sponsors and supporters

FSB – Franz Schneider Brakel GmbH

Deutscher Akademischer Austausch Dienst
German Academic Exchange Service

Bibliographic information published by the Deutsche Nationalbibliothek
The Deutsche Nationalbibliothek lists this publication in the Deutsche Nationalbibliografie; detailed bibliographic data are available on the Internet at http://dnb.d-nb.de

jovis Verlag GmbH
Lützowstraße 33
10785 Berlin

www.jovis.de

jovis books are available worldwide in select bookstores. Please contact your nearest bookseller or visit www.jovis.de for information concerning your local distribution.

ISBN 978-3-86859-552-9